Eliane Beaufils / Eva Holling (eds)

Being-With in Contemporary Performing Arts

Eliane Beaufils / Eva Holling (eds)

Being-With in Contemporary Performing Arts

Neofelis Verlag

Contents

7 // **Eliane Beaufils**
On Being-With

I Performing Participation

17 // **Katia Arfara**
X Apartments: Akira Takayama and the Precarious Condition of Togetherness

33 // **Narges Hashempour**
Theatrical Performances in Today's Iran.
Oscillating between Individual and Collective Being

49 // **Bernhard Siebert**
Survey on Stage.
Listening to the Audience in Kate McIntosh's *All Ears*

59 // **Gerald Siegmund**
Against Participation, or: From a Distance

Artist Talk

75 // **Interview with Heiner Goebbels**
Ensemble, Team & Polyphony
... But in Strong Artistic Experience One Is Always Alone

II Effects Between Scene and Audience

97 // **Eva Holling**
Lacanian Transference.
Co-Subjective Structures and Theatrical Interpellation

111 // **Eliane Beaufils**
Self-Play and Togetherness.
Sense-Making in *Before Your Very Eyes* and
Rhythm Conference Feat. Inner Splits

129 // **Marie Vandenbussche-Cont**
Nature Theater of Oklahoma.
A Theater which Calls Us to Remake (the) World

141 // **Chloé Déchery**
The Guest Performer.
Neo-Liberal Agency and Conflicted Authorship
in Contemporary British Theatre

Artist Talk

159 // **Interview with Ivana Müller**
A *Pas de Deux* You Cannot Dance Alone

III On and Beyond Partage: Theatrical (De-)Communification

181 // **Stéphane Hervé**
Testing Spectatorship at the Limits of Collective Experiencing

195 // **Isabelle Barbéris**
Conviviality, Parasitism and the Common Meal. Toward a Dramaturgy of "Preparation"

207 // **Leon Gabriel**
Scenes of Plural Constellations. *Partage*, Community and *Struction*

223 // **Marie Preston**
From Community-Based Art to the Art of Co-Creation

IV Note / Lookout

243 // **Kai van Eikels**
Performing Collectively, Performing Collectivity: What Does 'Together' Mean?

268 // List of Figures

Eliane Beaufils

On Being-With

> We know the scene: there is a gathering, and someone is telling a story. We do not yet know whether these people gathered together form an assembly, if they are a horde or a tribe. But we call them brothers and sisters because they are gathered together and because they are listening to the same story. We do not know whether the one speaking is from among them or if he is an outsider. We say that he is one of them but different from them.
> (Jean-Luc Nancy: *The Inoperative Community*[1])

This is how the French philosopher Jean-Luc Nancy tells the story of myths, in a movement that itself recalls the mythic tale: he transmits a scene that is intimately known, appealing to each of us. For the philosopher, the myth is a 'mouth' through which the community comes to speak and to recognize itself.

Literature knows this; and theater inherits the same scene, implicating our need for narration, sense and sharing. But these needs as well as the means to fulfill them are unceasingly put into question as sense is redeployed. This has led many contemporary philosophers to reflect

1 Jean-Luc Nancy: *The Inoperative Community*, trans. from the French by Peter Connor / Lisa Garbus / Michael Holland / Simona Sawhney. Minneapolis: University of Minnesota Press 1991, p. 86. French version: *La communauté désœuvrée*. Paris: Bourgois 1986, p. 109: "Nous connaissons la scène: il y a des hommes rassemblés, et quelqu'un qui leur fait un récit. Ces hommes rassemblés, on ne sait pas encore s'ils font une assemblée, s'ils sont une horde ou une tribu. Mais nous les disons 'frères', parce qu'ils sont rassemblés, et parce qu'ils écoutent le même récit. Celui qui raconte, on ne sait pas encore s'il est des leurs, ou si c'est un étranger."

on political difference: the difference between politics (or the *police* for Jacques Rancière) and the political, conceived of as a space of formation and articulation of new categories or perceptions. Some of them, like Alain Badiou or Rancière, consider theater as a privileged realm of thinking because of its particular capacity to self-reflect, offering itself as the locus of the questioning of sense and habitus. Is theater not

> an institution that is able to unsettle authorities that have been constituted elsewhere, that can criticize untenable ideological positions and dissolve patterns of order and doctrines of any kind [?] Theater – in accordance with a view widely held until recently by theater practitioners and commentators – is a critical practice[.][2]

But this critical vocation of theater raises concerns, because it has become difficult to refer to a common sense.[3]

Thus the main concern that animates Nancy's reflections on being-with until 2017 is precisely the question of how to make sense together now. Since the 1980s, he underlines that humans are first of all co-existent: they are obviously always together with others. But this being-with is far from being confined to a mere co-presence: "the thought of 'us' is anterior to any other thought [and therefore to any conscious co-presence ...] it is not a representative thought, but a *praxis* and an *ethos*"[4]. Being-with is, more than the horizon of our thinking, our condition. Humans can only make sense in relation to others. The meaning is "'meaning of Being': not only as the 'meaning of with,' but also, and above all, as the 'with' of meaning. Because none of these three terms [...] precedes or grounds the other, each designates the co-essence of the others"[5]. The philosopher comes hence to define being-with as a place: "the common does not present itself as the subject of sense but as its place", "nor spontaneous nor calculated", it is a place that enables "the movement thanks to what one gets out of

2 CfP for the 13th conference of the Society for Theater Studies: Theater als Kritik / Theater as Critique. http://www.theaterforschung.de/print.php4?file=inc_dates_auswertung.php4&ID=3770 (accessed April 03, 2017).

3 Ibid.

4 Jean-Luc Nancy / Daniel Tyradellis: *Qu'appelons-nous penser?* Zurich: Diaphanes 2013, p. 38 (transl. E. B.).

5 Jean-Luc Nancy: *Being singular plural.* Stanford: Stanford UP 2000, p. 22.

simple identity".[6] Nevertheless, the pitfalls encountered by the development of being-with are not few, especially as it is not conceivable to return to myths and communities.

Indeed, myths and communities go hand in hand, since the group speaks through myth and this speaking enables the identity settings within the collectivity and of each person towards the other. In giving the community an essence, myth gives one to the individual who recognizes him/herself as guided by narratives, principles and goals. In this way, Nancy casts the subject as relation from oneself to oneself, as transparent consciousness, into question. We are never anywhere other than "in between," in the relation – to the situation, from consciousness to consciousness – so that according to Nancy the human being has to be thought of starting from relation and becoming. It has somehow to be conceived of as *work in progress* and as endless process, similarly to every "community": that must not become an "*œuvre*", an "artwork"[7]. Obviously, the multiplication of totalitarianisms during the 20th century played a determining role in this awareness, and the philosopher warns us against the first of the myths creeping up on us: deploring lost communities, which have undoubtedly never existed as fraternally as we dreamt them. Rather, Nancy calls for a nourishing of the 'between', the sharing of meaning, which is also the sharing of singularities within the being-with. In fact, "as sense lies not in the unity of an 'all' [totalitarian or divine ...], sense lies in sharing and in the passage *between us*"[8]. Being-with thus designates an ontological as well as a symbolic process, which Nancy associates further with 'world making' in a time when the world is not thinkable any more as an entity or connected with an ordering.

If the failure of the Soviet regime has no doubt given a fundamental impetus to the philosophical reflections on community, the dysregulations / disruptions of the world order and the unabated conflicts

6 Jean-Luc Nancy: Un sens commun. In: *Libération*, 26.02.2015. http://www.liberation.fr/societe/2015/02/26/apres-charlie-retrouver-un-sens-commun_1210406 (accessed March 20, 2017; transl. E. B.).

7 This explains the title of his first book on the topic: *The Inoperative Community / La Communauté désœuvrée*, referring to the 'opus' / 'œuvre' that cannot be made.

8 "Comme le sens n'est pas assignable dans l'unité d'un tout [totalitaire ou divin ...], le sens est dans le partage et dans le passage *entre nous*." (Nicolas Poirier: Entretien avec Jean-Luc Nancy. In: *Le Philosophoire* 7 (1999), pp. 12–13. https://www.cairn.info/revue-le-philosophoire-1999-1-page-11.htm (accessed March 20, 2017; transl. E. B.).)

provided fodder for them in the 1990s, so that Nancy finds the key notions of 'political' and of 'communism' objectionable – communism should be "literary"[9]. The return of very conservative, identitarian movements in Europe, which can be related to the threat of terrorism or to the dismay provoked by the impacts of neoliberalism, makes being-with even more problematic. But the lack of global orders and of common reference frames seems the biggest challenge for the philosopher to take up, to the extent that he coins with Aurélien Barrau the concept of "*struction*". This concept is meant to be accountable for the large network within which we have to live today and which invalidated hierarchies as well as our coordinates and dichotomic distinctions between nature and technology, economy and politics, or body and mind.[10] Thus for both thinkers a being-with less engaged in an aleatory structure should be developed, one that departs more from sensing and feeling, and which is not essentially experienced in the mode of duty.[11]

The terribly complex dimensions of contemporary being-with have notable aesthetic and artistic implications. First, art has a particular dimension according to Nancy: since the 'between' cannot be accomplished, it can only inscribe itself. To inscribe relations and sharing means to expose the singular beings to one another, to show the openness of meaning and to expose this openness. The place of this inscription and of this exposure is above all literature, "the other of the sacred text (going back to the One)", or art, "what evades the assumption of a unified signification"[12]: art and literature live from an open sense.

9 Poirier: Entretien avec Jean-Luc Nancy (transl. E. B.). It is recalled that Nancy distinguishes like the other philosophers engaged in these discussions on being-in-common, most of all Claude Lefort, Alain Badiou, Jacques Rancière, Giorgio Agamben and Robert Esposito, politics (or the police for Rancière) from *the* political as a movement of sense in common. The political is the crucible of discussions that give birth to categories and institutions involved in politics ("the distribution of the sensible" according to Rancière).

10 Aurélien Barrau / Jean-Luc Nancy: *Dans quels mondes vivons-nous?* Paris: Galilée 2011.

11 Esposito shows that community is primarily founded on the 'munus', the duty as the etymology underlines. To the sharing of duty (com-munitas) Esposito opposes the im-munitas, the part of the common that liberates the modern individual from a single munus. See Roberto Esposito: *Bios. Biopolitics and Philosophy.* Minneapolis: University of Minnesota Press 2008.

12 "[La littérature,] l'autre du texte sacré (qui retourne à l'Un)", "[ou bien l'art] ce qui se soustrait à l'assomption d'une signification unie." (Poirier: Entretien avec Jean-Luc Nancy, p. 13 (transl. E. B.).)

They appeal to sharing in spite of the impossibility of a unified sharing, they interrupt sense, and they are also able to formulate a not-yet-communicated that is in suspension, echoing or rather responding to the others, readers or spectators. But if art is the place of the inscription, it is also "the index of the problem of sharing sense"[13].

We know that it would not suffice to consider live arts as oases of being-with, on the grounds that they put performers and spectators into relation, and that they want to keep awake the consciousness of sense in becoming between the stage and stalls, or rather between the stage and the different spectators. In conjunction with the becoming problematic of common sense – or with its necessary reflection in common – scenic arts have experimented with sharing processes of sense and of the senses, through frontal as well as immersive apparatuses. By now, performing arts have multiplied experiences of participation, happenings or delegated performances for fifty years. In theaters, directors constantly tested new performative or postdramatic forms, building on interruption and non-linearity, including for instance choralities and fictionalization of the spectator that wished to call out directly for the reflection of the spectators. But it is necessary to analyze the experiences in the light of recent critical books written on the topic.

Regarding participation, several scholars, in particular Claire Bishop and Juliane Rebentisch, underlined that one had to question participation-based projects, sometimes relying on preconceived intentions and lacking self-critical reflectivity.[14] It is not only a matter of instrumentalization, if not manipulation inherent to many participatory or immersive actions. One has also to consider the relevance of certain relational aesthetics: the communities constituted during the performances are often idealized, as if we waited for these moments to exchange significant words, so that certain performances seem to be situated in a post-apocalyptic universe where people no more enter in contact yet would be happy to do so.[15] Furthermore, it is important

13 "[L]'index du problème [du] partage du sens" (ibid., p. 14 (transl. E. B.)).

14 See Claire Bishop: *Artificial Hells: Participatory Art and the Politics of Spectatorship*. New York: Verso 2012; Juliane Rebentisch: Participation in Art: 10 Theses. In: Alexander Dumbadze / Suzanne Hudson (eds): *Contemporary Art. 1989 to the Present*. Hoboden: Wiley 2013.

15 See Dan Karlholm: Reality Art. The Case of Oda Projesi. In: *Leitmotiv* 5 (2005/2006), pp. 115–124, here p. 120.

to take into consideration the nature of the intersubjective relations woven during a participatory project, the part of personal, creative reflection, to which the performance appeals and which might go beyond the present moment. Is participation a way to generate sense if it has no finality? Might not the risk be to emphasize a simple, non-reflexive empathy, or on the contrary forms of resistance regarding a superficial and artificial consensus? Kai van Eikels points out the frequent reference to oneself, to processes of acknowledgment by others, or even to instrumentalization of the others; that means that one often becomes spectator of one's own performance rather than of the others, on a less open mode than during some frontal set-ups.[16] For Rebentisch, the most advanced performing art now reflects participation as a problem, not as a solution.[17]

That is the reason why this book does not focus on performances which are primarily participatory. It concentrates on performances that could enable a development of thought on common issues and somehow in common, trying in this way to develop an active being-with between performers and spectators. In *Performing Politics* and in *Social Works*,[18] Nikolaus Müller-Schöll and Shannon Jackson seem to indicate that performing arts can, surely not without difficulty, be laboratories of thinking in common in actions, concepts and percepts. This also implies communal reflection on the conditions of thinking. Many articles indeed show how theater is a thought-project, not only in being conceptual but in its openness or confusion, so that the indeterminacy appeals to the thought processes of the spectator. But the openness can in itself set the audience's imagination into motion without putting its categories into question in a movement of sense that might exceed the already thought or imagined. The second question is to analyze how it is possible to promote a dialogical art with the spectator.[19]

16 Kai van Eikels: *Die Kunst des Kollektiven: Performance zwischen Theater, Politik und Sozio-Ökonomie*. Paderborn: Fink 2013.

17 Juliane Rebentisch, conference "Theater as a Scene of Thinking", at the symposium *Thinking on/of Stage*, September 28, 2013 at Künstlerhaus Mousonturm Frankfurt (not published yet).

18 Nikolaus Müller-Schöll (ed.): *Performing Politics: Politisch Kunst machen nach dem 20. Jahrhundert*. Berlin: Theater der Zeit 2012; Shannon Jackson: *Social Works. Performing Arts, Supporting Publics*. London: Routledge 2011.

19 This dialogical dimension of theater represents for Hans-Thies Lehmann an "aesthetics of response-ability" in postdramatic theater. See Hans-Thies Lehmann: *Postdramatic Theater*, trans. from the German by Karen Jürs-Munby. London /

Which forms of appeal to thinking might induce an excess of narcissistic thought? Such an opening movement to a form of 'other of the thought' that Bernhard Waldenfels calls responsivity,[20] implies a conscience of the movement, and self-reflectivity goes hand in hand with the sense that appears, a sense that would unfold in an in-between, as a result of the 'common'. This kind of thinking may be linked to our common existence, our desires and investigations. It would exceed existing discourses and have an existential dimension – even more so, that it would involve the status of spectatorship in one form or another. Nevertheless, exceeding categories, objects and relations, always means to establish a reference to them. If a making-sense in common would be a laboratory of the in-common, how are the interrogations concerned with our relationships to others and our representations, how do they start from them – without confining us in a critical and defensive gesture? Or without letting us fall back into a mythologized co-presence? The activation of the spectator intended by multiple works has no doubt to be questioned on several levels: the symbolic level, the intersubjective level and the level of the sensible co-presence. The studies should also take into account the forms of spectatorial returns enabled by this activation, should they be critical, sensible or subjective.
Thus, this book focuses on three different points: the question of direct participation; the (co-)creation of the effects that emerge in theater situations – i.e. between stage and audience; and projects that work with different modes of partaking (*partage*) to question the preconditions of possible communities. The first part deals less with participation than with its being contested. The participatory projects that are presented are participations 'under conditions': in *X Apartments* studied by Katia Arfara, the penetration of daily but unfamiliar spaces in the Athenian outskirts is guided by a singular hearing and viewing, whereas the Iranian performances that Narges Hashempour introduces address different categories of people, so she identifies a form of collective identification which could as well occur in the most innovative and progressive works. Bernhard Siebert analyzes self-reflexive

New York: Routledge 2006, p. 185. He relates this to "a mutual implication of actors and spectators", which would be "an experience [...] not only aesthetic but therein at the same time ethico-political" (ibid., p. 186).

20 For an introduction to Bernhard Waldenfels' Analysis in *Antwortregister*, see Norm Friesen: Waldenfels' Responsive Phenomenology of the Alien, 2014. http://learningspaces.org/files/Waldenfels.pdf (accessed April 22, 2017).

participation advanced by Kate McIntosh, while Gerald Siegmund singles out the pitfalls of participation and shows that also frontal set ups can prove to be very instructive for conceiving the dialogicity between a show and the spectators.

The second part concentrates on projects that are not participatory nor even interactive but create genuine structures of being-with. As Eva Holling and Eliane Beaufils underline, they can promote complex forms of relations with the spectators. Eva Holling shows how every theatrical encounter is intersubjective, giving rise to theatrical interpellation by different kinds of Lacanian transference or foiling it critically, whereas Eliane Beaufils re-examines particular movements of sense that are liberated because the usual modes of subject recognition are diverted. But a subject can experience the movement of being-with as world making, as the Nature Theater of Oklahoma does for Marie Vandenbussche. Or one can grasp it through the difference in the text performances by very singular actors, who are invited by the British artists presented by Chloé Déchery to do so.

The third part deals with questions of 'communitification' in theatre – with forms of performance that wish to think and to act out togetherness and to negotiate the spectator's function from within. Stéphane Hervé presents many works which take care not to call for identification with the communities on stage, even at the expense of irritating spectators, whereas Isabelle Barbéris studies the critical dimension of polylogal or dissensual convivialities that are sketched out at the end of performances. Leon Gabriel highlights the awareness of *struction* in the works of Romeo Castellucci and Kate McIntosh. But being-with can also occur in the working groups of Marie Preston, whose unachieved videos of cooperation wish to interpellate non-group members.

Finally, Kai van Eikels reflects broadly on the bounds that may subsist, in the age of post-Fordism and a certain turmoil for artists, between artistic *poiesis* and strictly political *praxis*.

Between the sections, two interviews with 'polyphonic artists' also address the questions of being-with. Heiner Goebbels and Ivana Müller conceive theatrical works which are most of the time frontal but open the performative space to forms of co-creation with the spectators. In the interviews, they express their thoughts towards several 'beings-withs' on different levels in their artistic work.

I

Performing Participation

Katia Arfara

X Apartments: Akira Takayama and the Precarious Condition of Togetherness

The present article focuses on *X Apartments*, the urban project which was initially conceived by the German curator Matthias Lilienthal and which has been realized in different cities all around the world since its premiere in Duisburg in 2002. *X Apartments* will be critically approached as an exemplary urban intervention on the complex phenomenon of shared city space which brings new possibilities of coexistence and cohabitation into being. Lilienthal's idea is based on Jan Hoet's emblematic exhibition at the Musée d'art contemporain in Ghent in 1986 entitled *Chambres d'amis.* "Far from being a noncommittal tourist attraction, or another summer exhibition", argues Hoet in the exhibition's catalogue,

> *Chambres d'amis* deals with the idea of integration in a more subtle and cautious way. The meaning of modern art is not to be shouted from the rooftops. This is a cryptic and sensitive penetration. Art discretely penetrates realms that were for a long time unattainable: houses, space where people live![1]

Chambres d'amis was an attempt to reconcile the aesthetics with the everyday through privileging informal contact of contemporary, object-based works with the spectators. By inviting local residents (many of them art collectors) to give their already shaped space to

1 Jan Hoet (ed.): *Chambres d'Amis*. Exhibition catalogue. Ghent: Museum van Hedendaagse Kunst 1986.

the artists, Hoet attempted to link art with reality forcing "artists to incorporate elements of the homes and homeowners into the works"[2]. Initiated within the performing arts field, the project *X Apartments* shares, and, at the same time, expands and differentiates Hoet's visual arts concept: it is articulated around time-based performative interventions and installations that emerge site-specifically in urban neighborhoods from the interaction of the artists with the inhabitants, the surrounding environment and the specific sociopolitical context. The ambition of *X Apartments* is not only the transgression of old distinctions between the private and the public sphere, the ordinary and the extraordinary. Based in long term interdisciplinary research in the arts and in civil society, the project aims to open a critical discussion about the possibilities of socially engaged artistic practices to unveil contemporary controversies and homogenized perceptions of human geographies. Adopting the form of a constellation with multiple and formally diverse site-specific works, *X Apartments* remains open to endless possibilities and innumerable interconnections in order to create unexpected encounters and conjunctures between the real and the fictional worlds in an attempt to imagine notional shared spaces which lie beyond identitarian dictates and territorial thinking while simultaneously testing the limits and the potential of art's social function.
More specifically, *X Apartments*' hyper-dramaturgy is made up of time limited interventions in non-theatrical (private, public or semi-public) locations restricting the number of audience members to two every ten minutes and within a specific spatial order: every couple of audience members needed to follow a specific, carefully designed itinerary, determined by a printed map with a starting and an ending point. The project explores new models of spectatorship in various urban centers, all around the world, which stress audience involvement through an embodied dialogue between listening and viewing, imagining and experiencing, the mental and the material, the visual and the haptic. It temporally installs a complex situation that expands spectator's awareness, engaging him/her in an active perception of the three-dimensional space and, consequently, of the complex phenomenon of common space.

2 Avant-Garde Art Show Adorns Belgian Homes. In: *The New York Times*, August 19, 1986. http://www.nytimes.com/1986/08/19/arts/avant-garde-art-show-adorns-belgian-homes.html (accessed May 25, 2017).

X Apartments in Athens

This chapter will more particularly analyze the Athens episode which focuses on unseen or less known aspects of the Greek capital suggesting an alternative anthropogeography of the city. Co-curated by Anna Mülter and myself, Athens *X Apartments* took place in May 2015 within the frame of the 2nd Onassis Cultural Centre's annual Fast Forward Festival, which I initiated in 2014 and curated until today. The festival commissions and produces interdisciplinary site-specific works in public and private spaces across the city of Athens and its surroundings in an attempt to open a dialogue on critical social, cultural and political issues.

In *X Apartments* fifteen international and local artists from various artistic fields[3] intervened in apartments from the 1950s and 1960s as well as in houses from the pre-war year – buildings which testify to a rich architectural past of the city –, in empty spaces and homes full of memories and old objects, half-finished buildings and temporary constructions, semi-public spaces and sites of social exclusion such as an asylum. The project was based in an intense year long research period in collaboration with social networks, collaborative platforms and human rights initiatives, including educators, and vulnerable and marginalized groups. By interweaving with the urban fabric, *X Apartments* artistic interventions attempted to articulate a critique of the dominant narrative, which has locked the public image of downtown Athens into a discourse on overarching urban blight especially after the arrival of large numbers of migrants in the city center since the 1990s.

The project was articulated through two walking tours, two distinct itineraries in areas of Athens which have been recently traumatized by extreme social phenomena such as the violent attacks on migrants by members of the far right party Golden Dawn. One of the *X Apartments* tours took place in the densely populated area of Kypseli, due to the drastic shift in its urban identity and its high concentration of residents of multiple ethnicities. The other tour took

3 The project was based on the research of Prodromos Tsinikoris and involved the following artists: Anestis Azas (GR), Andreas Angelidakis (GR), Tzeni Argyriou (GR), Alexandra Bachzetsis (GR/CH), George Drivas (GR), Eleni Efthimiou (GR), Ant Hampton (UK/CH), Chris Kondek (USA/DE), Boris Nikitin (CH), Markus Öhrn (SE/DE), Akira Takayama (JA), Taldans (Filiz Sizanli & Mustafa Kaplan, TR), Syllas Tzoumerkas (GR), Doris Uhlich (AT), Daniel Wetzel (DE).

place around Larisis station, an area whose social identity continues to undergo constant transformation, and Kolonos, an old working-class Athenian neighborhood.

Each of the fifteen interventions operated both independently *and* as part of a whole within the restricted time frame of ten minutes. Participation was thus redefined as a complex relationship between the artistic practices, the environment, and the couple of spectators/visitors in an attempt to unsettle binaries such as activity and passivity, social efficacy and aesthetic legitimacy,[4] but also alienation and contemplation, audience and the 'stage'.

In their trajectories, spectators experienced site-specific situations while witnessing their aesthetic and social infrastructure. The project produces "a consciousness of artistic heteronomy and social interdependence together"[5], though the techniques by which each 'apartment' achieves such a coincidence differ. By limiting the number of spectators to two, *X Apartments* appeals to the voyeuristic desires that accompany the gaze into the private life of others, but it also deals with this voyeurism consciously. It puts spectators in an exposed position as the inhabitants (who are often performers as well) of the apartments look back at them too.

The spatial turn

X Apartments is an attempt to question the different sociopolitical issues which dangerously polarize and divide local and international civil society. Looking back over the last years, public art has increasingly challenged not only visual but also, more recently, performance

4 Shannon Jackson: *Social Works. Performing Art, Supporting Publics.* New York / London: Routledge 2011, p. 45. As Jackson points out, social public works are not anti-theatrical or *non*-theatrical. They rather introduce a new way to think about our relationships to one another and to the larger community around us. Social works are not against aesthetics but against aesthetic appropriation.

5 Ibid., p. 60. On the convergence of questions from both aesthetic and social domains see also Shannon Jackson: Working Publics. In: *Performance Research* 16:2 (2011): Performing Publics, pp. 8–13, here pp. 10–11: "Through social art projects that provoke a reflection on the opportunity and inconvenience of our enmeshment in systems of labour, ecology, ablebodiedness, social welfare, public infrastructure, kinship and more, expanded artworks might induce a kind of 'infrastructural avowal,' that is, an acknowledgement of the interdependent systems of support that sustain human beings, even though we often feel constrained by them".

artists, as it engages them to unlock alternative models of artistic production by intervening in unconventional spaces. This 'spatial turn' in contemporary theater and the visual arts implies a 'social turn', which provokes a shift both in curatorial practices and in aesthetics, revealing complex interactions between art, the communal and the political.[6] The term 'social turn' was introduced in 2006 by Claire Bishop[7] in the field of visual arts in order to characterize the expanded field of socially engaged experimental artists which have appeared in the public realm since the early 1990s, "when the fall of communism deprived the Left of the last vestige of the Revolution that had once linked political and aesthetic radicalism"[8]. These interdisciplinary practices are less interested in relational aesthetics rather than in the collaborative process of creation, and are often called by a variety of names: new genre public art, social works, connective aesthetics, dialogical art, collaborative or research-based art.[9] *X Apartments* is a socially engaged urban project articulated around an aesthetically defined artistic form, which can be perceived critically *as art*. It could be useful at this point to establish a clear distinction between two distinct 'genres' of social works: community-specific works and site-specific works. According to Claire Bishop, in community based social projects "the emphasis is on process over product" and the "artists use social situations to produce dematerialized, anti-market, politically engaged projects that carry on the modernist call to blur art and life"[10]. Unlike Bishop's homogenized definition of what she calls the 'social turn' in the arts, *X Apartments* claims an artistic quality and at the same time a new way to think about theater. Certainly it is an experimental artistic project

6 As Chantal Mouffe explains, the political is a dimension that can never be eradicated: "Politics' refers to an ensemble of practices, courses and institutions that seeks to establish a certain order and to organize human coexistence in conditions which are always potentially conflicting, since they are affected by the dimension of 'the political'." (Chantal Mouffe: *Agonistics. Thinking the World Politically*. London / New York: Verso 2013, p. 2–3.)

7 Cf. Claire Bishop: The Social Turn: Collaboration and its Discontents. In: *Art Forum*, 02/2006, pp. 178–183.

8 Ibid., p. 179.

9 Ibid. On collaborative art practices see also Maria Lind: The Collaborative Turn. In: M. L. / Johanna Billing / Lars Nilson (eds): *Taking the Matter into Common Hands. On Contemporary Art and Collaborative Practices*. London: black dog 2007, pp. 15–31, here p. 20.

10 Bishop: The Social Turn, p. 180.

reflecting anti-institutional and anti-formalist practices that emerged in the 1950s and 1960s especially in the United States.[11] Nevertheless, it does not aim to blur the distance between art and life through a participatory experience in long-term, open-ended situations; neither does it assume the recent orientation of art as activism.

Rather, *X Apartments* exhorts us to engage actively with the living conditions, allowing the invisible and the imaginary to 'contaminate' everyday life. With the tools of art and culture, the project attempts to overcome traditional perceptions (and uses) of private and public sphere. The distinction between private and public here is certainly maintained in the same way as the distinction between individual and citizen; nevertheless, these distinctions "do not correspond to discrete separate spheres. We cannot say: here end my duties as a citizen and begins my freedom as an individual"[12]. The blurring of the liberal and bourgeois gendered division between the private and the politically connoted public sphere constitutes one of the key dimensions of *X Apartments*. The project suggests a socially engaged authorship, which questions the regulative idea of the public sphere as "the terrain where one aims at creating consensus"[13]. At the same time, it critically expands the notion of spectatorship to an often inconvenient experience which remains open to the unpredictable and to the hazardous.

Akira Takayama's 'Home project'

I would like to further focus *X Apartments*'s analysis on the work of the Japanese artist Akira Takayama as an exemplary urban intervention on the condition of collaboration which operates in an expanded field of spectatorship while at the same time articulates a critical comment on the western and the eastern societies and their cultural and social particularities. Akira Takayama was among the artists who accepted our invitation to create works especially for the

11 I am referring here to the radical criticism of conceptual artists in the late 1960s and during the 1970s who attacked the absorbed, 'sleeping' spectator of Clement Greenberg's conservative modernism.

12 Chantal Mouffe: *The Return of the Political*. London / New York: Verso 2005, p. 72.

13 See Mouffe's criticism on the concept of the public sphere defended by Jürgen Habermas (Mouffe: *Agonistics*, p. 92).

houses and the sites in downtown Athens. Founder of the theater network Port B[14] in 2002, Takayama is one of the most socially engaged artists of his generation who continuously questions the concept of theater, challenging both its form and its content in an expanded field of relational aesthetics, which are placed in public or semi-public, in any case atypical, urban spaces. In *Tokyo Heterotopia* (2013) and *Yokohama Commune* (2014), his gaze was directed toward the 'Asia within' Japan, highlighting parts of Tokyo and Yokohama, which he considers as "heterotopias"[15], tracing the footprints and narratives of those who drifted there from all over Asia. Collaborating with architects, visual artists and scholars, he develops site-specific interdisciplinary works contributing to counter-hegemonic discourses on history and politics. His often invisible disruptions of the dominant social order attempt to re-imagine theater as a social and aesthetic event while giving voice to marginalized groups such as refugees, immigrants, the homeless.

Akira Takayama's first research visit to Athens, in the frame of *X Apartments*, took place in March 2015. After several meetings with social networks, activists, and inhabitants, he proposed to work on a project on homelessness. More particularly, Takayama proposed to explore the various aspects of homelessness in both Athens and Tokyo and their relationships with dominant living models. Resulting from the refugee reception crisis and the austerity program imposed on Greece by its creditors, the homeless condition in Athens is not (yet)

14 "B" stands not only for the name of Walter Benjamin but also for Port Bou in Spain, the place where Benjamin took his life on the run from Nazi agents. As Hans-Thies Lehmann argues, the name indicates an awareness of catastrophe like that envisioned by Benjamin in his famous angel of history, which has transformed both Takayama's thinking and his art long before Fukushima. Port B is not only a reminder of a suicide but also a reminder of the human disasters. (Hans-Thies Lehmann: Akira Takayama, Port B, Walter Benjamin (and the Theatre). In: H. T. L. / Tatsuki Hayashi / Matthias Pees (eds): *Evacuating Theatre. Akira Takayama's Rescue Plan for the Rhine-Main Region*. Berlin: Alexander 2015, pp. 240–246, here p. 242.)

15 "Heterotopia" is a term designating spaces that cannot be integrated into the regular distribution of territories, as they are "combinations of spaces that are normally incompatible." (Jacques Rancière: In What Time Do We Live? In: Marta Kuzma / Pablo Lafuente / Peter Osborne (eds): *The State of Things*. London: Office for Contemporary Art Norway / Koenig 2012, p. 34.) The term was dubbed by Michel Foucault in his preface of *Les mots et les choses* [1966]. Paris: Gallimard 2002, pp. 7–16. It was further elaborated in his seminal text Des espaces autres [1967]. In: *Architecture, Mouvement, Continuité* 5 (October 1984), pp. 46–49.

an act of civil disobedience and a refusal of domination structures as perceived in Japan, but, rather, an involuntary condition of marginalization and victimization that clearly demarcates the homeless as the *Other*. The comparison of the two distinct faces of homelessness in Tokyo and Athens in Takayama's project created a discursive platform open to critically challenging meetings and current debates in both capitals.

As the municipality of Athens declined FFF's request to construct temporary houses in a public square in order to avoid increasing the visibility of the homeless issue, it was decided to place Takayama's project at the abandoned Larissis train station, a *no man's land* area which divides Athens as both a natural and mental border. Due to a financial scandal, its construction was stopped in 2011. Today, the station is almost finished with all equipment already exposed, but remains unused and closed to the public.

In the second phase of the project, Takayama decided to conduct a construction workshop together with two homeless Athenian residents, Lampros Moustakis and Stelios Bachtsevanis, who were selected in collaboration with the homeless organization *The Raft*. In addition, Takayama decided to bring the homeless artist Tetsuo Ogawa from Tokyo, especially for the Athens project, in order to explore the local homeless living conditions but also the contribution of the 2004 Olympic Games to Greece's social crisis.

Collaboration as process

Collaboration is the main working method of Akira Takayama. It is an open-ended, site and time specific concept, which refers to various forms of togetherness.[16] For the Japanese artist, the preparation period is equally important as the performance period, the emphasis is given on the process *as well as* on the 'product'. I would like to quote Takayama here, from the unedited interview that he gave to OCC's documentation team at this occasion: "First of all we went around the station and collected the waste. Day and night we built the houses

16 Maria Lind marks the different connotations of terms such as "collective action", "interaction", "participation" emphasizing that collaboration is an "umbrella term" which has proved "to be a good instrument with which to challenge both artistic identity and authorship, and therefore to stimulate anxiety" (Lind: Collaborative Turn, p. 16).

and during this process we built also the relationship with each other. And now I feel that we are together"[17]. It is important to remark that even when Takayama isolates spectators through a process of "atomization"[18], reducing theater into minimum units such as the individual equipment of the i-Phone applications in *Tokyo Heterotopia* (2013), he nevertheless aims to create awareness of the pluralistic, heterogeneous society in which we are living by drawing imaginary communities.
By choosing collaboration as a process, Takayama relates his practice to the notions of collectivity and shared authorship. In *X Apartments*, not only does he choose to work together with two homeless people from Athens but he also invites a Japanese homeless artist, who lives in Yoyogi park, to equally participate in the whole process. The 'Home project' could not have taken place outside this dialogical structure. Takayama's collaboration, as a conscious process of creation, could integrate the broader discussion on the 'collaboration turn' in the arts that Maria Lind places in the middle of the 1990s, when the field of art has expanded and a kind of "neo-idealism" flourishes in the arts beside political "neo-radicalism". As Lind argues,

> this should come as no surprise; when politics in principle are completely steered by economics and the economy follows a capitalist logic, then culture tends to become an arena for ideological debate. Culture in general, and art in particular, then functions as a venue where the political is allowed to be enacted, if sometimes covertly. A situation then emerges where on the one hand, the political discussion in parliamentary democracies' public space is increasingly about ethics and morality, and on the other, art seeks out political phenomena that have long been taken for granted – phenomena like citizenship that either have been eroded or utterly transformed.[19]

Takayama relates to this collaborative turn, but he clearly takes his distances from the current affinities of contemporary art with activism.

17 Interview of Alaska Films' documentation team with Takayama in May 2015 (unedited).

18 On Takayama's theory of "atomization", see Kyoko Iwaki: The Politics of the Senses. Takayama Akira's Atomized Theatre after Fukushima. In: Barbara Geihorn / Kristina Iwata-Weickgenannt (eds): *Fukushima and the Arts. Negotiating Nuclear Disaster*. London / New York: Routledge 2017, pp. 199–220, here p. 216.

19 Lind: Collaborative Turn, p. 28.

Echoing Chantal Mouffe's argument for a pluralistic heterogeneous society, he argues that he cannot propose a system for building consensus: "It's like I've devoted myself to the work of listening just to voices, and the more I think about it the more it seems that I am not headed towards activism. It's like I am standing there in a stupor."[20] By expanding spectator's awareness of the everyday living conditions, he engages him/her into a new way of thinking our differences and our isolation, as individuals and as citizens living in the same, hybrid and conflictual urban landscape. In doing so, Takayama reappropriates Bertolt Brecht's concept of tiny theater, *Theaterchen*. As Takayama points out, "*Theaterchen* is pregnant with possibilities precisely because it is small, flexible, adaptable. I want to expand the possibility of theater by diminishing or, moreover, demolishing its form."[21] By integrating this minimum aesthetic unit into everyday life, Takayama aims at provoking a "daily tectonic shift of perceptions, which, when accumulated, may change the social fabric in the long run"[22]. Revolution for Takayama is not about becoming bigger, louder and faster, but about becoming smaller, subtler and slower.

Reframing the present

Considering information as an inherent quality of communication, Takayama decided to share some basic aspects of the project, and of the personal biographies of Lampros and Stelios with the audience by screening their 'portraits' on two monitors as a prologue to their visit. The questions (and the answers) in the presented interviews were very simple such as:

- What would you like most to have now?
- A job.
- *Tetsuo Ogawa, a homeless man from Tokyo, came to show you how to build a house with material that you found here. What do you think about the station?*

20 M. Cody Poulton: Antigone in Japan. Some Responses to 3.11 at Festival/Tokyo 2012. In: Geihorn / Iwata-Weickgenannt (eds): *Fukushima and the Arts*, pp. 127–143, here p. 140.

21 Iwaki: Politics of the Senses, p. 216.

22 Ibid., p. 212.

- The station is great. It is wide and we have space to work.
- *When you were homeless, what kind of house did you want to have?*
- Anywhere I could be safe inside.
- *What does home mean to you?*
- The smell of my mother's cooking, somewhere you can go to your room and have control over the TV remote.[23]

After those short video portraits, spectators split in order to separately visit the makeshift houses that Lambros and Stelios constructed by hand out of blue plastic sheeting and cardboard and wood found in the train station's broader area. Their tents vary in tenure, but they both have two chairs, a table and a clock which counts the time of the conversation that takes place between the homeless hosts and their visitors. During this intimate encounter inside the shelters, Lambros and Stelios are asking their guests about their notions of home, homeland and sense of belonging.

The audience meets again, shortly afterwards their encounter with Lambros and Stelios, at the tent of Tetsuo: here we sit on cardboard and we have an informal conversation about issues of homelessness and precarization in Athens and Tokyo.

Takayama divides his location into three different time-spaces, three "heterochronies" as Jacques Rancière (in reference to Michel Foucault's heterotopias) designates the "combinations of times that are normally incompatible"[24]. Time, or to be more precise the redistribution of time "that invents new capacities of framing the present,"[25] could be considered as the main dramaturgical device of *X Apartments*. The restricted time frame maintained the whole experience within the domain of the performing arts while clearly contaminating life with art – each encounter was not aimed at 'de-alienating' the audience – spectators never became the *Other*. They encounter the Others and, simultaneously, their own Self. As in his video installation *The City and*

23 Video interview of Akira Takayama with Lambros Moustakis, May 2015 (unedited).

24 Rancière: In What Time Do We Live?, p. 34.

25 Ibid., p. 36.

Fig. 1: Akira Takayama's installations at the Larissis train station, *X Apartments Athens*, 2015.

its Tower[26] (2016), Takayama attempts to critically approach the complex socio-political situation of homelessness and marginalization in contemporary urban centers through the eyes and from the words and the personal narratives of the encountered Others, coming from their 'peripheries'.

The 'drama' – if there is any – takes place between the artwork, the environment and the spectator, in other words within the 'gap' between art and life. In the restricted time frame of ten minutes, Takayama's 'Home Project' developed multiple comparative modes of perception in which spectators constantly shifted positions, differentiating between 'looking at something' and 'walking into something', observing and being observed, asking and being asked. According to the Belgian dramaturge Marianne van Kerkhoven, the dramaturgy, which emerges from this situation, is a "dramaturgy of perceiving" or a "dramaturgy of the spectator" who is both mentally and

26 In this work Takayama attempts to understand the city of Tokyo from the words and the impressions of foreign workers who may be employed to work on facilities for the 2020 Tokyo Olympics, together with workers from construction sites in the era of the 1964 Tokyo Olympics. The lives of these individuals become entangled with the life of the city of Tokyo (cf. Ozawa Keisuke: Where is the Other? Or, In Search of an Embedded Other. In: Araki Natsumi / Kim Sunjung / Ozawa Keisuke / Wu Dar-Kuen (eds): *My Body, Your Voice. Roppongi Crossing 2016*. Exhibition catalogue. Tokyo: Mori Art Museum 2016, pp.163–165, here p. 165).

Fig. 2: Lampros Moustakis in his tent with a participant, *X Apartments Athens*, 2015.

bodily engaged.[27] The blurring of the clear distinction between the private "seen as the realm of particularity and difference"[28] and the public defined as an homogeneous universalism oriented toward consensus,[29] urges spectators to think of their differences and particularities both as individuals and as citizens living together in contemporary multiethnic societies – in other words, to think *politically*. As Takayama points out in a recent interview, spectators are at the same time active and passive: "What is needed here is a theory of spectatorship and receptiveness that isn't pulled into the dichotomy of active-versus-passive. That kind of discourse has collapsed, I want to build a receptiveness in which that schema itself breaks apart."[30] The effect that Takayama desires is neither alienating nor assimilating the audience, but rather coexisting with the audience.

27 Marianne van Kerkhoven: European Dramaturgy in the 21st Century: A Constant Movement. In: *Performance Research* 14:3 (2009): On Dramaturgy, pp. 7–11, here p. 11.

28 Mouffe: *The Return of the Political*, p. 71.

29 Ibid.

30 Evacuating Theatre. Akira Takayama in Conversation with Dramaturge Marcus Dross. In: Lehmann / Hayashi / Pees (eds): *Evacuating Theatre*, pp. 247–253, here p. 251.

Shared spaces

I consider Takayama's work with the homeless people in an abandoned train station as an exemplary project of the condition of *togetherness* which lies at the very core of his work since the inaugural production of Port B in 2003. The three temporary shelters of Larissis Station were literally used as spaces for discussion and exchange: 3 microagoras of becoming-together, where multiple precarious conditions were overlapping – the precariousness of the homeless, the (ontological) precariousness of the spectators, the precariousness of the site, the precariousness of the whole *X Apartments* constellation. Takayama achieved the condition of togetherness exactly through this multilayered condition of precariousness in the sense Isabell Lorey analyzes in her essay *State of Insecurity* (following Judith Butler), where it is the term for a socio-ontological dimension of lives and bodies. Precariousness relates not to life itself, but rather to the conditions of existence. It is not what makes everyone the same but rather what is shared by all[31]:

> *Although* they need protection, living bodies can never be completely protected, specifically because they are permanently exposed to social and political conditions, under which life remains precarious. The conditions that enable life are, at the same time, exactly those that maintain it as precarious. All security retains the precarious; all protection and all care maintain vulnerability; nothing guarantees invulnerability.[32]

Takayama invites both performers and participants to equally participate in the dialogue and the verbal exchange about the broader notion of home, both physical and mental, real or imaginary but also about issues which are appealing contemporary Greek society such as precarization and povertization as well as the normalization of crisis. By creating a common space of mutual exchange (however partial and provisional), Takayama invites his audience and his co-creators to a common awareness of this "*shared* precariousness"[33], which does not

31 Isabell Lorey: *State of Insecurity. Government of the Precarious*. London / New York: Verso 2015, p. 19.
32 Ibid., p. 20.
33 Ibid.

exist beyond the social and the political.[34] Being welcomed by the three "experts", spectators are progressively transformed into visitors. Each visitor is invited to deal with a fragmentary picture of the 'real' world as a sample of a larger information system in which he/she is equally participating. By this 'sharing situation', visitors overcome the stigmatization of social precariousness as a dangerous condition which concerns the marginalized *Others*.

It is not by chance that Takayama takes his distances from the current collaborative turn which is often related with activist-inspired methods.[35] In a recent interview he insists on a clear separation between art and activism: "I am not an activist, so I am not involved directly in a situation. I am an artist. So I am always trying to make a space which is very un-political and un-economic but, afterwards, becomes political."[36] By avoiding being political in the literal, direct sense, he blurs the boundary between the ordinary and the extraordinary, confusing the senses of the audiences. As Kyoko Iwaki argues, "when the audience enters a world where the everyday and the theater are seamlessly integrated"[37], there is a possibility to gradually start mistaking the two realms, the ordinary and the extraordinary, the tangible and the imagined. Takayama wishes that the audience, however slowly, would literally start to take in their everyday lives as unfamiliar aesthetics principles. The political function of 'Home project' resides precisely in this decision to bring together two forms of reality: the iconic/poetic/imaginary and the raw/tangible/mundane. By clashing with the normative model of a homogenized collective identity, this encounter brings new possibilities of coexistence and cohabitation into being.

The small community of people who came together every ten minutes (in total, 25 couples of visitors every day) interrelated with the emptiness of the abandoned train station and the surrounding dense urban cityscape, opening to unknown, borderless mental landscapes. In other words, Takayama's multilayered urban intervention confronted the audience with an extended horizon of perception engaging them profoundly with their environment in a realm in-between the real

34 Ibid.

35 Lind: Collaborative Turn, p. 28.

36 Video interview for *X Apartments*' documentation team (unedited).

37 Cf. Iwaki: The Politics of the Senses, p. 216.

human presences and their 'representation'. It is interesting perhaps, to remark that Takayama's 'homeless homes' maintained a strong sense of the physical and the tactile floating between the formed and formless, inner and outer, serious and playful. The unexpected 'occupation' of the station enabled spectators/visitors to fully engage their imagination in an expanded theatricality within the unfamiliar, highly dispersed urban space of a chaotic metropolis such as Athens. Unlike his previous tour projects, which were transforming the city into an open virtual stage, the 'Home Project' was an 'analogue' project, which returned to the ancient Greek origins of theater when it was a public place for discussions and debates about politics and society. It is based on a discursive structure that enters both the sphere of politics and aesthetics, interconnecting various mediums, distinct personal trajectories, various interrogations on perception, both visual (optic) and tactile (haptic). The minimum units here were the three blue tents which encapsulated time blurring the boundaries between the ordinary and the extraordinary, the private and the public, the familiar and the unfamiliar. For Takayama,

> the audience members are performers; they are performing a Gestus in the Brechtian sense. There is a Japanese phrase saying truth comes out of falsehood. There is a point at which the theatre work's Gestus and the individual lives of the spectators intersect, and then a certain something that they had been doing as an act within the framework of this work becomes something that they actually do. It is in areas like this that I sense potential.[38]

So "what Takayama attempts to do in his own work is to be a 'theatre director' in the pre-modern sense, 'creating a path for people to go out into the real city'."[39]

38 Cf. Evacuating Theatre, p. 250.
39 Akira Takayama / Michiko Tsuda: Can Artists Return the Gaze of the Other? Confronting Censorship from the Bottom-Up. In: Artists' Guild + Arts Commons Tokyo (eds): *Our Feardom of Expression and Internalization of Censorship*. Tokyo: Torch 2016, pp. 85–89, here p. 87.

Narges Hashempour

Theatrical Performances in Today's Iran

Oscillating between Individual and Collective Being

Introduction

The essential elements for the establishment of every theatrical performance are two groups of members: the participants (the audience) and the performers, both of whom are physically co-present and mutually interact in a specific space and time with each other. In every theatrical performance, there is a constant power struggle and the participants are co-subjects in the performance, and as Fischer-Lichte says: "Each individual participant – even if to a different extent – co-determines the course of the performance as well as lets himself be determined by it, there is no one who would 'passively' take part in the performance."[1] This feature exists in every form of established performance, be that in a religious, ritualistic community, where "ritual and theatrical elements are closely intertwined"[2], or in aesthetic theater performances. However, each form of established theatrical performance also displays the social reality of the performance

1 Erika Fischer-Lichte: Culture as Performance: Theatre History as Cultural History. http://ww3.fl.ul.pt/centros_invst/teatro/pagina/Publicacoes/Actas/erika_def.pdf (accessed January 31, 2017).

2 Erika Fischer-Lichte characterizes religious plays as cultural performances in which "ritual and theatrical elements are closely intertwined." (Erika Fischer-Lichte: Theater und Fest. Anmerkung zum Verhältnis von Theatralität und Ritualität in den geistlichen Spielen des Mittelalters. In: E. F.-L. / Ingrid Kasten (eds): *Transformation des Religiösen: Performativität und Textualität im geistlichen Spiel.* Berlin: de Gruyter 2007, pp. 3–17, here p. 3.)

participants as well as the shifting historical concepts of culture, cultural norms and discourses through its specific theatrical elements and characteristics.

In order to determine how the dialogue or communication between participants in every established theatrical performance is created, the first thing to ask is which model of culture the established performance is based on and then, within this frame, to analyze how the relationship and communication between the performers and audience is established. Thus, the question would be: Will a specific attitude towards the participants in different models of culture determine the possibility of thinking in common and, if so, how are the specific strategies and aesthetics of the stage then utilized?

In this article, I will therefore examine the audience's status and role in two different theater performances based on two contrasting models of culture in today's Iran: one belongs to traditional, religious culture and the other to Iran's perception of developing modern culture. I define the post-revolutionary period in Iran as a liminal[3] time of being that oscillates between these two cultures, which is evident in almost every socio-cultural phenomenon in Iranian contemporary society, and of course also in the Iranian performing arts. To this end, I will first elaborate the function, role and status of the audience in Ta'ziyeh,[4] the Shi'a passion play, as a collective performance of Iranian

3 In accordance with Homi Bhabha's work, with 'liminal time' or 'in-betweenness' I mean a time in which a multitude of contradictions co-exist simultaneously; the complex and ambivalent oscillation between different binaries becomes possible. Moreover, there is no final meaning for a phenomenon, while every meaning of the phenomenon is in permanent change and transformation. It is a time of bridging between the past and present, historically different characters and events. It is also a time of breaking with past rules, while still looking for alternative ones.

4 Ta'ziyeh is a Shi'a cultural performance and mourning ceremony; a form of traditional public storytelling (*naghali*) and elegy (*marci-e sarayi*) accompanied by music (*museghi*), in which actors perform the death of Imam Hussein, the grandson of the Prophet Mohammed, and his followers' martyrdom on the plains of Karbala. In the sixteenth century, during the reign of the Safavid dynasty (1502–1722), Ta'ziyeh first grew popular. In the Qajar dynasty (1794–1925), Ta'ziyeh was further popularized. It was however subsequently banned during Reza Pahlavi's reign (1915–1941) because of the newly emerged discourse about modernity. During the reign of the Shah Mohammad Reza, particularly during the time that Iran hosted the Shiraz Arts Festival (from 1967), Ta'ziyeh became very much the center of attention again, not only for Iranian but also for Western avant-garde theater directors, such as Peter Brook. Since the Islamic Revolution of 1979 and the post-revolutionary

traditional, religious culture, within which the actors and audience are united as a community. Ta'ziyeh has survived until today in Iranian performance traditions through the employment of specific codes and symbols, habitual behaviors and its audience's faith and convictions. The other will be an example of a contemporary performance in Iran called *U-Turn*, which I saw in Tehran in 2010, as an illustration of Iran's modern culture, which is linked to at least 150 years of gradual transformation in all social and cultural spheres. I want to show how the re-enactment of authoritative speech acts from daily life in this performance, along with the other stage strategies, invites the participants to behave as individuals, not collectively. That is to say, the performance introduces a new mode of interaction between the performers and audience, creating a form of counter-community.

The Ta'ziyeh *Imam Hussein* (Tehran 2009): a community of collective identity

It was in 680 AD, during the reign of Yazid I, the second Caliph of the Umayyad caliphate, and in the plains of Karbala in present-day Iraq that the tragic death of Hussein ibn Ali, the Prophet Mohammed's grandson, and of his followers occurred. In Medina, Hussein ibn Ali was entreated by the Caliph's subjects to lead them in an uprising against Yazid I. Several letters composed by his subjects portray Yazid as politically oppressive and morally corrupt. Initially, Hussein dispatched scouts to report back to him. Then he assembled a caravan, including a number of close relatives, and left the Hejaz for Iraq. Yazid sent a huge force to intercept him and the caravan was surrounded. In the standoff, Hussein was ordered to offer an oath of allegiance (*bay'at*) to Yazid, which he refused to do, despite ten days of negotiations and sporadic fighting. Yazid I then denied Hussein and his followers access to food and water for three days in an attempt to force

period, Ta'ziyeh was identified by the Islamic government of Iran and became the symbolic representation of Islamic culture and identity. Ta'ziyeh performance is interwoven with everyday-life experiences, norms, conventions and other aspects of Iranian culture to the extent that most social movements in Iran involving protest or uprising against injustice and tyranny often associate themselves with the symbolic images of Ta'ziyeh. For example, in the protests of 1978, demonstrators identified themselves with Hussein's followers, Ayatollah Khomeini with Hussein, and the Shah and his supporters with Yazid.

them to bend to his authority. In the final battle, Hussein, along with most of his male relatives and supporters as well as some women and children, was killed. Shemr, the commander of Yazid's army, beheaded Hussein, who had already endured great suffering from his thirst. The remaining survivors were taken as prisoners, including Hussein's sister, Zeynab, a few women and children and Hussein's son, Zayn al Abedin, who was unable to join in the battle due to illness. These prisoners were put in chains and transported, together with the heads of the 'martyrs' held aloft on spears, to Yazid's court in Damascus. All along the route, crowds gathered to protest in the city markets. Hussein's surviving relatives, particularly his sister Zeynab and his son Zayn al Abedin, denounced Yazid for his cruelty to the descendants of the Prophet Mohammed.

The re-enactment of the main elements of the above story of the Shi'a Muslim passion play occurs in every Ta'ziyeh performance, including the one that I saw in Tehran 2009 in the *tekyeh* (specific large public courtyards for the performance) *Nafarabad*. Sitting around the circular-shaped stage, the audience surrounds the performers in the center. Women sit on one side and men on the opposite side, and together they engage in loud lamentation. The actor playing Shemr reads his speech from a piece of paper, accompanied by live music. When his role is over, he joins the audience and weeps with them over Hussein's headless body. Heaps of chopped straw in the corner of the stage represent the dust and sand on the scorching plain of Karbala. In moments of tragic tension, the heads of the audience and the actors are strewn with chopped straw. A copper basin brimming with water indicates the river Euphrates, evoking the torment of thirst suffered by Hussein and his followers. A red cloth represents the blood and wounds of the martyrs. The protagonists are dressed in black and dark green and carry or wear a small item, such as a green shawl or turban. The antagonists are dressed in brash red clothes and ostentatious jewelry. The actors have strong vocal ability and are professional singers.[5] The actor playing Hussein declares: "I am not Imam Hussein;

5 The Ta'ziyeh text is poetic, usually in verse, composed in a lyrical poetry style that is known as 'long meter' (*bahre-e tavil*), and the lines are chanted here by the protagonists and declaimed by the antagonists.

I am only playing his character."[6] A male actor whose face is veiled with a green veil and whose body is covered head-to-toe with a voluminous black garment to conceal his gender performs the female role of Fatimah, the daughter of Mohammed and mother of Hussein. He sings in a very elegiac, moving tone about the death of Hussein.[7] At one point in the performance, the actor playing Hussein circles the stage several times riding a white horse. This represents the journeys from one city to another. He never moves in a straight and direct line between two points. This is the moment of leaving for the battle at Karbala and saying goodbye to his children and family.

There are many other performative elements in this performance, which lasts for two hours, however, as the focus here is on theatrical communities, I will now turn to the active role of the audience and the occasional role reversal of actors and spectators in the performance as one of the ways in which the two groups operate together to create the performative experience. An old man covers his face with both hands and groans loudly, his tears running down his cheeks and fingers. Although he knows the whole story by heart, he still comes here every day during the Arabic lunar month of Muharram.[8] Another woman, covering her face with her black *chador*, weeps loudly and beats her breast. An old man carries a water bag on his shoulder and walks freely between the audience and stage, offering the people water to drink as a reminder of Hussein's thirst. When Hussein chants with his sister Zeynab to say goodbye to his children and family as he leaves

6 In Ta'ziyeh, the acting style is connected to the aesthetic principles of *tashbih*, a religious concept from the Iranian Shi'a tradition. Performers should not embody the characters they portray and they visibly read their texts from sheets of paper in order to hinder the illusion of a unity of performer and portrayed character (*tashbih*). The actors who play the saints or the antagonist make clear several times that they will follow the tradition of resemblance (*tashbih*). This is due to the fact that the characters (saints and enemies) are both viewed as absolute. Thus, according to traditional belief, in real life no human being could be as pure and holy as Hussein, or as completely evil as Shemr.

7 Since the use of makeup and masks in Ta'ziyeh is forbidden, here it is only the color of the veil that the actor wears and the tone of his voice that represent the female character he is playing.

8 The passion play was performed all year round, especially during the Arabic lunar months of Muharram and Safar. The first ten days of Muharram are the anniversary of the journey of Hussein and his family from Medina and the final battle on the plain of Karbala.

for the battle at Karbala, one of the audience members brings her baby onto the stage and lays the baby in front of Hussein. Hussein tears off a piece of his clothing, spreads the cloth out on the floor and places the baby on it. In this moment, the baby is symbolically transformed into the dead body of Ali Asghar, Hussein's six-month-old son who was killed during the Battle of Karbala, and the piece of white cloth becomes his grave. Hussein and his sister Zeynab then start reciting text in an elegiac tone to mark Ali Asghar's death.

It is clear from what I have described that a dynamic relationship between the audience and actors is one of the specific features of Ta'ziyeh.[9] This characteristic is also significant in other Eastern traditional theater forms, for instance in Indian Kathakali and Japanese Kabuki and Noh. Like in these other forms, the audience in Ta'ziyeh is familiar with the material being presented – in fact they are intimately familiar with all the details of the tragedy; however, the audience's role of participation in the Ta'ziyeh performance is different from those other traditional theater forms. The Ta'ziyeh audience is not there, as in other traditional theater forms, to evaluate how performers meet or exceed the standards of artistry that have been established by previous generations of expert performers. They are there to commemorate the story of Karbala and to weep with the performers during the performance of Ta'ziyeh as an expression of their common faith.

Therefore, despite the performers' task of provoking emotions through resemblance to the extent that the audience expresses sorrow by weeping, there is no necessity to establish adequate character backgrounds or descriptive and detailed psychological characteristics. Simple symbols are enough to evoke and remind the audience of the tragedy of Karbala. Thereby, in this circular space, essentially a theater in the round, it is possible that "on the one hand, the actor [who] is not performing at the moment lingers near the stage and cries over Hussein's innocence. On the other, the spectator [who] is moved by the play stands up and participates in the action as a member of the chorus."[10] Furthermore, when the performance of the actor (the *shabih* or the

9 This characteristic also attracted the attention of some of the most influential Western avant-garde directors in the late 1960s, such as Peter Brook and Jerzy Grotowski.

10 Parviz Mamnooun: *Ta'zieh: Schiitisch-Persisches Passionsspiel*. Vienna: Notring 1967, p. 115.

resembler) is finished, he joins the audience and accompanies them in the emotional display of mourning, weeping and chanting which the audience has already been doing throughout the play. The audience also contributes actively to the event of the performance through its vocal participation in weeping and repeating some words, in addition to entering the stage and eating and drinking, etc. As there is no distinct division between spectators and performers, the experience is intensified. Since it was promised that Hussein shall intercede with God for those who weep for him and his followers and will thus have the privilege of joining him and his circle on Judgment Day, the actors, be they protagonist or antagonist, as well as the audience deliberately work at producing this public display of weeping. Thus, the actors become actor-spectators and the audience becomes audience-actors, and at certain moments, the two groups become one. They are co-players in the 'communicative circle' of the event and the success of the event depends equally on both of them. Together, they establish a religious, ritualistic community where the performers and the audience gather because of their common faith and beliefs, ultimately strengthening their traditional identity. William O'Beeman views the active participation of the spectators in Ta'ziyeh as a function of paramount importance, aimed at re-commemorating their cultural structures and norms:

> [The] Ta'ziyeh performance offers the opportunity for the spectators [...] to renew their commitment to a religious and ideological order of which they are already an integral part. This ideological order does not limit itself strictly to religious dimensions but includes a political and nationalistic dimension as well.[11]

Hence, the time on stage is not used to develop the plot or the character or to make the dramatic characters readable for the audience. Rather it is spent by both the actors and the audience in displaying and identifying typological characteristics such as untruthfulness, mischievousness, honesty and loyalty so that, based on these, they may

11 William O. Beeman: Cultural Dimensions of Performance Conventions in Iranian Ta'ziyeh. In: Peter J. Chelkowski (ed.): *Taziyeh: Ritual and Drama in Iran*. New York: New York UP / Soroush 1979, p. 30.

identify themselves with any of the characters. Therefore, the dynamic interaction between the audience and the performers results in the formation of a community based on a common set of beliefs and values embodied by their religious faith. Furthermore, the repetition of the performance and its creation of a community of mourners also allow them to repeat and confirm their specific social and cultural roles. By involving themselves in the performance of Ta'ziyeh and taking part in conventionalized actions and interactions, actors and audience embody a community in which they constantly interact, ultimately strengthening their sense of belonging and identity. Finally, together, the performers and audience re-enact the process of life and death, a cycle that is universally experienced and thus shared by every member of this temporary community as well, further reinforcing their sense of common identity. (Fig. 1)

Ta'ziyeh performances are also based on a cultural model that displays homogenous and stable cultural meaning,[12] in other words, a model that attempts to stabilize and circumscribe the possibilities of experience for the different groups within that culture. That is to say, in Ta'ziyeh's involvement of complex cultural sign systems[13] such as

12 Here I am referring to Erika Fischer-Lichte's description of two models of meaning generation in culture: "The meanings [...] will exhibit a high degree of stability and homogeneity in a culture which, on the one hand, fixes and restricts the possibilities of experience within quite clear bounds for the different groups (e. g. children and adults, adults and old people, men and women, tribe and tribal chief, shaman and the non-initiated) and, on the other hand, successfully occludes outside influences." The other model of culture involves meaning that has contact with other cultures and is not restricted to rigid rules, "governing the possibilities of experience by the single persons and individual groups". These meanings produced are marked by "instability and heterogeneity in the meanings constituted in it. On the one hand, this latter culture will encourage the division of the complex of meaning to denotation and connotation, given that even it cannot get by without a minimum of mutually accepted meanings." (Erika Fischer-Lichte: *The Semiotics of Theatre*, transl. from the German by Jeremy Gaines / Doris L. Jones. Bloomington: Indiana UP 1992, pp. 2–3.)

13 Fischer-Lichte defines culture as a general concept that is generated by the human. Everything produced by the human signifies something, i. e. has meaning. She argues that the sum total of human productions constitutes a specific culture and functions as system. For example, social rules, religious customs, rules on clothing and many other cultural productions function as a system of the specific culture in which they are produced. These cultural systems do not inherently contain meaning; rather it is produced through the creation of signs. The users of the signs attribute the specific meaning to the signs created. Meaning emerges when the sign-user

Fig. 1
The Ta'ziyeh
Imam Hussein,
Tehran, 2009.

music, costume, acting style, architecture and dramatic text, it generates identifiable symbolic meanings that function for the performers and the audience simultaneously in the context of Iranian traditional culture. As the performers and spectators are members of the same culture and most likely share the same social experiences, convictions, common beliefs and perceptions of truth, the result is a communicative model of a fixed-sign system, through which stereotypes are performed and reinforced, and emotional bonds between performers and spectators are created. Ta'ziyeh is therefore a representation of collective being in Iranian traditional culture.

Thus, the underlying theatrical code as norm,[14] in the case of Ta'ziyeh, includes cultural symbolic stereotypes that carry momentous cultural significance. Codes, signs, costumes and props are all utilized to achieve cultural representation alongside theatrical symbolization. One important example is the idealized cultural and religious representation of gender; whether that may be physical representation

relates it to something within the context of the sign, which is historically and culturally determined. In her view, theater is one of the cultural systems and demonstrates the same features as any other cultural system: it generates meaning through its specific sign systems. Fischer-Lichte describes theater and performance as a theatrical text that is formed from different sign systems, in which the dramatic text is one of its signs. Thus in order to read and analyze theater, all of its sign systems should be regarded as part of the theatrical text. Ibid., pp.1–3.

14 Cf. ibid., p. 177.

(actors performing a female role wearing a black veil and covering their bodies and faces completely as the conventional embodiment of femininity) or character representation (portraying sympathetic characters in green costumes and objectionable characters in red costumes).
In Ta'ziyeh the symbols and icons create the participants' identities as performer and spectator. Moreover, traditional, religious participants share the common core of their identity, faith, behavior and attitudes in their culture and linguistic environment through the symbolic codes of the historical events of Ta'ziyeh. In fact, they link their contemporary sense of the world and its corresponding needs and problems to the historical story of Ta'ziyeh. Ta'ziyeh should therefore be regarded as a "cultural performance"[15], which illustrates the Iranian traditional, religious image and understanding of 'self'. I will now turn to a contrasting example of contemporary modern performance in Iran, in which the audience is more heterogeneous and from different parts of society while the stage strategies are aimed at provoking the audience's individuality rather than a collective way of thinking.

Hamid Pourazari's *U-Turn* (Tehran, May 2010)

In 2010, I visited a performance by the theater director Hamid Pourazari, who was born in 1968 and is well-known for working in unusual spaces with non-professional actors and people from the fringes of society. The performance, which I will now describe, was called *U-Turn* and was performed by young artists and Amir Kabir University students for one month in Tehran. (Fig. 2)
The audience buys their tickets from a car parked in front of Café Lorca. They then get into two minibuses, which drive a predefined route. During the drive, they hear female and male voices and narrations over the loudspeakers, voices and narrations of people they will meet during the performance. The minibuses come to a halt at the five-story circular car park belonging to Amir Kabir University. The audience gets out and receives their itinerary, consisting of numbered

15 Here I am referring to the theory of "cultural performance" elaborated by Milton Singer. See: Milton Singer: The Cultural Pattern of Indian Civilization: A Preliminary Report of a Methodological Field Study. In: *The Far Eastern Quarterly* 15:1 (1955), pp. 23–36. http://www.jstor.org/stable/2942100 (accessed January 4, 2018).

Fig. 2
Hamid Pourazari:
U-Turn,
Tehran, 2010.

parking spaces. Groups of four to five audience members are then separated into eleven waiting parked cars, which set off in four different directions. Over the next few hours, the audience is confronted with various stories inside and outside the cars and participates in events that make it difficult to tell who is an actor and who is a member of the public. When they have all experienced the different versions of the performance, the audience members come together again in a specific location, where an actress tells a story about her childhood during the Iran–Iraq War (1979–1987). As she tells the story through a loudspeaker, the actress leads the members of the public down into a tunnel, the ceiling of which gets lower and lower the further they enter, forcing them to stoop in order to be able to continue. The tunnel finally ends in a courtyard outside a car park building. A group of actors is playing drums. Other actors are throwing down photographs from windows. They are pictures of the audience, taken by hidden cameras during the car journeys. The members of the public collect the photos, get back into the waiting buses and are let out at Café Lorca again.

There are numerous instances of dynamic interaction between the audience and the performers in Pourazari's work. A young writer expresses her inability to complete the story that she is working on and asks the audience to find a solution. A young woman sitting in the back seat of a car speaks to her therapist on her mobile phone and asks the audience's opinion about the best approach. However, here I would like to focus broadly on just one example of the performance, where the actors re-enact and iterate socio-political speech acts from daily life which are familiar to the audience.

At the beginning, in the car park, several actors appear dressed as young paramilitary volunteer militia. They re-enact a situation familiar to the spectators from their daily lives, namely the enforcement of social and political rules, such as when public space is occasionally taken over by the militia for moral punishment or security reasons. For instance, a performer with a mask covering his mouth and a camera in his hand orders me to get into a car in which there are already three other people. I laugh at him and tell him that this is not the car I am supposed to take. Then, for a moment, a conversation inside the car grasps our attention. In the backseat, a young couple is fighting with each other. A frustrated young man asks the woman: "Are you satisfied with this situation now? Do you like what is happening here? Is this a theater?" In response, the young girl shouts back: "No! Stop talking."

I am unable to tell if they are actors or audience members. Suddenly the first performer comes back to me again and asks for my ID. I laugh again and respond: "It is in my bag and it is difficult to show you." He shouts at me: "Then how can I identify you?" At this moment, a woman inside the car calls out to him in an aggressive manner and says: "Don't shout!" The man responds to her in the same tone and says: "Cover your hair and look after your *hijab*, my sister." She responds: "I am not your sister and don't talk to me in such a loud voice!" He shouts even louder: "This is my voice!" Then he orders the driver to go and tries to force me to enter the car. I escape and run through the car park to follow my itinerary. As I am walking and sometimes running, I encounter other people who I assume are part of the play, who instruct me and other audience members (I assume) to move in one direction or another, not to enter a specific area, not to sit or stand and so forth.

However, during the course of the performance, I realize that, as a member of the audience, I have the right to include or exclude myself and to negotiate freely throughout the performance. Every time the actors address the audience – forcing them to follow instructions, telling them how they should move, which direction they should go, which car they should enter, or ordering them to separate from their friends – they are opening up a new space for the audience to discuss with others, be that the performers or other spectators, to move and behave differently. This creates new modes of interaction between the performers and myself, my "movements" and "different perceptual possibilities"[16] because both sides (actors and spectators) know that the re-enactment of these 'real-life' authoritative speeches does not carry the same legitimized meaning in the performance as in real life. These speech acts are re-enacted in a displaced manner: displaced from the specific authoritative socio-political conventions, laws and places where they are normally imposed. I feel, here and now in the performance, safe enough, as a member of the audience, to investigate the 'authority' of those speech acts and question them, which I do not do when confronted with the same speech acts in daily life.

Although it therefore may not at first appear like it, there is a consensus between the actors and spectators; however, it is not based on shared ideologies and common beliefs as it is in Ta'ziyeh. Instead, it functions as a temporal agreement between the actors and the audience to give the audience the agency to subjectively and intersubjectively engage in negotiation with and resistance against these social, authoritative speech acts. These 'displaced' and re-enacted authoritative speech acts are not seeking to affirm those that occur in daily life, rather they produce different effects and understandings which are specific to each unpredictable performance. One effect is to provoke the audience members into rethinking and reflecting on their own role and position, as well as their own individual relationship to those speech acts. Moreover, the actor's speech acts force the spectators into "new behavior patterns [...] often plunge them into crisis, thus denying the spectators the position of distanced, uninvolved observers."[17] Therefore, in the course of the performance, I acquire the agency to react differently, protest or follow the actor's instructions and orders, which I could not do in everyday life. I thus realize my own role in those speech acts by taking certain actions and responding in a certain way in everyday life. Moreover, the performance creates

16 See Erika Fischer-Lichte: *The Transformative Power of Performance: A New Aesthetics*, transl. from the German by Saskya Iris Jain. New York: Routledge 2008, pp. 107–108.
17 Ibid., p. 50.

a space for the possibility of resistance and makes me responsible for the function of the speech acts. In the course of the performance, the 'real' power that those speech acts are based on is therefore undermined and subverted.

In the two theatrical performances described above (Ta'ziyeh and *U-Turn*), the audience is a co-actor in the performance, creating a dynamic relationship between the stage event and the performance participants. The interchangeability of audience and actor is characteristic of both performances. However, as they are based on two different cultural systems of meaning, how they utilize specific stage strategies and aesthetics is totally different in each of them. In Ta'ziyeh, the performance is constructed from cultural symbolic orders about which both sides of participants are in agreement. These orders are shared by the two groups of members of the performance: spectator and actors. In contrast, in *U-Turn*, there is no symbolic order known by both sides, rather the performance emphasizes the subjectivity of the audience and his/her subjective experience in the performance. In Ta'ziyeh, the interchangeability of audience and actor allows the actors to interpret the meaning of what they are producing in real time, together with the audience; thereby they both present and reflect upon themselves at the same time. They are united as one. Every individual element in Ta'ziyeh refers "to the theatrical code underlying [...] the performance [...], a code which foresees a certain meaning being attributed to each element used."[18] In *U-Turn*, however, the specific rules and spatial arrangements in the unconventional space of the Amir Kabir University car park, in combination with different acting strategies such as re-enacting everyday speech acts, produces an individualized and subjective mode of experience. This is further emphasized when the spectators are forced to move and act differently in the performance; each participant experiences the performance's elements in a variety of ways. A spectator sitting in the car experiences one specific atmosphere, while another spectator walking through the car parks encounters another. The audience therefore does not "all perceive the same thing at the same time."[19]

18 Fischer-Lichte: *The Transformative Power of Performance*, p. 177.
19 Ibid., p. 62.

It can thus be concluded that the aesthetic of Ta'ziyeh's theatrical performance displays the social and collective identity of the audience while, in contrast, the aesthetic of *U-Turn*'s theatrical performance illustrates the individual identity of each audience member. Moreover, in Ta'ziyeh, tensions between the individual and the collective being as a whole are reduced, while in *U-Turn,* these tensions are increased. Based on different systems of cultural meaning, these two theatrical performances in today's Iran embody a complex and ambivalent oscillation between different binaries in a society that is currently going through a liminal phase in its development. This permanent oscillation between those binaries is of great complexity, demonstrating a deeply paradoxical ambivalence in a wide range of social, political as well as artistic phenomena.

Bernhard Siebert

Survey on Stage

Listening to the Audience in Kate McIntosh's *All Ears*

1.
Are you sure you are really interested in the preservation of the human race once you and all the people you know are no longer alive?
2.
State briefly why.[1]

These questions mark the beginning of Max Frisch's *Sketchbook 1966–1972*. It continues as follows:

3.
How many of your children do not owe their existence to deliberate intention?
4.
Whom would you rather never have met?
5.
Are you conscious of being in the wrong in relation to some other person (who need not necessarily be aware of it)? If so, does this make you hate yourself – or the other person?
6.
Would you like to have perfect memory?
[...] 16.
Are you convinced by your own self-criticism?

1 Max Frisch: *Sketchbook 1966–1971*, transl. from the German by Geoffrey Skelton. New York: Mariner 1974, p. 4.

[...] 20.

Do you love anybody?

[...] 23.

What do you need in order to be happy?

24.

What are you grateful for?

25.

Which would you rather do: die or live on as a healthy animal? Which animal?[2]

We are confronted with a questionnaire designed by Swiss writer and architect Max Frisch. But whom do these questions address? Are they "autocritical" – an expression proposed by Frisch himself? Or should they be considered mere sketches for another text, a dramatic text, maybe, in which those questions would be clearly asked within a dialogue?

A difficult situation. Frisch put this questionnaire at the beginning of his *Sketchbook*, published in the 1970s. (Helen and Kurt Wolff published the English translation by Geoffrey Skelton in 1974.) Having prepared his questionnaire for actual readers, Frisch, who died at the beginning of the 1990s, wanted us to be confronted by these intimate and introspective questions. Before talking about himself, Frisch wanted to show what a text can do, namely: ask, question, confront. He doesn't give us the key, nor indeed any answers. There's no premeditated reading of what could lead up to a certain typology. In his *Sketchbook*, this questionnaire is actually the first in a series of eleven texts. Every single one of these questionnaires has a specific topic: be it religion, homeland, friendship, hope, or humor. By interrogating us, Frisch also interrogated himself. It is surely a kind of *autocritique*, but we could also ask who really has the authority here, who is asking these questions. Is it the text? Is it Frisch? Is it ourselves, the readers? Since Frisch consciously decided to put those questions at the start of the book, this might also be a means of indicating that we are about to cross a border here, that we oscillate between the public mode and the private mode, that a published journal isn't a private diary any

2 Frisch: *Sketchbook 1966–1971*, pp. 3–4.

more. With this, Frisch turns his journal into something different. He asks us to read it attentively, to ask ourselves questions, to find our own answers.

In 1988, the publishing house Suhrkamp took the eleven questionnaires from Frisch's *Journal* and published them in a collection called *Fragebogen*, "questionnaire". Those small books have known a huge success, and they've been republished again and again. The title, *Fragebogen*, offers perplexity on multiple levels: Firstly, in German, the singular and plural forms of the term 'Fragebogen' are the same. Second, the term *bogen* is polysemic. It signifies a piece of paper, but it also signifies an arch or a bow. If we decide to stay with this signification of the bow, we could think of using this book of questions to shoot questions, like arrows, at different dialogue partners: from the author to a reader, from a reader to the author, but possibly also from one reader to another. Those questions are used, by the way, by the German weekly newspaper *Die Zeit*, which presents it to German personalities – much like Marcel Proust's questions are used in *Regard* and other newspapers. Frisch's exercise here is to transform the test into a text. Inspired by investigative sociological or psychological surveys published in magazines, for example, Frisch makes a literary text out of them, which doesn't really annihilate the question of authority inherent to the questionnaire. And, by the way, this questionnaire exercise isn't really that far away from a survey, and here, we'll get closer to the main topic of this paper. For the survey also is an investigative method.

It's necessary to ask about Frisch's reasons for implementing questionnaires into his diary *Tagebuch*. The supposed reasons have always been seen as a kind of moral initiative, as offering a pause to the audience for reflecting upon what happens in life, allowing for a moment of hesitation. We could also say that it expresses a wish to get to know his audience. This is, more or less, a survey method designed to draw a portrait of a readership. These are some of the questions authors ask themselves – for whom am I writing, whom am I addressing? Who reads me? For whom am I readable? Who's to be found on the other side of my artistic production? Through his questions, the author asks himself about his readers. In another part of the journal, written in 1948, Frisch talks about theater, as he brings up the notion of the theatrical: "[…] the word 'theatrical.' What does this stand for?"[3], he asks, and he responds:

> Theatrical diagnosis: Do the things I see and the things I hear bear any relation to one another? If not, if the point being expressed lies exclusively in the words, enabling me (if I wished) to close my eyes, then the stage itself is lying fallow, and what I perceive on it at this point (since naturally I do not close my eyes) is not a theatrical situation, but an irrelevant spectacle, a seemingly haphazard gathering of speakers, epic, lyric, or dramatic.[4]

"A seemingly haphazard gathering of speakers"! In quite the same manner that Frisch is asking himself questions about his readership, Kate McIntosh also asks herself questions concerning her audience or her audiences in her piece *All Ears*, created in Brussels in 2013. Readers and spectators – this is the very question of this book: About whom do we talk when we talk about an audience, or about audiences? This is a recurrent question, if we believe Nancy Delhalle in this respect when, in her recent publication *Le Théâtre et ses publics*, she stresses the fact that "as an art that's live and that's concerning life (*art vivant et du vivant*), theater, in the course of its history, has asked itself the question about the audience without interruption"[5].
As we enter the space of *All Ears*, Kate McIntosh sits at a white table in the left half of the space. She regards us attentively and takes notes. She waits, her arms relaxed against the table, sitting on a small stool. As soon as the spectators are seated, she takes the microphone placed in front of her. Without saying hello and without hesitating, she asks a first question:

> Just wondering, uh, how many people can whistle? I'm looking for whistlers, it … it could be something really simple like a kind of a [*whistling*] kind of thing, maybe, or, ah, maybe you know how to do the real, proper

3 Frisch: *Sketchbook 1966–1971*, p. 179.

4 Ibid., p. 181.

5 "[…] en tant qu'art vivant et du vivant, le théâtre, au cours de son histoire, s'est sans cesse posé la question du public." (Nancy Delhalle: Un lien pour le temps présent. In: N. D. (ed.): *Le Théâtre et ses publics: la création partagée*. Besançon: Les Solitaires Intempestifs 2013, pp. 29–38, here p. 29.)

> kind of wolf whistle. […] So if you know that you can whistle, ah, could you just raise your hand up in the air pretty clear so that we can see that. Ah. Perfect, right. Can you hold your hands up for a moment? We actually have thirty-seven whistlers. Thanks.[6]

Us? Whistling? What's happening here? Whistling, isn't this forbidden in theater spaces? And, to be honest, why does the performer want us to do it? The stage is almost empty, the audience lights remain on. To the right-hand side of McIntosh and behind her, we see different materials: strings, wood, chairs, sorted and arranged in a strange manner. We ask ourselves what this might be used for, and which turn this piece might take as is starts with such a simple question. But, as does Frisch, McIntosh lets other questions follow:

> Could we say that we have any punctual people here tonight? Is there anyone who likes to be on time? […] Maybe you were early tonight, if you know that's you, could you raise your hands now? […] Okay, that's 23, that's actually slightly less than yesterday, I think. Yeah, okay, that's a drop from yesterday.

Who has been dining alone in the last days? Who has seen ghosts? – Ah, no, this question wasn't to be included in this piece, McIntosh tells us. Where's South? Who's always late? Who knows some other person in the room but happens to have forgotten their name? Who has stolen something in his life – "just make a coughing sound"? Who has once been a member of a music band?

But the form of this survey quickly changes because, suddenly, McIntosh doesn't want her audience to raise their hands any more:

> Don't indicate for this, just think it through quietly for yourself. Perhaps now you're getting some sense of who's actually here tonight. I'd like you to think about people who you might have noticed. Is there anyone that interests you? Are there any people that you're drawn to or that you, you might

6 *All Ears* (Premiere: May 24, 2013, Pact Zollverein Essen, concept, performance: Kate McIntosh; artistic advice: Pascale Petralia, Tim Etchells). I have seen the piece on November 3, 2013 at Künstlerhaus Mousonturm, Frankfurt am Main. Thanks to Kate McIntosh for giving me a recording of the show.

wanna know more about? Are there some people that you really don't like the look of? Were you're like, ah, I'm gonna get stuck in a conversation with that person? It is linked to this thought, um, did you make a good choice of seat? [...] If you could change your position now, would you?

For a moment, we've become a mute audience again. No gesture, no mumbling – the spectators listen to the performer's words. But we're thinking of the others, we're referring to the others present – co-present – with us in the theater space. Everyone is on their own, we're all ears, but for the others, my responses, my reactions are not visible.

Tout ouïe, all ears. A little bit later, McIntosh shows her mastership in directing the audience when she gives directions without announcing them and without having prepared them. During the questions at the beginning of the piece, McIntosh had asked who finds it pleasant to listen to the sound of rain at night. A certain number of people had raised their hands. Now, she asks these persons (she calls them "rain people") to take a relaxed position and to close their eyes. As soon as their eyes are closed, McIntosh directs the others without words: With only her gestures, she divides the audience into three parts – left, center, right – and makes them produce sounds with their hands and legs. Slowly, we get the impression that these claps and clacks produce the sound of rain that starts falling lightly at first, but becomes stronger and stronger, only to get light again at the end – then, with a sign by McIntosh, people are asked to stop the sounds.

Many more things follow: the spectators will pull certain strings and throw balls on stage while McIntosh is off-scene, not without having left written instructions for the audience. As she comes back, she has changed her clothing and now wears a large microphone which signals to us that she is recording the sounds – sounds of a mute audience, of a thinking audience. Then, she asks the spectators to imagine that they are imprisoned in the theater space due to a problem with the doors' locking mechanism. After this, she switches off the light and puts on her sound recording of the rain that has been produced by the audience some minutes ago. This scene, which ends the piece, is also a moment of introspection for the spectators, who ask themselves: What has happened during this hour of theater? What has it made of us? Have we become a different audience?

"How can putting together different singularities give room for a being together (*être-ensemble*)?"[7] This has been one of Eliane Beaufils's questions for this research project. She asks how it is possible to take the individual into account while at the same time developing an *être-ensemble* (being-together) and an *être-avec* (being-with) as defined by Jean-Luc Nancy, among others.[8] Isn't that exactly what Kate McIntosh does in her scenic installation? McIntosh shows us that there is a problem: She has no difficulties in working with the audience, her piece *All Ears* works, and nevertheless, she doesn't know anything about how the different audiences in the different evenings are composed. If, obviously, it is always different spectators who are watching the show, it seems that there is no need for a special audience for the show to work, as it works all the time with *any* audience. And, if the audience is so exchangeable, how can it be taken seriously? Kate McIntosh has organized her own research day, or, let's say, research evening, to confront herself with the question of the audience, and to confront us, as an audience, with that question.

In this work, we literally have the possibility of changing places. "Who'd like to change places?", McIntosh asks at a certain moment. But actually, we can't really change places in the scenic dispositive. Even if we change our seat, we'll stay spectators, we stay at our places. "That space where the king and his wife hold sway belongs equally well to the artist and the spectator,"[9] Michel Foucault writes in *The Order of Things* when looking at Diego Velázquez's *Las Meninas*. In art, it seems that the place of the one who gazes can also be the place of the object as well as the place of the subject of the work: McIntosh is the artist of *All Ears*, but she puts herself on stage as both spectator and researcher. We are those who watch her, but at the same time we are also those who are being watched, while we gaze upon each other. We do all this without even accounting for the fact that we, too, are going to make theater.

7 "Comment la mise ensemble de singularités peut-elle donner lieu à un être ensemble?"

8 Cf. Jean-Luc Nancy: *Being Singular Plural*, transl. from the French by Robert Richardson / Anne O'Byrne. Stanford: Stanford UP 2000.

9 Michel Foucault: *The Order of Things. An Archeology of the Human Sciences*, transl. from the French by R. D. Laing. London: Routledge 1970, p. 15.

McIntosh isn't alone in stressing the spectators' exchangeable position: in Rimini Protokoll's *Situation Rooms* (2013), the audience takes on different roles, one after the other, to better understand the global arms market. The spectators, equipped with a tablet computer, move within the set following a route indicated on the screen. In his version of *Le Sacre du Printemps* (2007), Xavier Le Roy directs us as if he were an orchestra conductor, and the instruments' sound comes out of loud-speakers under our seats. There are similar examples in works by Philippe Quesne, Monster Truck, Frédéric Gies, Nicolas Stemann, Cuqui Jerez, or Ivana Müller, among others.

Kate McIntosh, nevertheless, announces her very own position in the title of her piece when she says that she herself is *"All Ears"*, as if to indicate that she's taken an alert position in which she takes notes and thinks. She collects statistic data. She directs and listens at the same time. And, as journalist Melanie Suchy puts it, "Kate McIntosh choreographs us, as well as our thoughts".[10] She takes demographic tools and makes choreographic ones out of them.

Can "All Ears" give us ideas for thinking about the question of being-together? What Kate McIntosh does, of course, is to show us how easy and yet how absurd it can be to make a research object out of the audience. What do we want to know? What evidence do we want to produce? Which epistemological system do we want to tap? It is easy to say that it is important to know well the place from which we speak, from which we start a survey. The place of observation is part of a dispositive, and it gives us a certain authoritarian power. It also questions the research dispositive we'll have to use to access sensitive data. But what McIntosh does is that she takes this survey dispositive and puts it on stage, all the while keeping certain roles in function.

Her piece thus also plays with the position of authority: Even if a part of the audience refuses to participate, there seems to be no way of escaping this survey dispositive. Refraining from voting keeps the audience in the game all the same. And even if many of the questions aren't very interesting, on either a sociological level or concerning introspection, they make us wonder what relationship they have with the overall dramaturgy. We could say that this is exactly why these

10 Melanie Suchy: Kate McIntosh: 'All Ears'. In: *tanz* 07 (2013), p. 44.

Fig. 1
Kate McIntosh:
All Ears, 2013.

questions are innocuous – because they have no implications, they merely allow everybody to become aware of the manipulation with a certain ludic distance.

Artistically, Kate McIntosh lets us take part in the research she does to better understand the relations between the audience's space and the stage. The dispositive of the survey does not simply serve to give her a prefabricated method of controlling the audience, it is rather by using this system that she strings together several public survey ambiances. She makes the multitude of strings that connect subjects and objects in the theater space visible, audible and perceptible.

And, like Frisch, in a certain sense, she opens her work sketchbook to give us a glance into what she is questioning herself, as an artist, and what she would like to ask, about us, together with us.

Gerald Siegmund

Against Participation, or: From a Distance

In August of 2004, to open the fifth International Summer Academy at Künstlerhaus Mousonturm in Frankfurt, Jacques Rancière was invited to give his now famous lecture on "The Emancipated Spectator."[1] Please forgive me if I begin my contribution to this year's summer laboratory at Künstlerhaus Mousonturm in Frankfurt with a reference to the *genius loci*, even though the exact *locus* of Rancière's lecture was in the big theater space next door from where I am speaking.[2] Apart from the fact that Rancière was "there," it seems appropriate to start with this reference, because we are, eleven years later, still occupied with the same questions that Rancière and many others before him have asked since the heyday of the 1960s social protest and the explosion of forms and types of theater and dance that accompanied it in one way or another.

The problem of spectatorship and of how to deal with the spectator, looker or viewer in a theater situation, still haunts every performance – so it seems. It touches at the core of what theater, performance or dance are, want to be, and, most of all, what they want to achieve. Where to place or not to place the spectator asks for special attention and individual solutions on the side of the artists. At the risk of being

1 Cf. Jacques Rancière: *The Emancipated Spectator*. London / New York: Verso 2009.

2 This text originally was a lecture held at Künstlerhaus Mousonturm in September 2015.

redundant in such a long-standing discussion, it may still be worth taking another look at the problem of participation and making a few further remarks on the subject.

My lecture is somewhat polemically titled "Against Participation", a title that may recall Susan Sontag's essay "Against Interpretation" from 1964,[3] in which she emancipated the spectator long before Rancière by absolving him or her from having to detect meaning in a work of art. He or she might as easily have an experience that provides insights into *how* our world is made instead of forcing him to find out what it means. As with Sontag's notion of interpretation, it is thus only a certain type of participation, and not participation as such, that I object to for reasons I will start to elaborate in what follows.

1. Looking is an activity

The central argument of Rancière's lecture holds that throughout its history, theater is only considered to be 'good theater' when it overcomes theater. For its critics, theater is only valid when it stops being theater. And theater stops being theater when spectatorship is abolished.

The criticism of theater already starts with Plato's exclusion of the theater from his ideal state. Since theater incites the people of the polis to leave their assigned places and cause disorder within the natural order of things, theater has to be excluded from the ideal state. With a different focus, the same anti-theatrical argument can be found in Jean-Jacques Rousseau's *Letter to D'Alembert* and, in the second half of the 20th century, as Jörn Etzold has pointed out, in Guy Debord's war on spectacle.[4] Traditional theater, as philosophers and artists alike argue, provides the spectator with false images and illusions that shield him or her from seeing the world as it really is. Theater is considered detrimental to knowledge. Apart from being fooled by illusion, the spectator is also condemned into passivity: The spectator is being cut off

3 Cf. Susan Sontag: Against Interpretation. In: S. S.: *Against Interpretation and Other Essays*. London: Penguin 2009, pp. 3–14.

4 Jörn Etzold: *Die melancholische Revolution des Guy Ernest Debord*. Zurich / Berlin: Diaphanes 2009; for a recent collection of essays on the anti-theatrical argument cf. Stefanie Diekmann / Christopher Wild / Gabriele Brandstetter (eds): *Theaterfeindlichkeit*. Munich: Fink 2012.

from his capacity to act. He or she is the passive recipient of images that alienate him or her from direct human interaction, which is considered to be the touchstone of a true community. Turning passive spectators into active participants, turning the worship of consumer idols into the participation in and the production of what is considered to be the self-presence of life or the social, this must be the aim of the theater if it wants to be socially and politically relevant. Emancipation promises knowledge and agency.

For Rancière, in the first half of the 20th century, Bertolt Brecht and Antonin Artaud are two examples of the overcoming of theater by theater itself. For Brecht, illusion must be overcome by a learned understanding of the social conditions that, outside the 'theater proper', stimulate the spectator to act for change. For Artaud, the passive body of the spectator must be consumed and transformed by energies that bring him into contact with his full physical and mental capacities.

From all the anti-theatrical arguments throughout history, a remarkably consistent list of oppositions can be compiled which marks the 'demarcation line' between good and bad theater:

Bad Theater	**Good Theater**
Passive	Active
Illusion	Action
Identification	Agency
Drama	Movement
Individual	Public
Transcendental	Relational
Imagination	Here and Now
Aesthetical	Ethical
Representation	Presence
Distance of false images	Self-possession of a community
Death	Life

In this list of oppositions, one term of the binaries is obviously valued higher than its complementary term. One is good, one is bad; one is emancipatory, one is deficient.

"Emancipation," however, as Jacques Rancière claims in his counter argument, "begins when we challenge the opposition between viewing and acting"[5]. It starts from the opposite principle, the principle of equality:

> Emancipation begins when we challenge the opposition between viewing and acting; when we understand that the self-evident facts that structure the relations between saying, seeing and doing themselves belong to the structure of domination and subjection. It begins when we understand that viewing is also an action that confirms or transforms this distribution of positions. The spectator also acts, like the pupil or scholar. She observes, selects, compares, interprets. She links what she sees to a host of other things that she has seen on other stages, in other kinds of places. She composes her own poem with the elements of the poem before her. [...] They are thus both distant spectators and active interpreters of the spectacle offered to them.[6]

For Rancière, the work of art belongs to the sphere of what we call 'reality.' As such, it operates on the same level as the political that divides the sensible matter in which we are grounded in a different way. Art redistributes the hegemonic "configuration of domination and subjection,"[7] thereby liberating the subject to see and hear differently. It allows for perspectives, points of view, and knowledge hitherto unseen or unheard of. This is the politics of aesthetics. By calling the performance a poem, Rancière bestows a certain autonomy on the performance that is created by its form. Thus, the performance itself possesses an 'inner distance', something irrecuperable in and by the performance itself, something absent that we may not possess, hold or understand, something that escapes us while we experience it, something that creates a distance from everyday activities and points of view we may hold. Rancière uses the term "a third thing"[8] to

5 Rancière: *The Emancipated Spectator*, p. 13.
6 Ibid.
7 Ibid.
8 Ibid., p. 15.

characterize the performance as an aesthetical experience. The performance as a "third" neither belongs to the performers or artists nor to the spectators. Although I strongly believe that the production process of a performance shows in the performance itself, there is no guarantee that just because the artists had a good and satisfactory working process, the performance as an aesthetic experience will be successful. Works of art resist the logic of cause and effect. Their outcome is unpredictable; their occurrence is an event. If the performance is a "third," then the distance between production and reception will be as inevitable as the distance between the spectator and the performance. The performance is something to which performers and spectators alike refer without being able to control.

What Rancière wrote in 2004 had already entered the literary criticism discussion in the 1960s and 1970s. My reference to Susan Sontag's "Against Interpretation" is a case in point. Rancière's "third" is what critics like Roland Barthes or Wolfgang Iser in Germany and the US most emphatically called a "text." A text is also written by the reader, it is a "writerly text," as Roland Barthes puts it.[9] A text is composed of many different elements and materialities that trigger the reader's or spectator's desire to play with its signifiers that are irreducible to any authorial intention. Iser saw the act of reading as a performative act that involved the reader in the text itself by means of his or her faculties of imagination and understanding.[10] He or she is implied in the text, his gaze or mind wanders through the text, actively constructing its world.

2. History

Each form or type of theater developed its own notion of spectatorship by assigning the audience a specific place within the architectural space of the theater. Theater and performance distribute their spaces according to what they want their audiences to do, which in turn defines what type of theater they are. Most famously, the bourgeois theater imagined and created an audience that sat behind the much

9 Cf. Roland Barthes: From Work to Text. In: R. B.: *Image – Music – Text*. London: Fontana 1977, pp. 155–164.

10 Wolfgang Iser: *The Act of Reading. A Theory of Aesthetic Response*. Baltimore: Johns Hopkins UP 1980.

maligned fourth wall in the relative dark, while the actors on stage pretended not to notice their presence. In times of political upheaval and revolutions, the bourgeois theater invented the absent spectator – and this absent spectator is the 18th-century version of the passive spectator that still haunts us today. But the fourth wall was not invented to turn spectators into passive beings. On the contrary: It came into being as a device to trigger the imagination and to create points of views. It enabled the spectators to imagine and understand social situations. It put them in a position to analyze the actions of individuals and their emotional reactions to these actions. It enabled the theater to become a tool for calmly observing society's fabrication in an analytical way in order to be able to go beyond the Here and Now. In short, the imagination that was set in motion by the invention of the fourth wall was meant to transform and create rather than to affirm the social.[11]

With the advent of performance art in the 1960s, the erstwhile radicalness of the fourth wall was long forgotten and buried in mere convention. Thus, the question of what to do with the spectator and how to address him or her became paramount again. The absent spectator was replaced by the visible spectator. In 1962, Susan Sontag, in her analysis of the new form of the Happening,[12] underlined that Happenings aimed at abolishing the distance between stage and auditorium to physically attack the audience. Thus the audience was placed on stage and turned into a scapegoat sacrificed and waiting to be transformed in the sense of Artaud to become performers themselves. But this renewed focus on audience participation did not primarily mean that members of the audience were physically involved in the *action* of happenings. On the contrary: While most Happenings, such as the famous first Happening by Allan Kaprow *18 Happenings in 6 Parts* in 1959 or Happenings by Robert Whitman such as *The American Moon* in 1960 or *Flower* in 1963, did away with the traditional proscenium stage and placed the audience within the performance space

11 Cf. also Gerald Siegmund: Der Einsatz des Spiels. Theater als Dispositiv der Wahrnehmung. In: Gerda Baumbach / Veronika Darian / Günther Heeg (eds): *Momentaufnahme Theaterwissenschaft. Leipziger Vorlesungen*. Berlin: Theater der Zeit 2014, pp. 187–198.

12 Susan Sontag: Happenings. An Art of Radical Juxtaposition. In: S. S.: *Against Interpretation and Other Essays*, pp. 263–274.

itself, they did not ask members of the audience to give up their position as observers of the action unfolding in very close proximity to their own bodies.

So participation, then, did not mean *agitating* the audience. It meant opening up other channels of reception: physical, sensual, acoustic, haptic. It meant drawing attention to the materiality of performance elements to the detriment of a closed narrative and meaning. Participation meant making an aesthetic experience for which, phenomenologically speaking, you need to experience the situation while knowing that you are experiencing it. There is a certain dialectic involved in the theater situation, a dialectics of being in and out at the same time when being in also means being out and *vice versa*. For many participatory performances today, this aim is still a valid goal of the performance.

However, if following Rancière, seeing from a distance is already a productive activity, then why do so many performances today insist on diminishing or even abolishing the gap between performers and spectators? Nicolas Bourriaud, once again making use of my chart of 'good' and 'bad' art or theater and inscribing himself into the more than two-thousand-year-old tradition of anti-theatrical prejudices, famously holds that art which develops what he calls *relational aesthetics* functions as an antidote to our increasingly alienated life in our societies of the spectacle.[13] Art provides possibilities of meeting and exchanging without the mediation of objectifying digital images. People look for spaces in which to come together and to interact, which are becoming increasingly scarce in contemporary consumer societies. Art therefore compensates a social loss or lack. It provides experiences that the real world is no longer able to provide. Turning spectators into participants therefore serves to legitimize theater, dance and performance as socially and politically relevant: 'My art is socially relevant. It makes people act instead of providing them with an escapist idea that is socially irrelevant.' It is easy to see that Bourriaud's argument engages in the very same logic that Rancière criticizes. It also – and this is another criticism that has been brought forward against relational aesthetics – overlooks the fact that art is still art and not social work. Within what Rancière calls the "aesthetic regime," even art

13 Nicolas Bourriaud: *Relational Aesthetics*. Dijon: Les Presses du Réel 2002.

works that cease to be art works aiming at pure relationality cannot help but be produced, sold, and perceived as art works. The overcoming of the audience-performer divide can only work productively once the split between audience and performers has been established and *continues to exist* for the relational work to produce its specific effect. This means that the exchanges from subject to subject provided by relational art take place within the confined institutional spaces of museums, galleries, or theaters where they are real and *not real* at the very same time. To put it bluntly: relational aesthetics is a luxury entertainment for the elite few of art consumers, a past-time that will not affect or change social problems.[14] This brings me to two more fundamental criticisms against participation understood as social compensation:

1. You cannot do away with the spectator, however hard you try.
2. Performances that pretend to do so fall prey to two fallacies:
   a. the fallacy of power and
   b. the fallacy of the Here and Now.

Let me continue with my first point against participation, the 'eternal spectator.'

3. Spectatorship forever

Doing away with the proscenium stage and the separation of stage and auditorium does not automatically abolish spectatorship in favor of communal acts of participation. Rather, whenever we deal with questions of the theater, which for my purposes here include performance and dance, there will always be spectatorship. Spectatorship as well as performing automatically emerge as *functions* or *symbolic positions* whenever the cultural practice of theater is called upon. The theater is thus a situation that emerges as soon as spectators and performers emerge. It emerges when the two parties meet as audience and performers. Performers and spectators occupy two structurally different, yet in Rancière's sense equal positions in the playing out of theater that they share.

At first sight, Bertolt Brecht's most radical idea of a theater without an audience – his Learning Play (*Lehrstück*) – seems to offer an alternative to this structural dilemma. A Learning Play is aimed at those who

14 Juliane Rebentisch: *Theorien der Gegenwartskunst*. Hamburg: Junius 2013, p. 62.

play it, i.e. only those who play in it will benefit from it by learning. There are only players in the Learning Play, so spectatorship is abolished. But at a closer look, this is not the case at all. In *The Measure Taken* (*Die Maßnahme*) for instance, the control choir serves as an audience. The four activists perform for the choir and in front of it. Second, the change of roles between the performers implies that they themselves are always observers of their own former roles and actions. They demonstrate to *others* – the choir, to themselves and to the other players – both as performers and as spectators of their performing. Thus, spectatorship in the Learning Play is distributed equally on stage and between the performers who switch from performing as acting to performing as observing and, by implication, distanced critical reflection. Rudolf von Laban's movement choirs that LIGNA revitalized in their piece *Tanz aller* in Römerberg Frankfurt in 2015 is another case in point. Like the Learning Play, the idea originated in the late 1920s to educate and teach workers or people in general, to instigate social change. The knowledge that we are part of a performance event immediately brings about a distance to one's dancing.

Therefore, spectatorship is always part of the deal unless theater stops being theater and becomes therapy, pedagogy, social practice or political activism. However, this is not to say that theatricality is not at work in all of these activities. Of course it is – from the staged carnivals of street protests that put moving and dancing bodies on display to the therapeutic function of role playing and performing, of masking and unmasking the self in therapeutic practices, theatricality is an inherent and foundational principle of almost all cultural practices. But all these activities have a directly ethical or pedagogical function. They are aimed at and against something; they strive for a cause and hope to be directly effective in bringing about change.[15] But theater, whenever it is called upon by an institution or by artists, is not pedagogy. Next to its social dimension of bringing people together, it also has an aesthetic function. The aesthetic function of theater always openly puts on display its own construction mechanisms that prevent any

15 For an interesting perspective on the role of the dancing body in political protest cf. Oliver Marchart: Dancing Politics. Political Reflections on Choreography, Dance and Protest. In: Gerald Siegmund / Stefan Hölscher (eds): *Dance, Politics, and Co-Immunity*. Zurich / Berlin: Diaphanes 2013, pp. 39–58.

performance, one step removed, from becoming *directly* effective as a social or political practice.

We should therefore take the position of the spectator seriously. The spectator brings something to the performance that the performer alone cannot bring: he or she brings *trust* in that which the performers have to *offer*. If artists pretend to have nothing to give, there will be nothing for the spectators to engage in and to create. The spectator *values* that which the performer gives and that is what turns theater into an act of recognition and acknowledgement. Theater relies upon the mutual trust that the performer offers something that I as a member of the audience do not have. The spectator, on the other side, will bring something the performers do not have without the active presence of the spectator: value.

To reformulate Rancière's position in Lacanian terms: the mutual engagement and trust in the emerging situation only comes about when both the members of the audience and the performers do NOT know what it is the other knows or has or what he or she is looking for.[16] Both spectators and performers are equal in the sense that they are not in possession of themselves and their knowledge. Spectators assume the performers know, but the performers will only get an idea of what it is they produce once they have engaged with the audience as audience and not as agitated performers. This, rather than the notion of participation, is the ethical dimension of theater: trust, value, and acknowledgement. The question of knowing more or less inherent in any theatrical situation brings me to my second objective: the question of power.

4. The fallacy of power, or: we are all equal

In most cases, participation in performances unfolds along the lines laid out by the production team of the show.[17] It is the production team and the performers that define the rules of the game the

16 Eva Holling has developed this idea in relation to the psychoanalytical concept of "transference", cf. Eva Holling: *Übertragung im Theater. Theorie und Praxis theatraler Wirkung.* Berlin: Neofelis 2016.

17 Marvin Carlson has pointed this out in relation to the participatory performances of the British group Punchdrunk; Marvin Carlson: Immersive Theatre and the Reception Processs. In: *Forum Modernes Theater* 27 (2012 [2016]), pp. 17–25.

spectators have agreed to play in. But these rules pre-define what I am allowed or expected to do or not to do in order to bring the performance about. Power, thus, is not equally distributed. Communication still remains directed communication. It creates a situation in which my agency, however open the situation may be, is restricted by force. Performers who do not assume their position of power often mask it as complicity or, even worse, equality. As Slavoj Žižek once remarked, power only becomes obscene when nobody wants to assume it. In such an unclear, diffused state, I have no choice but to feel manipulated, always sensing that the performers know more about the situation than they are ready to reveal. Doing away with spectatorship, which is impossible, therefore does not resolve the question of power inherent in the theater situation either. Power relations will not go away just because performers pretend we all have equal opportunities to make choices and to make decisions.

One possibility for being honest about power relations is to address them in the performance itself. Once they are out in the open, they change their nature and become material to play around with in the performance: they become negotiable. There are quite a few participatory performances that do address the question of power in their work: *Situation Rooms* by Rimini Protokoll, for instance, or most of Gob Squad's more recent performances. At one point or another, these performances reveal that our actions as participants have been filmed and observed all along by an uncanny third party. Entering the field of play of the performance, power relations may be unmasked, played around with, discussed, and negotiated.

5. The fallacy of the Here and Now, or: the double address

Masking power relations is not the only trap into which participatory performances fall. The second danger lurking in participation is the reduction of the performance to the fabled Here and Now, the immanence of the situation that is brought about by performative acts in which everybody participates. The fallacy here is that there never is only a Here and Now.

Theater never addresses its participants only in the Here and Now. Rather, the Here and Now only ever is the common ground from which to start the performance. It is not the *aim* of the performance.

If it is the aim of performance, it will most likely also be the *end* of performance. The fact that performance or theater always transcends the Here and Now is already inherent in the notion of address that is specific to theater.[18] Even when performers address members of the audience directly, they do not address only them. The words are at the very same time and with the very same address directed to something and someone else, something larger than the individual addressed, something that must remain absent, an empty space within the performance, the place of not-knowing. Performers address the act of speaking or dancing at the same time that they address individuals in the auditorium. There is a rift that goes through theatrical address itself, a gap between the actual person addressed and the *means of address*, i.e. language and movement. It speaks to you, but at the same time it only ever speaks to itself.

Historically, this double address (addressing the audience and addressing the form it creates) was underlined by the poetic function of language, the theatrical dialogue. Either in verse or in a form that would often make use of rhythm or metaphors, it assumed a form that transcended the everyday and mundane function of daily conversation. It paid homage to the absent God that Jean-Luc Nancy places at the beginning of theater.[19] Theater is no longer a religious ritual, but a social practice that exposes men to other men, co-emerging with each other and yet separated, hesitating between presence and absence, in which the words of the absent Gods still resonate. The function of the Gods has been assumed by language as the only means to form a social (political, juridical) order. In dance, ballet or any other movement vocabulary served the same function. Movement languages are artificial ways of speaking or moving that channel a subjective expressivity through a general, objective form, which in turn serves as a public

18 Cf. Helga Finter: Nach dem Diskurs. Zur Ansprache im aktuellen Theater. In: H.F.: *Die soufflierte Stimme: Text, Theater, Medien. Aufsätze 1979–2012.* Frankfurt am Main: Lang 2014, pp. 559–573.

19 Jean-Luc Nancy: *Nach der Tragödie.* Stuttgart: Legueil 2008; J.-L.N.: Theaterkörper. In: Nikolaus Müller-Schöll / André Schallenberg / Mayte Zimmermann (eds): *Performing Politics. Politisch Kunst machen nach dem 20. Jahrhundert,* Berlin: Theater der Zeit 2012, pp. 158–171; J.-L.N.: Theaterereignis. In: Nikolaus Müller-Schöll (ed.): *Ereignis. Eine fundamentale Kategorie der Zeiterfahrung,* Bielefeld: Transcript 2003, pp. 323–330.

address. Thus speaking or dancing on stage always includes a third party that is made palpable in the *way* of speaking and moving. Form, thus, is the contested placeholder for things that cannot be said, while they can only be said in the specificity of the form.

The address inherent in the form of moving and speaking opens up the act of speaking by means of form trying to capture that which must remain absent in speaking and in the Here and Now. Here, acts of memory and imagination are set in motion, acts that leave the Here and Now and open the situation up to things remembered and things imagined, things worth keeping and things utopian, potential situations that inform und nourish the situation just as our being together does. Thus, to neglect the issue of double address means to reduce the performance to the Here and Now; it means to tie it down to the brutality of the factual and the banal without hope for change or transformation.

6. Questions of freedom

If my objections to participation depend upon the premise that we call a specific cultural practice "theater," then why not stop referring to performance practices as theater in order to do away with power relations and this muddy idea of double address? Here is why we should not stop considering theater and dance as aesthetic and therefore as opposed to merely social or pedagogical practices: Giving up the aesthetic means giving up a *singular place* from which to speak in a unique way about the world and our relations with and in it. The aesthetic is a practice that allows us to *risk* knowledge, received opinions and hegemonic social practices. Rather than mirroring our social world, it allows us to gain insight into how our worlds are constructed, reflecting the possibilities of change. It suspends judgment and puts us in a limbo state where we cannot decide what is right or wrong, good or bad, pleasant or unpleasant. It puts the dancing and performing body at risk because it undoes what this body has learned socially. Reducing theater to its social dimension deprives us of our freedom that resides in the aesthetical force that, for philosopher Christoph Menke, is pre-subjective and human. Drawing on force, human beings can play and transcend their social limits by doing something that they do not normally do.[20] Maybe this is why we should keep art. Despite being a real body of flesh and blood that acts and dances, the body on stage always is at the same time an imaginary body that develops a *possibility* to move and act, a possibility that undoes and risks itself at the very same time it occurs. It is an imagined body that transcends the immanence of the social here and now.

Participation may help the process of unlearning or, as Rancière puts it, of redistributing the sensible, just as sitting in the dark watching performers in front of you may help to bring this risk of the unknown about. There is no general rule of what is a successful artistic strategy. My polemical title "Against Participation" here reaches its limits. Participatory performances are not deficient as such. Their success depends upon whether they aim at a consensus or a realized social utopia, or whether they instigate dissensus by keeping the process of reception open. Questions of spectatorship in theater always arise in times of political crisis in which the need for a 'new' theater to heal, counter or work on that crisis seems to be most prominent. Just as the fourth wall as a result and instigator of the political changes of the late 18th century did not suffice the social upheavals of the 1960s, the question remains whether the strategies of participation developed in the 1960s (the conflation of life and art as a continuation of avant-garde practices before World War II) suffice for our political and social crisis today. *In order to associate you have to dissociate*. In order to be able to re-think and re-combine images and practices, you have to cut lose and open up spaces of indeterminacy, spaces for memory and the imagination. Today, in our thoroughly mediatized and digitalized societies, where even bodies are consumed and abolished by a swipe over the touch pad, maybe we need more time to reflect and to re-connect with what we have lost. We need to undo ourselves by remembering und imagining. We need to take a step back to regain time by stepping back and engaging from a distance.

20 Christoph Menke: *Die Kraft der Kunst*. Berlin: Suhrkamp 2013.

Artist Talk

Interview with Heiner Goebbels

Ensemble, Team & Polyphony

… But in Strong Artistic Experience One Is Always Alone

Lorenz Aggermann / Eliane Beaufils / Eva Holling: Dear Heiner Goebbels: first we'd like to ask you, if the concepts of 'being together' or 'community' play a role in your work? And if so, in which ways, and has that maybe changed over the years?

Heiner Goebbels: I'd like to answer to these notions, first of all, only from the perspective of production, because I think that a spectator is always alone in a strong artistic experience, in the moment of being affected, even if he or she is sitting amongst 1,000 people. When a whole audience laughs during a show, I most certainly do not. Reacting together is a kind of affirmation that has nothing to do with artistic experience. It is, rather, a misunderstanding on the side of many spectators (who are not to be underrated or reduced to this, though) and especially from the side of theater makers who produce a theater that is based on recognition – which is an anti-artistic strategy, as John Dewey[1] has put it: recognition has nothing to do with Art, but the theater, which is full of clichés and stereotypes 'to show us a mirror of reality', is based on it. An artistic experience can only be an experience with something unseen, something strange, something different or something that is positioned outside yourself. This is not an experience that you have easily 'in common' or together with others. It would be of no use to have it together anyway, because then it

1 Cf. John Dewey: *Art as Experience*. New York: Perigee 1980, esp. pp. 35–58.

wouldn't affect you personally. The Being-Together, the community, the familiarity would predominate your experience at the expense of an experience that touches or affects you deep inside.
Of course, we could discuss the notion of experience longer, but experience – as Philippe Lacoue-Labarthe[2] develops it in his book on poetry from its etymological roots – always has to deal with traversing, with risking, with danger and irritation. Maybe one could, facing a danger, reassure oneself not to be alone, but I think when the danger – or the unknown, or the artistic experience – finally has got you, moves you (and I mean this not in a pedagogical way but as real pleasure), it is an experience that one goes through alone.
When you mention the concepts of community or being together (*être ensemble*), I am more interested at the level of production. There it has a great potential. In the 1970s and 80s, I have been working in German city theaters, and there was, and still is today, the notion of an *ensemble*. It held a great significance at that time because in Frankfurt it was a structure of self-administration: the actors discussed the theater's program, they discussed the distribution of the roles, they declined offers, and as such the actors became producers in a way. But now, from what I have experienced in theater, it is utter mockery to use the term *ensemble*, since the actors are totally excluded from practically every decision, be it in casting, in the work of the director of the production or of the institution. I know stories from other directors – and have experienced it myself – that when you are invited to work at a theater, you are not even allowed to speak to the actors of your choice beforehand: not until 14 days before the rehearsals start (I think this is the time limit, that at least I know from those stories) it is allowed to contact the actors. The actor I chose to work with in Zurich (and told the leading team of the theater half a year ahead) was not even informed of this until one week before the rehearsal. Then of course he said: "For God's sake, I'd really love to do it, but that is too difficult, I cannot make it, when you just tell me a week before." So, it is still a common practice to not even enable the actors to participate in planning and preparation – and this is why the use of the term *ensemble* in theater is a delusion.

2 Cf. Philippe Lacoue-Labarthe: *Poetry as Experience*. Stanford: Stanford UP 1999.

In opposition, I experienced the concept of *ensemble* as a very productive one particularly in times of the Sogenanntes Linksradikales Blasorchester or in my cooperations with the Ensemble Modern[3] who actually do not have an artistic director. Therefore, they invented a very complex structure that has a lot to do with collaboration and coexistence and not only with a kind of 'positive' community; of course there are many conflicts, but nevertheless every musician in the Ensemble Modern contributes to important decisions: what is to be played, where it is to be played, how long the rehearsals will be, who the conductor will be, and so on. It makes a huge difference to work with such an *ensemble* that decides for itself in comparison to other groups where other people make decisions for the group. All the projects I did with Ensemble Modern couldn't have been created in the form they have been with any other, not self-determined group, because the Ensemble Modern projects were strongly based on difficulties, on resistances, on cooperation and on unusual structures – like taking over unfamiliar roles, accepting to play other than the familiar instruments, or performing together without a conductor. I could only do all that because the musicians were ready for this, wanted it and decided by themselves to work with me. From this moment on they could not blame anybody else when problems appeared – they have to accept or solve them together.
When I am told, for example, to play in Moscow and then I get up at 5 o'clock in the morning, head to the airport, find myself in a Moscow traffic-jam with heavy snow for two hours and after that I have a rehearsal until midnight, I usually blame the one who organized all that – including the weather … But when I agreed to that risk myself, I find myself surrounded by happy faces until midnight who want to get things done and work with great motivation. Of course this also deeply touches the musical structure, the ambition to master difficult challenges, the critical cooperation between the different groups of instruments etc.
There I experienced an *ensemble* in a very positive way – and it has nothing to do with the absence of conflicts, rather it has something to do with rules determining how to deal with the conflicts in a civilized

3 For any information about the work and the cooperations of Heiner Goebbels visit https://www.heinergoebbels.com.

way. And of course there will be conflicts between individuals who all are soloists, who have their ambitions and their own ideas of aesthetics. So this is a contemporary notion of *ensemble* that lives up to its demand, because decisions are taken together in form of majority votes; you have to commit to it and accept it democratically. When 15 people vote for a project and four people vote against it, those four nevertheless participate in the project. I have found this kind of cooperation to be an experience that can make you happy, again and again.

Perhaps I have known another notion of *ensemble* by being able to consistently re-gather the same team for my own projects over the last 20–25 years. I've been working with costume designer Florence von Gerkan and with set- and light designer Klaus Grünberg for ca. 20 years, with my sound engineer Willi Bopp and with assistant and dramaturg Stefan Buchberger for 27 years. This is a team that is not bound to me by contract – nor me to them – but a team that gathers as a self-determined one again and again. That will probably change one day, sometimes a biography strikes a new path, but until now this constellation is a rather stable one – that also would be a positive concept of *ensemble*. Or with the French actor André Wilms for instance: Together we realized four productions in 25 years and more than 500 shows all around the world. This also is a kind of *ensemble*, where we are bound together only by the desire to do a common work. Perhaps here something like a community emerges, but one which is determined by art. We are not 'friends' in a common sense, but it is a community that is communi-cated by this 'third thing': producing art together. "Me-ti said that the relationship between two people will be a good one if a third thing is present in which both are interested."[4]

And now it gets interesting, because this kind of community formed by self-determined individuals produces something together which actually emerges independently. That is to say, when I am working on a production like *Max Black* or *Stifters Dinge*, I provide (*ich stifte*) a basic idea and make the production possible, give a core and perhaps also a form to it – and that is how I understand my concept of composition: to compose all theatrical means. But, all the particular material that

4 Bertolt Brecht: *Me-ti: Book of Interventions in the Flow of Things*, ed. and transl. from the German by Antony Tatlow. London / Oxford: Bloomsbury 2016, p. 160.

comes together in the piece can be produced independently: Klaus Grünberg might work on a certain idea while I'm working on another, and at one point, we try to put them together and we realize: this image and this text are a bad match, but that image goes together with that music very well. That means the material is often developed independently and then it is pulled together in my compositional procedure.

I often call that *polyphony*, Vielstimmigkeit: many voices come and speak together in a process comparable to music, as simultaneous but independent voices (*selbstständig geführte Stimmen*), all working on something different – the sound engineer works on sound ideas, the light designer works on light ideas, the pyrotechnician works on fire ideas etc. Those voices are the voices of people working together in the team. On a second level, those voices are materialized in the work: as light, sound, or fire. In the end you might not be able to determine who exactly 'did this or that', but you probably can feel the independent voices in the texture of the theatrical composition. You can feel or notice if a piece is produced hierarchically or if it consists of different voices that are of the same value and not organized in a hierarchic relation. You can tell that from the things on stage, from the theatrical means. On a third level of this *polyphony*, it is possible to look at those voices and listen to them from various perspectives. I can watch a production like *Max Black* because I like fire, or because I like Paul Valéry's texts, or because I'm interested in music, or because I love the actor, or maybe because I have a background in Fine Arts and therefore I enjoy those strange images that emerge. This is a kind of *audience polyphony* that answers to the complexity of the production in an individual way. The polyphonic community of producers, that work together on the same subject but not necessarily on the same materials (or means, or even concepts) corresponds to a certain complexity in the artistic work. The artistic complexity answers to a community of heterogeneous perspectives – and voices – in the audience.

So, I understand that you don't have different concepts of Ensemble, Community or Polyphony, even if you work in different 'functions'? I imagine that in your function as composer, you are working alone, and in your function as director, you are working together with people?

Well, those functions sometimes overlap. When I am composing for a big orchestra, I am in fact mostly sitting here alone at my piano or at my computer – but even then there are moments of cooperation. Sometimes in rehearsals there are musicians or conductors who defend the composed notes against myself, when they say: "But here it is written like that!", and I answer "I don't care, because what you were playing is much better than the notes written on the paper." Those are moments of feedback, but in the work for orchestra, most of the composition takes place separately. That is why I don't like it that much, and the last time I worked like that, was 15 years ago.
With smaller ensembles like the Hilliard Ensemble, London Sinfonietta, the Orchestra of the Age of Enlightenment, Carmina Slovenica or the Ensemble Modern we often work and develop things together. In such early workshops I behave more like a director, proposing things like 'try something else', 'try moving to the corner', etc. I only go back to the isolated loneliness of being a composer *after* such a workshop to take as many experiences as possible into consideration. This is also how I work in theater: I try to consider all theatrical means at the same time, I never work only on a text first or with an actor alone. I always work simultaneously with all material at once: light, sound, text, images, space, etc. It is a huge (also financial) investment to be able to work like that, but I try not to abstract some means from others. Therefore, I do not necessarily need a strong concept beforehand; very often I don't have one and I definitely do not have a prefigured 'vision' of what the piece will look like. I have a starting point, a question or a subject, which I share with my team, and then we try to approach it from many sides.

Well, I imagined that 'composing' would be somewhat different…

When we started *Stifters Dinge* for instance, me and Klaus Grünberg were only asking ourselves if it is possible to create a piece without anybody – a performer, actor, singer, dancer… Klaus wanted to work with water and I suggested to try working with pianos, because I knew how to 'play' them via remote control programs. We started with one pool and two pianos, and after a year and a half there were three pools and five pianos; everything was developed in the process.
Yesterday, I was invited to a discussion with Gunnar Hindrichs to Musicology Studies at Goethe University in Frankfurt talking about

the "tendency of the material" which is a concept by Theodor W. Adorno[5] that I even discover in theater. While he referred to the interrelation of material, that a 12 tone row has its own rules, for me, "the tendency of the material" also means to watch the surface of water for three weeks and then seeing more and more possibilities to react to it and deal with it, to recognize its ecological implications, to throw something in it, to see how bubbles are produced – and to discover further possibilities, like the potential to build music around this material.

In the process of my productions I never actually have a vision in advance. Therefore it was a big surprise when I invited some of our students from Gießen to attend the working process for *Hashirigaki*. While the students often approach their work conceptually, my team and me were simply playing around for a week with texts by Gertrude Stein, with colors, with music from the Beach Boys – and the students were astonished and maybe even disappointed. They probably expected us to have everything in mind beforehand and therefore we would be able to explain every move. But we couldn't. I mean, I can explain it now, but at the time, I could not.

Basically, I always try not to be satisfied with what I have and with what there is, but to turn it into something else. This was and is the 'motor' of my work: to react to the things we have, to the 'tendency of the material' and to discover it, accept it or turn it into something else. In the end I am the one who is the most surprised about the result, because I never anticipate it.

I'd like to ask you another question concerning what you've said about ensembles, particularly from your, let's say, historical experience with the model for collective participation in decision-making ('Mitbestimmungsmodell') at the Schauspiel Frankfurt. Why was this model given up even if its aesthetic output was quite convincing? Why do you think the structures in theaters today may be even more authoritative than they were at the time?

I was very young at the time of the *Mitbestimmungsmodell*, in my mid-twenties, and I only witnessed the end of it. Today, I would be

5 Cf. Theodor W. Adorno: *Philosophy of New Music*, ed. by Robert Hullot-Kentor. Minneapolis: University of Minnesota Press 2006.

more able to analyze the situation and why it failed, but other people like Karlheinz Braun would be more suited to respond to that question. I suppose that the institutional conditions finally get in the way of such concepts as the *ensemble*, like the fact that the curtain has to be lifted every night and that there has to run a different play every evening in the German repertoire system. This is how I experienced it back then. I think that a self-determined model has to produce in its own way and cannot fulfill institutional structures that were developed 100 years ago, because decisions have to be made quickly; you're not free to leave the stage empty for three weeks or to rehearse something new without knowing what will come out of it and if it will be good enough to have it premiered next year. This is not the logic of a repertoire theater (*Stadttheater*), but Schauspiel Frankfurt is one of those.

In other contexts, I consider it possible to work in a self-determined way, in teams such as Forced Entertainment or in groups coming from Gießen like Monster Truck. But as I said, it has to have an influence on *how* people are working together. And there is an incompatibility. Models of self-determination won't work out in the structures of an institutionalized theater system, because the system itself is already built to be hierarchical.

Musicians then may seem to have stolen the idea of codetermination, or maybe they even had it before – I think the Wiener Philharmoniker had it before, didn't they? –, because in music it is easier to compensate or to balance the conditions: things are more predictable, roles are more predetermined. I experienced it with the Berliner Philharmoniker, they also have a *Mitbestimmungsmodell*, where the musicians decide what is being played, who will become the next conductor and so on. But there can be complications, because an *orchestra* is in fact not an *ensemble* and therefore cannot be dealt with as such. It makes a big difference if I am one of five drummers being able to realize myself with great pleasure, or if I am the 16th violinist sitting in the back row at music stand n° 8. These positions have different motivations and capacity for curiosity, it can even be a different constitution of subjectivity and potential. In an orchestra basic democratic problems can appear, because all the string players together hold the majority, since everyone has a vote. So, the strings section functions as a persistent element when it comes to decisions – this shifts the power structure, which is rather particular. So I understand that their democratic model works differently than it does at Ensemble Modern, where everyone is a soloist, able to realize him- or herself in a specific way and therefore they are also different characters. In the end, I think the *Mitbestimmungsmodell* in Frankfurt failed because of the institutional structures and not because of the people who were involved.

Here is a question regarding the 'ensemble' of independent means and materials, that is to say the heterogeneity, in your work: does this have something to do with resistance for you? Because working in this way seems to be resisting conventional forms to allow the production of something innovative and exceptional – is this maybe even a form of critique?

Spontaneously I'd say that this sounds quite 'pedagogical' to me. The aesthetics that we produce in our intuitive and independent work is above all a need. We don't do it because we want to be difficult. It's just, when something is fitting too easily, it is simply not interesting to us. Our way of working results from the pleasure of tension between the things we put together. We seek tension because we cannot intentionally invent or conceptualize it, we can only find it. Tension for me is basically a musical category, the counterpoint between what we see and what we hear. And in our work we seek this counterpoints until we find them. But we seek tension not in order to be against something or to present mind-altering images, this is not the motivation. It is just a joyful process of seeking a power balance that doesn't bore us even after the 20th rehearsal – and that is a need. We do not criticize, we're looking for something that attracts and surprises us.
You know, I rarely understand why something is working, maybe the others don't understand either. But when something is working, everyone suddenly knows it. In such a moment, everyone agrees. There is something about a community in such moments that works like a corrective and all of us realize it. It is the same when I am working with students. If something doesn't work, there are a hundred reasons why: the music was too loud, the light was too dark, the performer weak, the text was stupid... whatever. But when it works, we all agree, even if we all look at it from different perspectives and with a different taste. This is exactly what happens in my own productions too: the

artistic research comes only to an end when you realize that the relations between sound, text, image, and light are 'somehow' working. You also mentioned more conventional forms: I think when you're working in a 'conventional' way you can establish rules and laws for it. You know certain things, for instance that the actor has to be up front to be visible and that the light has to follow him etc. Such hierarchic laws are even teachable, because you can canonize them. But if you are willing to question those conventions, and if you do not want to produce 'sense' in the first place, but to invite sense 'to take place', you have to play around and try. If you want sense to happen while you're perceiving and to open up a tension that makes this possible, you cannot make up in your head – you have to seek for it in an experimental way. You always start from scratch when you're trying to find something that you haven't seen before.

I agree, resistance and critique in this context sounded too intentional; but actually we have come to a crucial point with this, namely the practice of composition. Speaking about this, you also mentioned the notion of resonance – which is rather oscillating and can be used on several levels. You also just mentioned that everyone agrees when something is working: would you call that a kind of resonance to something when everything and everyone vibrates together?

Normally, I am careful with the notion of resonance because it has such a specific meaning in music referring to the sound board of a piano. It is possible, of course, to use it metaphorically, but I am a little astonished that I'm said to have used it. In speaking about musicality and about composing elements in theater, I'd rather use different terms to express the two dynamics in my works.
On the one hand I try to think music in a visual, scenic way – when I am staging concerts – and on the other hand I try to think theater in a musical way. But that does not have much to do with music in a narrow notion; it has to do with the fact that I am not interested in a theater that believes in the successful transmission of a message. When Jean-Luc Nancy is talking about music he explains that musical fragility is a consequence of the non-articulation of a sense (a meaning), which at the same time is mounted, presented and withdrawn: "Musical fragility (fractality, discretion) resides in the inarticulatedness of

a sense always both extended – offered – and withheld."[6] You cannot say that music makes no sense, but you never know exactly what it is. This is the endless attraction of music.

And this is the point of music I am actually trying to transfer to theater: to be able to see a play in the same way I am listening to music: to feel that there is something that concerns me, but I cannot exactly define what it is. And then I see it another time and I am affected again, but somehow differently. Theater can be an art form like Fine Arts or music: to insist on a vagueness and on the "riddle character of art"[7], and not to submit its elements to deliver a statement. This is the crucial point for me in the distinction between 'making music with theater' and 'making music for music's sake'. I don't think "oh, how nice it is to be able to hear the steps of the actor", but in the *ensemble* of all elements, in the result, there has to be this potential of a 'sense that happens' which is not produced or defined intentionally and one-dimensionally. Theater can be a play with sounds, words, significations but should never appear as narrowing-down to one form of interpretation. That is why I work from the basis of musical principles. And I can do so because I am a musician – but I am not expressing myself musically, I am using it as a *tool* to find theatrical forms that open up a space for imagination and sense to happen.

Maybe this is a peculiar concept of resonance that differs from a musical understanding? There is a definition of resonance by Albrecht Wellmer[8], who claims that every medium, every art form holds a kind of 'immanent hole' that refers to other forms of expression, so that language can refer to musicality, musicality itself refers to images and an image might refer back to language or whatever. Thus, there are always interferences – and I would call them resonances – of other media in one particular medium. And I see that happening strongly in your work…

6 Cf. Jean-Luc Nancy: *The Sense of the World*. Minneapolis: University of Minnesota Press 1997, p. 86.

7 Cf. Theodor W. Adorno: *Aesthetic Theory*, ed. by Gretel Adorno / Rolf Tiedemann, transl. from the German by Robert Hullot-Kentor. Minneapolis: University of Minnesota Press 1997.

8 Albrecht Wellmer: *Versuch über Musik und Sprache*. Munich: Hanser 2009, p. 24.

You can define it in such a way, but somehow I dislike the notion. When I am working with a text or a language that is already musical in itself, like Gertrude Stein or Samuel Beckett, I of course chose them because they have a transition (*Übergang*) to other media, so to speak. But I don't see the notion of resonance in there. Do you mean that someone who listens to a text or language is reminded of music?

Well, I don't know if it is a reminder, for me it is more a kind of re-adjustment of perception. As I can actually 'hear visually', I can also perceive images in a linguistic way. So I think this re-adjustment or re-functionalization of perceptional principles that questions the perceived and that cannot be captured by sense or meaning, works by a kind of resonance.

Yes, here I would agree.

And as you were mentioning musical texts and language, are there also nonmusical ones? It seems you also came across the like?

Funny, that you ask this, because not long ago I was asked the exact same thing. I'd say: yes, there are indeed many nonmusical languages. Languages, which don't have a body, which only follow a concept – that has a lot to do with missing the body.

... and it is the body that resonates ... ?!?

There we go!

These remarks on the body and its resonance lead me to a question regarding technical procedures. I consider it most peculiar, in a very positive sense, that in your work body is given to such procedures and also to things. They are equivalent to all other procedures of your theater and they are not hidden: on the one hand the people executing the processes and on the other hand all the various mechanisms and objects that contribute to the composition. In the end, the theater can even reveal itself as a machine, as in Stifters Dinge ...

Right, but there are always people behind the procedures and I am sure that you can feel that. The audience senses how the technicians have influenced the piece, and are not reduced to 'executors' of a 'vision' the director believed to have had … So the relation is very intense; especially the one to the objects in *Max Black*. You instantly realize the care and competence the props were selected with. You don't meditate over that, you just instantly get it.

I would also like to speak about fear and danger: with reference to Stifters Dinge, André Eiermann mentions a "dangerous openness"[9]*, that you also bring up in connection to Rimini Protokoll's* Call Cutta in a Box. *What do you like about this phrase?*

I quoted that from someone else – I think it was Gernot Böhme.[10] The elemental thing is, when you are perceiving something, you don't know exactly what it is. You cannot take possession of it. On the contrary, it takes possession of you because it emits something that you cannot name. That can be dangerous for the subject. I think this was the interesting point for me in this phrase.

You just mentioned musicality; but in some texts you also refer to the notion of the 'poetic' or to a 'poetical logic' with regard to composition. And from what you have said it sounded to me that sense and meaning is brought up in your work, but without putting a controlling force to it. Would that also be a poetic way of working?

This notion is quoted from Friedrich Hölderlin's "Remarks to Antigone",[11] and I understand it as an aesthetic tool of production. Only last week I tried to explain it to my students: it has something to do with finding a way to get from one picture to the next, or from one word to another, or from an image to sound, from one movement into

9 Cf. André Eiermann: *Postspektakuläres Theater*. Bielefeld: Transcript 2009, esp. pp. 238–265.

10 Cf. Gernot Böhme: Acoustic Atmospheres: A Contribution to the Study of Ecological Aesthetics. In: *Soundscape. The Journal of Acoustic Ecology* 1 (2000), pp. 14–18.

11 Cf. Friedrich Hölderlin: Remarks on Antigone. In: F. H.: *Essays and Letters on Theory*, ed. by Thomas Pfau. Albany: SUNY Press 1988, pp. 109–118.

the next scene. When I make theater, I hardly work inside the scenes because they develop very quickly – but I am busy for weeks to find ways of transition from one to another. When this is not solved in a poetic way, we as readers, listeners, or beholders, start to ask too many questions. We find ourselves at a point where something ends and something else is going to start, and in this *caesura* we have too much time to ask (stupid) questions. When I succeed in linking these two segments (or words or images or scenes) in a way that prevents that kind of questioning, it might be the result of a poetical logic. Then you do not inquire about logic, because it is solved by poetry, i. e. by sound or by the relation between sound and light, by the rhythm of the transition. The reader of Hölderlin's poetry is convinced that the words within fit perfectly together, although they might have nothing to do with each other; this is only because of rhythm and sound, because of poetical logic. When I transfer this to theater, or to film, when I succeed to turn the caesura unrecognizable or into a healthy rupture, then I'd say it is a successful moment of poetical logic.
I was told that by a magician one day. In my early days as a student, I played the piano for a magician in his show. 20 years later, he saw one of my pieces and said I do the same thing he does: 'you distract the people and suddenly there is something unexpected happening. This is magic.'

But isn't there after all something that comes from a certain resistance? From the resistance against an explaining logic?

Well, yes. Certainly, you do not want to reproduce clichés. But this goes without saying. We already didn't want that in the Linksradikales Blasorchester.

... Which is not to be diminished!

No, of course not. I learned a lot from it concerning collaboration and co-existence in composition processes. All the processes of (aesthetic) opinion making can be collective ones that you can rely on. And you do not have to insist on your ego. I experienced all of this back then already. It was incredibly enriching – and also very relieving – that decisions were made by many.

Would this also be a political component for you? On the one hand, working collectively became a model of success, but on the other hand, many things in the art market are still based upon concepts of the genius, the cult of celebrity and so on ...

This can be quite destructive with such external pressure. The hunt for 'gang leaders' was also a problem for the Linksradikales Blasorchester, particularly when some journalists tried to identify the dominant persons within the group, claiming 'now we know who it is!' That press damaged the collective. I also worked with set designer Michael Simon on two projects for which we were both equally responsible as authors and directors, but someone wrote in an article "Heiner Goebbels and his stage designer". Michael instantly stopped our collaboration because of that, even if it was not my fault, and decided from then on to work alone as a director. Now I prefer to say quite bluntly that it is me who starts a project and stages it, that I make it possible by finding coproducers and funding, that I collect the team and give a core idea, like I already said. I am finally the one responsible for the composition, and for bringing all the elements together, and that is why it operates under my name. Then it is simply clear – and it would also not be possible anymore to 'hide' that fact anyway ...

But are you generally interested in the question of the relation between art and the political?

Well, that is actually a new topic. When you don't understand the political in a narrow sense (of message), then it concerns the way something is produced. And 'the political' can also be linked to what Hans-Thies Lehmann calls "wahrnehmungspolitisch"[12] – politics of perception. It is – again – the question what kind of potential you open up to the audience, and I have already stressed, that this strongly depends on *how* you work. Some of my works may express the political more obviously – like *Eislermaterial* or *Landschaft mit entfernten Verwandten* or my work *Eraritjaritjaka* with the texts by Elias Canetti, because these texts are highly political by themselves. Others touch the political in a more subtle way, but I don't really care anyway. *Stifters Dinge*,

12 Cf. Hans-Thies Lehmann: *Postdramatic Theatre*, transl. from the German by Karen Jürs-Munby. Abingdon / New York: Routledge 2006, pp. 184–186.

which was only planned to be a theater-experiment, was perceived as an ecological and ethnographic piece; which is totally okay, but wasn't our first intention. I believe that the greatest chance for the political to emerge is to not intend it, because it would easily be obvious, dominate the perception, and people would be 'turned off' at once.

And the spectator couldn't detect potentiality anymore.

The audience must get the possibility to explore, to be able to detect something, to link it productively to their own biographies and experiences – or not. Therefore it must not be exposed by the producers – that wouldn't work.

You also spoke about the audience being affected. This 'being affected' seems to focus neither sense nor sensibility alone; and you also mentioned that you choose voices for your works that affect you ... To affect, to touch ... does this have something to do with emotions that come up in your work?

Wait, emotion is something different ...

Yes, that is why I was hesitating to use that word. I was somehow searching for a common denominator ...

I'd rather not use the term emotion. Even when emotions are produced. I cannot negate it. I saw many people crying in *Stifters Dinge* – curiously always at the same moment: when it rains. That wasn't my intention, but I certainly worked on this emotion in an unconscious way. The piece of music you hear while it is raining is a piece I practiced when I was 13 years old, the slow second movement from Bach's *Italian Concerto*. But back then I studied the full concerto and the third movement, the fast one, was a very successful part of my first (and last) public concert in the German Palatinate region – afterwards I quit piano lessons. So I have a close biographical relation to this music. Maybe there is also something in the light, there is the interview with Claude Lévi-Strauss, and it is raining – all this seems to have an emotional effect, which I didn't realize. That is to say, I do not avoid emotional moments, I also allow them in my working process, but the emotions that are triggered within the audience are not

mine – I've never cried during this scene … I also believe that these emotions might be very different, because the audience's perspectives on the simultaneity of Bach, Lévi-Strauss, and the rain can be diverse. One might not realize that there is a piano during this talk, while another person only listens to Bach, and a third one is looking at the falling raindrops, as if they have never witnessed anything like that in real life before.
I think that there is no such thing in my work as an orchestration or staging of emotions. There are, in fact, even people who say that *Stifters Dinge* is a cold piece because there is nobody on stage. But I have often been addressed by people of the audience after other works, like that couple at the Ruhrtriennale for instance, who saw many of my productions and said "Mr. Goebbels, it is a wonderful program, but the people on your stage never touch each other, they are always so alone …" And I replied: "Yes. Like in real life." But the two of them stood there arm in arm and just could not understand what I meant. So it might even be an emotion that I put on stage and they were maybe afraid of, that one could end up alone some day. But anyway, I am more interested in creating a tension and distance between people on stage than pretending to form a community …

I wonder if 'intensity' wouldn't be a suitable notion to express that? Because what you just mentioned talking about Stifters Dinge, the moment when rain, music and the voice of Lévi-Strauss come together, they all have the same intensity in their particular means.

This indeed brings me back to the notion of resonance: if you are listening to the speech melody of Lévy-Strauss you find resonances between his intonation and phrasing and Bach's music! But I only realized that afterwards. I placed the music in a way I liked it, but I noticed only after the 50th time, that there are structural resonances between the length of a Lévy-Strauss-sentence and the length of a phrase in Bach's melody.

I just wrote the notion of intensity down for myself because earlier you also spoke about joy, which seems to be a strong stimulus in your work. Is this joy maybe a quest for intensities? Or what would be your vocabulary?

It is the joy you feel when you discover something you don't know yet!

Would you on the other hand agree to the statement that you cannot find or compose something new, especially in music?

You cannot discover new sounds, but in the composition of materials already invented you can perfectly create something new. This is even possible with a piano piece which is 300 years old.

It is obvious that the human in your work is often present in an absent way. Therefore, the general question of the human gains importance. Maybe you would be so kind to outline a bit why you are tempted to put it on stage more absently?

Well, this merely is a trick! For me there are two 'main presences': on the one hand an acoustic presence that always comes along with a corporeal absence, I'd say; and on the other hand there is the presence of the spectator. In *Stifters Dinge*, there are 150 protagonists in the auditorium, and they are motivated and addressed in different ways; and they only become protagonists of the show because they miss something or because they do *not* see something they were expecting. Their imagination specifically 'happens' in the tension between the seen and the unseen.
As a matter of fact, when I started to create theater I really tried to avoid certain things in my work – there the notion of critique would fit. In my first works, I did not know what I wanted to see, I only knew what I did *not* want to see. That is why I told the musicians in *Schwarz auf Weiß* to turn their backs to the audience. Or at the beginning of *Die Wiederholung*, there is someone on stage doing nothing for 15 minutes because I had not seen something like that before. The negation or prevention of what disturbed me in theater led to such images that deal with absence. I did not go to a rehearsal saying that I want to do something with absence, I rather tried to find something I can stand and enjoy looking at. When I am looking at a back and have no clue who is talking – and *Schwarz auf Weiß* starts with a quote from Maurice Blanchot: "qui parle?" – I find the tension I was searching for.

The enigmatic and the beautiful are two components that, for me, go together in your work. Is that because this combination provides the strongest impulse to think?

No, that is also one of those needs, namely to do something utopic. I was never interested in showing or denouncing the world as such on stage, even if that is an intention of many theater makers. I, for my part, was always interested in seeing something I'd been longing for. There is this wonderful late interview with Heiner Müller I only read a few years ago that one could apply to the works I did in the 90s. He describes why the strange is the beautiful: because it is not found in reality.[13]

Yes, I think I read the article "The Utopia of Form" ("Utopie der Form") where this is mentioned, but there it is not linked that much to longing. To utopia, yes, but not to longing…

Yeah, it is a big word, probably too big. I have no problems living without – as you see I am fine, I don't necessarily have to work, and I do not long for working, so let's just forget the word.

Ok then; just one final question: does the intellectual provide an important frame of context for art? I mean, is it a frame of context for the way you are working? Or are the two completely separated?

They are, indeed, separate things. There is a kind of synchronization of thinking and doing as I already sketched in my diploma thesis on Hanns Eisler, which also grounded the Linksradikales Blasorchester. But the more I worked artistically, the more important it was to free myself from conceptual thinking. I often thought about concepts, but then I tried to forget them, and to compose or work intuitively and physically. Then of course the conceptual thinking did not get lost – you build up a framework of criteria in this conceptual phase and this framework also persists when you are no longer aware of it. But in

13 Cf. Heiner Müller: Utopie der Form. In: H. M.: *Werke*, vol. 12: Gespräche 3. 1991–1995, ed. by Frank Hörnigk. Frankfurt am Main: Suhrkamp 2008, pp. 802–803.

order to achieve artistic solutions that are interesting, I have to free myself to give a chance to the unconscious. That is most important. The freer I feel to explore things in a relatively unreflected way, the better the result. But this does not exclude long stages of conceptual reflection before. But I think – and this is important for a conclusion to this talk and also for the future of the Institute in Gießen – it does not work to make a concept in a seminar, enter the rehearsal stage, and then form a piece out of it. It only works when you read an interesting text in the morning and in the afternoon you work on something completely different. Then some unforeseen synapses might occur that you cannot explain. Then it can get interesting… There is no direct way from theory to practice at all. Again and again we reach the chance of being 'unintentional'. But of course there is a way in the opposite direction: when I reflect on the things I've done, I benefit a lot from my formation. But in the artistic process the intellectual is only productive when it is independent.

Thank you so much for this lovely and inspiring talk!

(*Interview translated by Eva Holling*)

II

Effects Between Scene and Audience

Eva Holling

Lacanian Transference

Co-Subjective Structures and Theatrical Interpellation

Talking and thinking about 'being-with' in theater brings up questions of who is involved, in what togetherness, and what possible mutual influences there are. Obviously, concepts come to mind, such as Philip Auslander's 'liveness,' Erika Fischer-Lichte's 'co-presence' and Hans-Thies Lehmann's 'theatron-axis' or 'situation as power center of theater',[1] all focusing on theater as an art form that gathers people in a shared space and time. But interestingly, none of these concepts focuses intensely upon the specific quality of their particular 'co' – it seems that specifying the participants of their theorized togetherness is not their main goal, whether they be individuals, humans, persons, subjects ... ?

This contribution proposes to examine this gathering as one of *subjects*, even if Jean-Luc Nancy speaks of the "impossibility of being common as subject."[2] Basically all concepts of community in theater discuss the relation of stage and audience, which means: all involved people are confronted with functions they must fulfill and with places in

1 Cf. Philip Auslander: *Liveness. Performance in a Mediatized Culture.* London / New York: Routledge 1999; Erika Fischer-Lichte: *Ästhetik des Performativen.* Frankfurt am Main: Suhrkamp 2004; Hans-Thies Lehmann: Shakespeare's Grin. In: Judith Helmer / Florian Malzacher (eds): *Not Even a Game Anymore. The Theatre of Forced Entertainment.* Berlin: Alexander 2004, pp. 103–117, here p. 107; H.-T. L.: Die Inszenierung: Probleme ihrer Analyse. In: *Zeitschrift für Semiotik* 11:1 (1989), pp. 29–49, here p. 42 (transl. E. H.).

2 "L'impossibilité d'un être communautaire en tant que sujet." (Jean-Luc Nancy: *La communauté désœuvrée.* Paris: Bourgois 1986, p. 42.)

which they are put. Their common presence is always framed by theater and its institutional and 'dispositivical' conditions, so theater in a way provides a certain space to create subjects and to distribute places, so that it always has to be taken into account as the frame for the encounter, as a 'third' in the co-presence of stage and audience. Thus, the question would be to ask exactly how that encounter, that frame, that space where 'it' happens is determined and how subjects are created within it.

This necessarily involves determining a concept of 'subject'. Lacanian subjects for instance – to introduce the approach of this text – are not the same as Nancy-ian ones, and that is why it is perfectly possible to sketch a co-subjectivity in theater. For Jacques Lacan, subjectivity is always to be seen in relation to others and Others, and while Nancy defines his subject as "objectivable et productible"[3], for Lacan, a strict subject is characterized precisely by its impossibility of being objectified, distinguished and communicated.[4]

Now a perspective that takes the psychoanalytical concept of *transference* into account offers the possibility of retracing structures that determine inter- or co-subjective relations, which Lacan called "rapports"[5]. With his approach to the theory of transference, which is one of love and desire, it is possible to analyze ways of theatrical impact and effectiveness, that is to say: practices of *theatrical interpellation*.[6] Therefore, it is necessary to briefly summarize what can be understood by transference and why it is a concept that works not only in psychoanalysis but in all spaces where subjects co-exist.

3 For Nancy, the subject belongs to the idea of an operative community which he rejects. In there, a common being would be seen as objectifiable and productive "[...] dans des lieux, des personnes, des édifices, des discours, des institutions, des symboles : bref, dans des sujets." (Ibid., p. 79.)

4 Jacques Lacan: *The Seminar of Jacques Lacan VIII: Transference*, ed. by Jacques-Alain Miller, transl. from the French by Bruce Fink. Cambridge: Polity 2015, p. 144.

5 Cf. Jacques Lacan: Intervention on Transference, transl. from the French by Jacqueline Rose. In: Juliet Mitchell / Jacqueline Rose (eds): *Jacques Lacan & the École Freudienne: Feminine Sexuality*. New York: Macmillan 1982, pp. 61–73, here p. 62.

6 Cf. Eva Holling: *Übertragung im Theater. Theorie und Praxis theatraler Wirkung*. Berlin: Neofelis 2016.

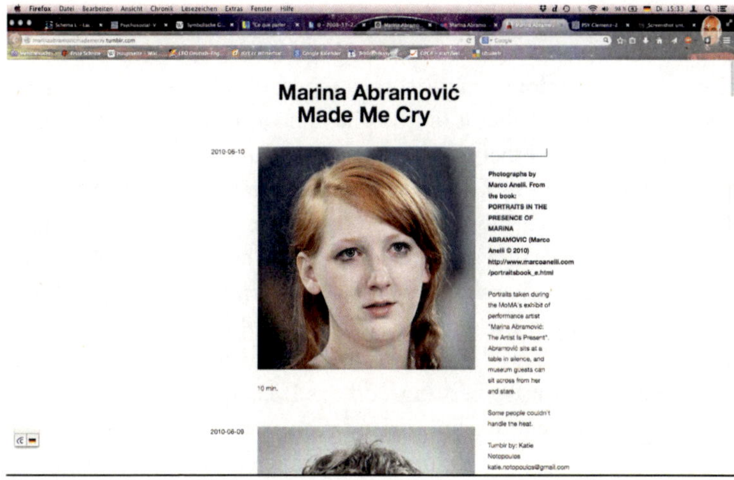

Fig. 1: *Marina Abramović Made Me Cry*, Screenshot.

"Be careful": transference and its impact

To show on what a transference-based perspective might focus, the blog *Marina Abramović Made Me Cry*[7] is a suitable object of research. It shows various portraits of visitors who attended the big exposition *Marina Abramović: The Artist Is Present* in New York's Museum of Modern Art in 2010. Each person shown in these portraits is crying. Mario Anelli, the photographer, took the pictures while the subjects were sitting across from the artist. Marina Abramović conducted the long-durational performance with the same title (*The Artist Is Present)* as part of the exposition, in which she invited people to take a seat at the opposite end of the table where she was sitting for as long as the visitors chose to stay. Many of them began to cry while sitting there. A transference-sensitive perspective on this might ask: why is this? And the reply might be: Firstly, those crying people are expressing something called "prise des spectateurs" by Enzo Cormann,[8] which means that the visitors are somehow 'taken' in and by this situation (the noun 'prise' comes from the verb 'prendre' which means 'to take').

7 http://marinaabramovicmademecry.tumblr.com (accessed January 7, 2017).

8 Enzo Cormann: Fantasme Malentendu. In: E. C.: *À quoi sert le Théâtre?* Besançon: Les Soutaires Intempestifs 2003, pp. 33–37.

And secondly, this 'prise' can be considered a result of a *rapport* of subject to subject, which is essentially influenced by transference.

Transference therefore structures the rapport of subject to subject, and psychoanalysis describes it on the one hand as resistance against the analysis and on the other hand as its most useful tool.[9] Sigmund Freud first mentions it in his *Fragment of an Analysis of a Case of Hysteria*, describing "new editions or facsimiles of the impulses and phantasies […] that replace some earlier person by the person of the physician" or "psychological experiences revived as applying to the person of the physician at the present moment."[10] Because of this substitution it is also called 'misalliance'[11], and it is maybe good to keep that in mind, because it highlights something 'odd' (as Lacan puts it[12]), something inequivalent in the intersubjective relation.

Lacan modifies Freud's definition of transference especially with regard to its connection with the past: For him, the impact of transference on *present* intersubjective structures is much more important than its relation to bygone experiences or to repetition compulsions. He claims that transference turns every present in something partly fictional, because subjects tend to 'mis-take' what they see and to build up phantasms, especially when it comes to relations with other subjects. Lacan's focus thus lies on a mutual *supposition* as the basis for interaction. And therein lies one of the biggest differences with the Freudian approach because Lacan's transferences are not affects or emotions but a structure that expresses itself *in* emotions.[13] Emotions and affects "constitute a perception"[14], as Lacan says, but they are not

9 Cf. Sigmund Freud: Transference. In: S. F.: *Standard Edition*, vol. 16: Introductory Lectures on Psycho-Analysis. London: Hogarth 1963, pp. 482–501, here p. 496.

10 Sigmund Freud: Fragment of an Analysis of a Case of Hysteria (1905). In: S. F.: *Standard Edition*, vol. 7: A Case of Hysteria, Three Essays on Sexuality and Other Works. London: Hogarth 1953, pp. 1–122, here p. 106.

11 Transfert (psychanalyse). In: *Wikipedia*. http://fr.wikipedia.org/wiki/Transfert_%28psychanalyse%29 (accessed January 7, 2017).

12 "I am looking for some equivalent for the word impair, for the subjective oddity of transference, for the oddity that it contains essentially." (Lacan: *Transference*, p. 1.)

13 Cf. Lacan: Intervention, p. 71.

14 Jacques Lacan: *The Seminar of Jacques Lacan XI: The Four Fundamental Concepts of Psychoanalysis*, ed. by Jacques-Alain Miller, transl. from the French by Alan Sheridan. New York / London: Norton 1998, p. 154.

the structure itself; they only make the impact of that structure perceivable. That is why the tears of the Abramović-sitters can be taken as a hint that transference is active in this constellation.

Now, to understand a bit more of this theory, it is helpful to look at the two main factors in Lacan's concept, namely the *agalma* and the *sujet supposé savoir* (subject supposed to know). Lacan finds the notion of *agalma* in Plato's text *Symposium*. In this text, a certain Alcibiades sees precious things in Socrates, and the Greek word for this treasure is *agalma*, a term often used to designate statues of gods. The *Symposium* provides us with a nice image for seeing-value-in-people: a satyr-shaped box that contains a treasure when opened. Alcibiades claims in one of his speeches that Socrates is like such a box; he looks like an old buffer from the outside but contains precious value on the inside. He sees *agalma* in Socrates, and following Lacan, this is the main constellation of transference. It is in fact an (over-)valuation of another person: one imputes value to another, and this is precisely the structure of love and desire. Hence, transference theory is one of the occasions for Lacan to develop his famous *object a*, the precious object *a*-galma that lies inside the box.

This intersubjective structure of valuation is characterized by several conditions and brings consequences for the people involved. First of all, the over-estimating or admiring mis-taking of other people makes fiction and imagination the main agent in transference. "The subject in transference pretends, fabricates, constructs something"[15], states Lacan, clarifying that transference is a fictionalization of the people one looks at and speaks to.

Additionally, Lacan identifies as desiring subjects those who are able to see treasures in others. In transference, "there is revealed a structure in which we can rediscover what we ourselves are capable of articulating as altogether fundamental in what I would call the position of desire."[16] Thus, it is desire that turns the eyes into seeing ones, that makes them see the preciousness, that changes the gaze and allows one to over-estimate the Other. And that is where and why the smart Socrates in the *Symposium* attempts to unmask this process by saying:

15 "[W]e arrive here at the point where transference appears as properly speaking a source of fiction." (Lacan: *Transference*, p. 149.)

16 Ibid., p. 144.

"Be careful, at the place where you see something, I am nothing"[17], as Lacan paraphrases. Socrates intends to restore an equivalent level of value between him and Alcibiades, to bring the hidden process of over-estimation to light and to make it clear that he is no more valuable than the counterpart in this dialogue (in this attempt, Lacan recognizes the work of a psychoanalyst). But the desiring subject, Alcibiades, on the other hand, wants to keep up the inequivalent relation because he sees the opportunity to benefit from the richness of the 'agalmatified' Socrates.

In this way, the structure of transference installs a disparity,[18] something uneven in the intersubjective rapport. And for Lacan, this constellation can finally lead to a constellation of power because it "involves [a] falling under the influence of the commandments of the one who possesses"[19] *agalma*. In this logic, the desiring subject is willing to follow the one in which it sees *agalma* because it is convinced of the value that lies in the words and actions the agalmatified person expresses while being also convinced that parts of this value can 'rub off' on subjects who are ready to receive it. Therefore, transference comes always with a potential for power and authority. The desiring subject's interest in such potential benefits is responsible for its voluntary *assujettissement* (as Louis Althusser says[20]), as in Alcibiades' falling under the influence of Socrates: he does what Socrates says, because he is convinced that Socrates and his words are precious. Hence, this is a structure that allows one subject to have influence over the other.

With the concept of the *subject supposed to know*,[21] Lacan goes a step further and specifies his theory of transference by qualifying *agalma* as *knowledge*: the desiring subject supposes that the Other is a knowing person; the precious thing supposed to be inside her or him is knowledge. With this move, the focus of Lacan's theory of transference shifts mainly to the potential of authority and power in the

17 Lacan: *Transference*, p. 134.

18 Cf. ibid., p. 11.

19 Ibid., p. 121.

20 Cf. Louis Althusser: Idéologie et appareils idéologiques d'État. (Notes pour une recherche). http://classiques.uqac.ca/contemporains/althusser_louis/ideologie_et_AIE/ideologie_et_AIE.pdf (accessed January 7, 2017), p. 11.

21 Cf. Lacan: *Four Fundamental Concepts*, p. 232.

transferencial rapport. With the core of knowledge, the agalmatified person now receives, above all, the function to be followed and to be believed in – and in this, transference shows itself as a major subject in psychoanalysis and at the same time as a major subject in the analysis of intersubjective relations, in structures of desire and power and of fictionalization which serves as the psychic groundwork for those structures. That is why a perspective emphasizing 'transferencial' phenomena focuses on the positions from which subjects address each other,[22] determining what they see in each other, and asks if there is any power-relation or distribution of authority. This also questions the *functions* that subjects have in intersubjective rapports, making *fiction* and *function* what is at stake in intersubjectivity.

Transference outside of psychoanalysis: Abramović, Bourdieu, Althusser

One of the most important aspects of the structure of transference is that it embodies itself, or incarnates itself, as Lacan says, in the involved subjects. Transference reveals itself on a body-level (by affects – tears –, words, behavior) but also 'puts' *agalma* in the interiors of bodies. To return to the pictures of the people sitting at a table with Marina Abramović, we can see the bodily effects of some kind of transference: it seems that those people have accepted her as their *subject supposed to know*, that they are taken by the possibility of sitting face-to-face with a person full of treasure, and that the tears reveal this esteem. All emotions coming up seem to be related to The Artist, even if they might not all be caused by her.

This diagnosis and the potential of intersubjective influence that lies in transferencial encounters demand an awareness of the possibilities of how such a constellation can be exploited – meaning exploitation of the basic human need for love and attention – and by whom: in this case, obviously, by Marina Abramović and, by extension, the Museum of Modern Art as the institution that organizes the exposition in which the encounter takes place. All those visiting people benefit from transference. Because they want to sit with the Artist, they buy their tickets, they do their own advertising, they even line up every

22 Cf. ibid., p. 233.

day and camp in front of the museum to ensure that they will get in. Transference is thus used here for a specific goal, and the institution even intensifies it by putting the performance right in the middle of the museum, so that a whole community of adoration and worship for a collectively-shared precious subject can form itself around the table. And this community is even more reinforced by people hired by the institution to film and to take photographs. There is a security service as well as a surveillance system called "marina cam" that streams permanently into the web. And all this can be called collective acting out of transference: worshipping Marina Abramović.

Lacan also reminds us that if there is "no analyst in view, there may be, [...] transference effects that may be structured exactly like the gamut of transference phenomena in analysis."[23] So a definition of transference that claims that such processes usually happen naturally between people emphasizes that transference is not reserved for psychoanalytical constellations alone. If there is a "natural model"[24] of transference, as Lacan puts it, then it is interesting and important for *all* intersubjective rapports. That is why transference can provide reasons for integrating the desiring subject into interpretations and analyses of theory, art and theater that deal with questions of intersubjectivity and co-subjectivity.

For instance, transference allows for the re-reading of theoretical concepts, such as the 'symbolic power' by Pierre Bourdieu and the 'interpellation' by Louis Althusser. Both concepts need transference for their effectiveness insofar as power is always transferred by other subjects onto potentates or rulers in their willingness to believe and follow. Those who want to speak with *symbolic power* are dependent upon ears that hear the 'richness' of their speech, meaning the supposed value, as Bourdieu puts it: "Discourses are not only [...] signs designated to be understood, decoded; they also are signs of richness destined to be valued, appreciated and *signs of authority*, destined to be believed in and to be obeyed."[25] And the *interpellating* voice is also

23 Lacan: *Four Fundamental Concepts*, p. 125.

24 Ibid.

25 Pierre Bourdieu: *Language and Symbolic Power*, ed. by John B. Thompson, transl. from the French by Gino Raymond / Matthew Adamson. Cambridge: Polity 1991, p. 66.

just as dependent upon accepting ears and emerging subjects who are ready to turn:

> [T]he hailed individual will turn round. By this mere one-hundred-and-eighty-degree physical conversion, he becomes a subject. Why? Because he has recognized that the hail was 'really' addressed to him, and that 'it was really him who was hailed' (and not someone else).[26]

The belief in the hailing voice is always a phantasm with an enormous impact on reality, always a mis-take, as Cormann puts it in his explication of the being-taken spectators: "this prise, isn't it always misunderstanding, understood-for-oneself, in the secret certitude that it's me and only for me"[27] (referring to what has been spoken). Misunderstanding influences subjects in the here and now – or it might even turn them into (theater) subjects in the first place. But speaking of theater and audiences, a subject in the function of a spectator always has to be seen as a representative of the public, as Erika Fischer-Lichte reminds us.[28] So mis-takes, misrecognitions and phantasms in theater are never only private or personal ones.

Apparently, there are several ways to deal with the natural sources of transference: on the one hand, an exploiting one that interpellates individuals, turning them into subjects for a prefigured, ideological goal (and this is the tendency in *The Artist Is Present*); but on the other hand, there are also experimental practices to be considered that do not exploit but that interrupt active transferences, playing with them, seeking for the occasions where interpellation can and must fail, where resistance arises and subjectivity becomes non-ideological or at least questionable. Art and theater would be the places to find such practices.

26 Louis Althusser: Ideology and Ideological State Apparatuses (Notes towards an Investigation). In: L. A.: *Lenin and Philosophy and Other Essays*, transl. from the French by Ben Brewster. New York: Monthly Review 2001, pp. 127–186, here p. 174.

27 Cormann: Fantasme, Malentendu, p. 37 (transl. E. H.).

28 Cf. Erika Fischer-Lichte: *Semiotik des Theaters. Eine Einführung*, Vol. 1: Das System der theatralischen Zeichen. Tübingen: Narr 1983, p. 16.

Theater's co-subjectivity: a space for transference towards a gorilla

So, if intersubjectivity is postulated here as theater's basis, and subjects are seen as desiring ones, how can theatrical co-subjectivity be described and how is it structured? What functions do theatrical subjects have and how are they fictionalized? Of course, there are no general answers to those questions, only ones that can be applied on a case-to-case basis.

On a theoretical level, Jacques Rancière gives a good example of how transference and theater can be discussed together, coming from his popular theory of the *Ignorant Schoolmaster*.[29] In a 'transferencial' regard, the 'master' always remains a master, a subject who is supposed to know, no matter how democratic his teaching methods might be – only that he doesn't exploit his position. When Rancière expands this theory to theater (in his *Emancipated Spectator*), he unwillingly develops a concept of theatrical transference by questioning the subjectifying methods of theater makers towards audiences. He understands theater as an intersubjective and collective process[30] in which he criticizes the functions that are distributed among people in pointing out "embodied allegories of inequality"[31]. With this notion, he highlights a "network of presuppositions"[32] acted out as "a priory distribution of the positions and capacities and incapacities attached to these positions"[33]. The *Emancipated Spectator* deals mainly with the distribution of activity and passivity which means at the same time knowing and not knowing in theater, where the audience often is supposed *not* to know and thus passive. Indirectly, this is the diagnosis of theatrical transference, when a theater wants to destroy the distance between stage and audience by putting it up in the first place: the presupposed distance is acted out and comes to life only in this action and the

29 Cf. Jacques Rancière: *The Ignorant Schoolmaster. Five Lessons in Intellectual Emancipation*, transl. from the French by Kristin Ross. Stanford: Stanford UP 1991.

30 "Theatre emerged as a form of aesthetic constitution – sensible constitution – of the community." (Jacques Rancière: *The Emancipated Spectator*, transl. from the French by Gregory Elliot. London / New York: Verso 2009, p. 6.)

31 Ibid., p. 12.

32 Ibid., p. 7.

33 Ibid., p. 12.

presupposition of its existence. Thus Rancière asks, "if it is not precisely the desire to abolish the distance that creates it?"[34] A passive audience does not exist just like that, it is a supposed one, a fiction, seen as such and then interpellated, created. Hence, theater and its interpellated subjects practice their mutual fictions and transferences in their special rapport and in every new encounter.
To give an example, a little moment from Forced Entertainment's *Bloody Mess*[35] can show some interpellating methods. Shortly after the beginning of the show, the performers are sitting on chairs in a row on stage. They pass a microphone around, addressing the audience. Richard starts:

> Well, good evening. Before we start, I think some people had a few things that they wanted to say. I know that for myself, I'm hoping that tonight you'll see me very much as the romantic hero of the piece; strong, sensitive, caring, manly and well, very virile.[36]

Everyone then continues to present him- or herself, mostly with their names and by expressing how they would like to be seen by the audience during the show (only Cathy hopes that everybody missed her name when she was called by it, because she desires to stay enigmatic). They formulate images, figures that shall emerge in the audience's gaze. When Claire's turn comes up, she states:

> Hello, I'm Claire, and I hope that during this evening's performance, I hope that you won't be able to take your eyes of me, that you might be distracted by other things going on, but your gaze will return to me again and again. You'll be like a helpless moth drawn to a burning flame. And there'll be a feeling that starts in the pit of your stomach and spreads through your body like an infection, and you'll realize that you are utterly consumed by physical desire for me.[37]

34 Ibid.
35 Forced Entertainment: *Bloody Mess* (Premiere: May 07, 2004, Kunstenfestivaldesarts, Brussels).
36 *Bloody Mess*, performance text, p. 9.
37 Ibid.

Fig. 2: The Gorilla in Forced Entertainment: *Bloody Mess*, 2004.

This is particularly funny because Claire is going to wear a gorilla costume during the show that covers her whole body – so she'll have a kind of precious inside contrasting with a weird outside.

In this scene, the (mostly funny) effects emerge from fictionalizations on several levels: The actors fictionalize themselves by creating images of how they want to be seen and of what they want to achieve during the evening. But these images clearly depend upon the gaze of the spectators: they wish for the audience to see certain *agalma* in them and only the audience is able to fulfill that wish. Claire expresses it quite directly: she starts speaking of a hope, but quickly falls into an imagined future where the audience *will* do as she desires (which, by the way, is a desire for desire and therefore exactly Lacan's theorization of desire). In doing so, Forced Entertainment openly fictionalize the audience – or better: they fictionalize the fictions of the audience. A play aiming to benefit from transference in an exploitative way would use identification (*Einfühlung*) without exposing it. But this show plays openly and consciously with it, making the gap between the address and the addressee perceivable, a practice that should therefore be called experimental.

Fiction, as shown in this short argumentation, plays an important role in transference as well as in theater, and Tim Etchells stresses the importance of fictionalization for the work of the group. They "start with the basic [...] notion of presentness. And then [...] processes of fictionalizing, flirting, lying, pretending what you speak of can take us on journeys away from the here and now."[38] Fiction therefore needs a present from which to differ, and one method of working with transference in theater is thus a perceivable mis-taking of this present, as Etchells puts it: "We talk about these as processes of misrecognition – and as a fictionalization of the audience. Putting the audience in a fictional place by addressing them wrongly."[39] This can also be seen as a 'fake interpellation,' a game with Althusser's "Hey, you, there!"[40], referring to his interpellating policeman on the street. Theatrical subjects in the audience are interpellated from the stage (and vice versa) and the question arises: what ears will be hearing that? Will the spectators 'turn round' and in which direction? What will they do with these crazy demands? There is no ideological intention or prefigured *telos* in this interpellation, or better: there is an open one. The addressing itself is the main thing from which to start.

Transference is thus the source for co-subjective creations that always happen when people gather. *The Artist Is Present* and *Bloody Mess* show different ways of dealing with the willingness-to-receive (of the spectators), caused by transference. Abramović and the MoMA do not interpellate their visitors in an open way without *telos*, for even the basic artistic setting of the performance is designed as such. On the contrary, security systems ensure that admiration is only acted out in predetermined ways.[41] And what the visitors perhaps pre-imagined when they turned to the MoMA is confirmed: admiring the artist.

38 Can you trust the people sitting next to you? Interview with Tim Etchells / Dagmar Walser. In: *Passages. The Cultural Magazine of Pro Helvetia* 57:3 (2011), pp. 20–23, here p. 20.

39 Tim Etchells in an Interview with Adrian Heathfield: As If Things Got More Real. A Conversation with Tim Etchells. In: Judith Helmer / Florian Malzacher (eds): *Not Even a Game Anymore*, pp. 77–99, here p. 83.

40 Althusser: ISA, p. 23.

41 Nino Klingler describes some reactions on not-predetermined actions that happened during the performance: "Dissense is treated quite straightforward: spectators who do not want to accept the exact predetermined position vis-à-vis Abramović and therefore performatively express the uncertainty factor 'human being' are already after a split second dragged away from their chair by the security service. A young woman, obviously a big admirer of Abramović's work, tears apart her dress and wants to pose naked. After her expulsion she wails: 'But I thought the audience was part of the work!' Right and wrong: the audience is only part as

Forced Entertainment on their part play openly with the fact that there are mutual suppositions and expectations in theater by exaggerating them and playing them out offensively and always in an identification-breaking way. In their practice, they do not appeal to "a version of His Master's voice issuing positive prescriptions" but rather to the other side of the "shifting line" in the interpellation voice, or as Mladen Dolar describes it: the "excess of the voice" that "does not tell us what to do and does not offer a handle for recognition and identification" and therefore aims at "an opening, a pure enunciation compelling a response, an act, a dislocation of the imposing voices of domination."[42]

Theater can therefore be the place for the failure of interpellation that always happens and can therein create a place for co-subjectivity where subjects can question their fictionalizations and functionalizations, in other words, their co-subjectivity. In conclusion, a transferencial approach invites a questioning of the interpellations and treatments of subjects and asks whether they are exploiting or experimental; it is interested in the functions and fictions of intersubjective relations created in theater and claims that theater should be aware of its network of presuppositions. Transference that is acted out finally reveals itself always as a political act. The Rancièrian 'distribution of the positions and capacities and incapacities attached to these positions' is intersubjective, a socio-politics of theater and of art in general.

long as they accept the predetermined role." (Nino Klingler: Die Ausweitung der Affirmationszone. In: *Critic*, February 13, 2012. http:// www.critic.de/lm/marina-Abramović-the-artist-is-present-3661 (accessed August 29, 2014) (transl. E. H.).)

42 Mladen Dolar: *A Voice and Nothing More*. Cambridge / London: MIT Press 2006, p. 122.

Eliane Beaufils

Self-Play and Togetherness

Sense-Making in *Before Your Very Eyes* and *Rhythm Conference Feat. Inner Splits*

The evolution of the performing arts has mostly been related to the history of the performer's status, even in recent studies dealing with conceptual forms of performance.[1] During the 1960s and 70s, attention was often given to 'mythical' performers like Marina Abramović whose performing processes could be linked to Jerzy Grotowski's actor play theory, but in these cases as well as in others, to be a performer also meant to reflect upon the subject's inscription within the symbolic order. Emancipation from these orders was at the core of practical performance research, either conceived as a rebellion against symbolic oppressions in the emblematic works of Performance Art or later on as "autobiographical fantasies"[2], lecture-performances and other half-representational forms, where performers distanced themselves in various ways from their former experiences. Yet for Fernando de Toro, the focus on the performer falls short because postmodern performances do not primarily concern the performers but rather deal with a topic or a set of questions.[3] While the performers can bring autobiographical elements into play among numerous other elements, the

1 Cf. Philipp Schulte: *Identität als Experiment. Ich-Performanzen auf der Gegenwartsbühne*. Frankfurt am Main: Lang 2011.

2 Cf. Marvin Carlson: Performing the Self. In: *Modern Drama* 39,4 (1996), pp. 599–608.

3 "La performance théâtrale postmoderne ne performe pas une parole ou un spectacle, mais une problématique." (Fernando de Toro: Chapitre 4. Performance: quelle performance? In: André Helbo (ed.): *Performance et savoirs*. Bruxelles: de Boeck 2011, pp. 65–102, here p. 82.)

work does not concentrate on them. In the following pages, I would like to focus on two very different works that can be categorized as "thematic postmodern performances", but which are centered on the topic of subjectivization. Moreover, I would like to provide support for my analyses from Judith Butler's theory of subjectivization as performative identities. These performances regarding subjectivization take a playful turn that also needs to be questioned. While indeed seeming to undermine the discourses that constitute us, conspicuous play also transcends the conceptual mode and builds on what constitutes the performers' outside of discourses. One may ask if this movement opens up a particular space of thought for the spectators that enables them to rethink their own use of discourse. What constitutes us may consequently be linked to that which binds us to others. I will show how playful performances appeal to what binds us to others and to our capacity to reinvent the sense of discourses as well as the production of sense. Such performances engage a process of being-with, as coined by Jean-Luc Nancy,[4] between the spectators and the performance: a movement of sense, which also means of sense-making, as sense always needs to exceed the individual and to be collective. The self-reflexive deepening of sense-making in these performances can be thought of as a prelude to every common movement of sense, even if the kind of sense at stake should be specified further.

Performative identities *Before Your Very Eyes*

The performance *Before Your Very Eyes*, created by the theater collective Gob Squad,[5] appears very relaxed. It presents children aged from 6 to 14 in a glass cube situated within a black box. The two-way

4 Cf. Jean-Luc Nancy: *The Inoperative Community*. Minneapolis / Oxford: University of Minnesota Press 1991.

5 Gob Squad: *Before Your Very Eyes* (Premiere: April 28, 2011, HAU 2, Berlin). This theater-performance was instigated by Theatre Campo in Belgium, which held a series of performances by children (rather than with them). Adults were not authorized to enter the scene, and the children spoke in their Flemish mother tongue. I saw it on September 8, 2012 at Künstlerhaus Mousonturm (Frankfurt am Main) and on a video recording by the group. Gob Squad (Johanna Freiburg, Sean Patten, Berit Stumpf, Sarah Thom, Bastian Trost, Simon Will) created the concept, the set and directed the young actors, who are Maurice Belpaire, Zoë Breda, Ramses De Ruyck, Fons Dhossche, Tasja Doom, Robbe Langeraert, Aiko Vanparys.

Fig. 1: Looking at/like teenagers in Gob Squad: *Before Your Very Eyes*, 2011.

windows allow them to not be disturbed by the presence of the audience. The children start by representing themselves playing, and then each in turn dances enthusiastically to the music of Queen's *Don't Stop Me Now*. An off-voice guides them afterwards in an enigmatic way: after asking embarrassing questions about death, it orders them to "grow up!" The children start to imagine and enact themselves being teenagers. They try to dress up as adolescents do in their eyes, adopting specific – rebellious! – attitudes. Later on, they project themselves as young adults, eventually becoming adults in their forties and even seventies. They perform a parody of life, a concentrated presentation of social roles as defined by Erving Goffman: typical and ritual behaviors of teenagers and adults are nailed in a few words and attitudes.[6] (Fig. 1)

But they are also led by this quasi-divine and ubiquitous off-voice, so that their play parodies a performative construction of identity, relying on discourses that can be perceived as 'voices', and that are incarnations of power. The children measure themselves according to their representations of adolescents and adults, and this in fact sends the

6 Erving Goffman: *The Presentation of Self in Everyday Life*. New York: Anchor 1959.

spectators constantly back to their own representations: they are confronted with their clichés of normative injunctions that echo those of the children. This becomes very clear when, during Zoe's 40th birthday party, Tasja pretends to admire Zoe's horribly failed hairdressing while Ramses poses as a wine connoisseur. Beyond the teenager and adult rituals that are pinned on, Ramses and Tasja show the hypocrisy of the norms and the vanity of the roles. This has to be related to other key moments. The children are invited to answer questions they composed two years earlier. At the beginning of the project, they had imagined questions which they would have liked to ask themselves in the future. For instance, we see the cool and blasé teenager Ramses watching video footage of himself as a younger child addressing his older self, who is so profoundly irritated by the sensitivity and enthusiasm of his previous self that he interrupts the viewing and rebels against the apparatus. Such confrontations of possible or past selves happen regularly in the course of the performance. These moments introduce a friction in the easygoing show. The performers display a self-distance in relation to their 'true' past selves and react to the "psychological rest", arousing what Butler (following Sigmund Freud) calls "melancholy", because it comprises all that one had to reject or repress in his/her life in order to construct him/herself as an adolescent or to show him/herself to be an adult: in fact, one has to reject potentialities of him/herself so that s/he may better identify with categories and constitute him/herself as an (intelligible) subject. In consequence, the rejection of potentialities goes hand in hand with a loss, a melancholy. In so far as the adolescents constrain themselves to seemingly blasé or 'anti-sentimental' reactions, they suppress these kinds of rejections. The difficult relation to the psychological rest is parodied in the performance, while the affirmation of identity caricatures the habit of 'behaving as expected'.

For Butler, parody remains a major form of subversion, even if her initial theoretical reflections required some nuancing.[7] In fact, *Before*

7 The Parody (of the Drag-Queen for instance) remains a good way to show how norms were naturalized. See Judith Butler: *The Psychic Life of Power. Theories in Subjection*. New York: Routledge 2001, p. 146; Nicole Balzer / Katharina Ludewig: Quellen des Subjekts. Judith Butlers Umdeutungen von Handlungsfähigkeit und Widerstand. In: Norbert Ricken / Nicole Balzer (eds): *Judith Butler: Pädagogische Lektüren*. Wiesbaden: Springer 2012, pp. 95–124, here p. 109.

Your Very Eyes represents the possibility of a critical acknowledgment of clichés as well as a liberation through laughter: in the staged ages and rituals with which everybody can identify, one may recognize the strength of discourses incarnated by the adult's off-voice and the forceful power behind them. At the same time, one may also recognize the correlative strength of the psychological rest that everybody must regularly surmount as well as the necessity of going back to the inner self. Moreover, if children can appropriate the attitudes and reflections that guide adults – maybe more than some spectators would like –, then the subjectivization process appears far too simple. The transmission of adult norms is manifest as well, most pointedly since the children founded their imitation games on interviews conducted with persons around them.

But these recognitions may not be particularly distressing, as they are founded on a parody that does not implicate very many real experiences and since the ones accomplishing the parody are not particularly developed as characters. On the contrary, such recognitions may be thrilling and liberating, especially since many processes feed into the comical. The comic effect occurs mainly due to caricature and acceleration: the children metamorphose in a few seconds "before our very eyes". The performance is so easily accepted by the spectators[8] that one may wonder if it can be called subversive. Does it not permit the spectators to accommodate the mechanisms of voice and the automated behaviors they may often adopt simply because they bring a smile, giving them the impression that they are being liberated from them by recognizing them? The laugh of superiority also enables spectators to anchor relations of power over and manipulation of the children in the pretext that they are merely playing – as usual – but in a golden

8 The reviews are all very glowing. See for instance Matthias Weigel: Spieglein, Spieglein an der Wand. In: *nachtkritik*, April 28, 2011. https://www.nachtkritik.de/index.php?option=com_content&view=article&id=5557:before-your-very-eyes-ua-gob-squad-spielt-am-hau-berlin-mit-erwachsenwerden-und-den-altersschablonen&catid=55&Itemid=40 (accessed April 04, 2017): "a playful and cruel theatrical happiness"; Pascale Anja Dannenberger: Hereinspaziert. In: *Frankfurter Allgemeine Zeitung*, September 09, 2012: "contaminating joy of life"; Petra Hallmeyer: Tolstoi für den Laufsteg. In: *Süddeutsche Zeitung*, March 23, 2016: "The most beautiful of their plays". Many spectators express their enthusiasm, like Prospero (blogger on *stagescreen*): "it was the most beautiful and truthful show of the year" (comment to Weigel: Spieglein, Spieglein an der Wand).

cage or a laboratory box. The reality is that most of the young actors have no desire to become actors in the future,[9] and that the experience does not seem to be quite so exhilarating or liberating for them.

From the constitutive outside to sense-making

The limits of the performance are linked to the fact that the performative identities remain somehow exterior to the performers: they are hypothetical and arbitrary. They are related to childhood. But the performance is also powerful because of these limits. It facilitates the shifting from the question of the subject to the question of collective being or to the Big Other (Jacques Lacan).[10]

In fact, the most revealing episode of this manipulative farce is no doubt the moment when the children are commanded to "grow up"! This interpellation sounds absurd, but it reveals the injunction grown-ups make regularly and implicitly to children: be big boys or girls, show yourself responsible, grow up, become subjects. Parents and educators never would allow themselves to express it in such terms and they would never consider themselves to be manipulators, despite being the main perpetrators of these discourses. Hence, the spectators'[11] strong implicit involvement is also due to the fact that they are called into question as manipulators and conceivers of these discourses that the children pick up on and perpetrate.

As the children cannot have had the majority of the experiences they present and recall, there is a double distance inscribed in the quasi-determinisms within which they operate, and this distance nurtures the consciousness of the margin, where all real possibilities still exist for them. There is no destiny, and nothing is tragic for them or for the spectator. Everything is play, and moreover, everything is likely to be a play. Everybody can be a playing subject. The virtuosic young actors reveal ways of distancing themselves from the modes of

9 I refer to an interview with Bastian Trost on May 16, 2014.

10 Lacan calls the symbolic system the Big Other whereas other people are "little others". The Big Other thus interferes in our relation to an object or to a person, it mediates every relation.

11 If one considers the descriptions and reactions of journalists to be representative for the spectators, as well as my impressions regarding the audience at the Mousonturm.

subjectivization they show. This partly meets the principle of active subjectivization according to Butler – being active by shifting or subverting the use of discourses. But it goes far beyond this. The aesthetic experience signals a possibility that escapes Butler. In her eyes, minor beings can only be "oppressed and unintelligible" subjects, for as long as they are unintelligible, they cannot constitute real subversive subjects[12]. When the performance appeals to their play, they are nevertheless interpellated as the playing subjects they are. This is no doubt a key element of the show. It indeed has performative effects as it causes the children to mature and partially become subjects.[13] Moreover, the children open another horizon when they participate in a play of performative identity. The discourses become less a sum of references with which one must deal in a somehow restrictive though 'active' manner than they constitute elements one can constantly rearrange. Such a radical rearrangement would correspond to the idea of resistance developed by Butler, were it not much easier, freer and less critical than Butler conceives it.[14] The resistance here looks more like a constructive self-technique.[15] Of course, there are multiple reasons why children play with discourses and disrupt them: they have less identity to defend, they target less recognition – which is the main motivation of subjectivization for Butler.[16] But most of all, children build on their personal experiences by recalling objects of attachment and key

12 "To be oppressed means that you already exist as a subject of some kind [...] To be oppressed, you must first become intelligible." (Judith Butler: *Undoing Gender.* New York: Routledge 2004, p. 30.)

13 Some journalists and spectators cannot believe how professional the children are, which induces a tension. See for instance Matthias Weigel: "They play children's plays but with the stage presence of grown-ups. They ask adult's questions and are commanded all the way." (Weigel: Spieglein, Spieglein an der Wand.)

14 Every agency involves a sort of subversion for Butler because the subject "resignifies" norms by using them individually, so that they evolve. But resistance goes further. Resistance is an act of "critical desubjectivization" for Butler: it is a very active subversion, where the person can put fundamental norms and his/her identity into play. See Butler: *The Psychic Life of Power*, p. 130.

15 Even if Michel Foucault did not think of this kind of process, one can use the term he coined in Luther H. Martin / Huck Gutman / Patrick H. Hutton (eds): *Technologies of the Self. A Seminar with Michel Foucault.* Amherst: University of Massachusetts Press 1988, pp. 16–49.

16 For Butler, recognition is a key principle for the subject, as it is for Hegel. The subject needs to be recognized to be itself, and to persist in this being (Spinozian *conatus*). But this recognition will only work under certain conditions. For the

moments in their existence. They prompt the adolescent and the adult they are pretending to be, starting from what they are, not ontologically but constituently. These personal experiences in fact constitute essential, vital references, and they come back to these until the end of the path: to remember the first love letter, the joy of dancing or the teddy bear doctored by the mother with a bandage, means to be filled with events that mean something, that incarnate meaning. Sense cannot be separated from emotions; emotion is a sign of sense because it testifies to what is existential for a person,[17] including the joy of dancing and of feeling one's energy. Neither can sense be dissociated from experiences. What carries the performance away, enabling it not to be reduced to a series of clichés, relates consequently to that energy, that sense that exceeds all mastery and all mastered thinking. The performance does not (only) 'enable the spectator to become child again' and to distance him/herself from the dominant discourses, it also allows the audience to see what reaches beyond the subject and the more-or-less conscious discourses. One can suppose that what affects the spectators also has an effect on them and is eventually the sum of all the components that cannot be reduced to discourses nor be completely manipulated: the strength of personal stories, of emotions, of spontaneous dancing. Many critics evoke the existential, if not cruel dimension of the show.[18] The play and the stories told constitute the outside shell of the power embodied by adults, and they largely expose this part of oneself that one does not claim as subjectivized but that still

subject's desire is not only to persist in his being, but to live in a world of representations that acknowledges and recognizes this possibility of being and that reflects it. Cf. Balzer / Ludewig: Quellen des Subjekts, p. 120.

17 For Butler, affect is that which enables something (object, experience, category) to become yours. Moreover, "in Spinoza [she] found the notion that a conscious and persistent being responds to reflections of itself in emotional ways according to whether that reflection signifies a diminution or augmentation of its own possibility of future persistence and life." (Butler: *Undoing Gender*, p. 245.)

18 See Matthias Weigel "a playful and cruel theatrical happiness" (Weigel: Spieglein, Spieglein an der Wand); Petra Hallmeyer: "[performance] changing between wonderful lightness and very sad melancholy" (Hallmeyer: Tolstoi für den Laufsteg).

contributes to determining one as a subject, called the "constitutive outside"[19] by Butler.

In a way, this performance calls for an exploitation of the constitutive outside, inviting the audience to explore other forms of subjectivization that are also performative ... less intelligible and more sensible forms of affirmation. The intelligible recognition that is for Butler the main spur of the becoming subject seems able to lock in the subject, similar to the way the children are imprisoned in their cage. Moreover, if recognition is only founded on intelligibility and not on the psychological side, the relation to others may fall within the order of give-and-take, like Tasja and Zoe confirming each other's appearance and role. The constant re-arrangement of sense and the being-with are rendered difficult in that case. Butler writes that "something exists that makes the subject beyond the discursive techniques of self in the subject" but does not specify what this would be like.[20] To claim that one should recognize the "constitutive outside" and that this recognition binds somebody to the others in an open manner is an indirect invitation to break the cage: to be open to a being-with outside a frame, be that frame institutional, geographic or even rational (if rational means that you only have to take into account what is intelligible and not what causes sense, what gives an impetus to the movement of making sense and constitutes one of the foundations of sense making and of a subject who wishes to make sense).[21] The performance lets the audience not only feel a deep bond with the children, but it also sets in motion a questioning that is indebted to them. It lets the spectators feel that they situate themselves often in relation to others as if they embodied a constraint whereas the recognition of oneself and joy are linked to the recognition of the other in a broader manner, as well as to self-recognition as a being filled with experience and emotion, and

19 "The subject is constituted through the force of exclusion and abjection, one which produces a constitutive outside to the subject, an abjected outside, which is, after all, 'inside' the subject." (Judith Butler: *Bodies That Matter*. New York / London: Routledge 1993, p. 14.)

20 Interview with Butler in Hannelore Bublitz: *Judith Butler zur Einführung*. Hamburg: Junius 2005, pp. 142–152, here p. 143.

21 Butler seems also to underline this constitutive dimension of the others in her latest works. Cf. Balzer / Ludewig: Quellen des Subjekts, p. 121.

as a playing, experimenting subject. Does it set in motion a being-with towards the children and, beyond them, with the members of Gob Squad? The performance becomes the place of a sense opening (about recognition) which is also a 'subject opening'. It shows how much the recognition of sense may be indebted to a 'common place' more or less beyond the frames, cages and subjects.[22]

Against discourses: the call for disobedience

Conspicuous play is also a matter of great importance in the second example, which nevertheless appears to be more complex.

Rhythm Conference Feat. Inner Splits starts with a rhythm, a kind of coming into a rhythm of the three performers, who begin to shake.[23] The main performer, Anneke Bonnema, starts with a sort of jarring movement which sets her whole body into vibration; with open arms, she seems to listen to her body and to come to meet the spectators. No meaning can be attributed to this jarring, and the performers are absorbed in their bodies and their listening. Many people in the audience also look affected by this presence, not knowing what is happening other than their own diffuse response to the affected body. The following message sounds very clear and cryptic at the same time: "We have to separate ourselves from ourselves. We have to leave. We have to say goodbye." Will it be a matter of de-subjectivization, or is it about a more radical departure: death? The performers wear a weird pointy white hat and a white dress; they present themselves as "angels of disobedience". They appear to look inside themselves for something that extends beyond their intelligible being – a source of disobedience? For Butler, disobedience lies in putting constitutive principles of the subject into question. In questioning themselves, the performers show

22 Again, the reviews seem to testify that the show raises existential questions, and this is also due to its ambiguity (joy and melancholy, children and grown-ups).

23 MaisonDahlBonnema: *Rhythm Conference Feat. Inner Splits* (Premiere: December 19, 2014, Kaaistudios, Brussels). It is a work of MaisonDahlBonnema, a company within the Needcompany. The performers are Anneke Bonnema, Hans Petter Dahl and Catherine Travelletti. The musician Nicolas Field has composed a partition for the drums and accompanies the show most of the time. I attended the premiere and also a rehearsal on June 21, 2014, followed by an exchange with the performers, as well as with Jan Lauwers and Elke Janssens. Parts of the show were already presented on several Needlabs.

their weakness and the weakness of the norm. Yet the next assertion is: "We will tell you the whole story". What story? May disobedience mixed with storytelling be a mere denunciation?

Then, Hans Petter Dahl gives hand signals as if they are about to intone a discourse in chorus, and the performers start to cry, yet without any sound. This scene is repeated three times. Hans Petter speaks then, while the drums on stage accompany him; but one cannot say that he speaks according to the rhythm of the drums for the sounds are regularly discordant. One may get the impression that he enumerates all possible miseries on earth: murder, child labor, women's deportations, child rape, or exploitation of children as criminals and the risk of their execution.[24] Anneke takes over with another list: free radicals to avoid, yoga classes to take, memory exercises to do, nutriments to eat, food to prohibit, news to be listened to, work to finish, loads of norms to take into consideration that pile up and paralyze us under the weight of obedience. For five long minutes, these hammered words seem to sum up all normative discourses. Their accumulation would be oppressive without the drums, which somewhat foil the personal resonances of what is said, but every word, every expression of the norm and of misfortune is likely to affect the spectator, especially as it sounds like the tip of the iceberg, the colossal and derisory summary of lives and efforts one must take into account.

This time one can see what is at stake: disobedience stands against the form of conference cited in the performance's title, against norms, and even against the "whole story": against history or against the sum of discourses that crush people under their weight. The performance aims at any rate to generate consciousness of this sum of knowledge and the pressure of discourses without succumbing to them and without reproducing another (meta-)discourse. What may enable the listeners to escape the sentences and to not be crushed under the weight of grief, loss and melancholy is, on the one hand, the drums that shatter every rhythm and every speech and, on the other hand, Anneke's body. The performer starts to shake while listening to all the miseries and atrocities; her body becomes a sounding board that is far from receiving the effect that is attached to the words but that expresses and repels what is bad even while receiving it. It is an anti-trance in

24 In the text given to me by Anneke Bonnema, this list fills several pages…

response to an overload. It increases and returns the overload like a string or a chord, perhaps close to imploding in "*inner splits*". While somehow hosting the atrocities, taboos and norms through language, the body also enables a discharging of them. At other moments, Catherine and Anneke cry, echoing each other by shouting, "I scream", "I cry". As it is not possible to cry all the time, the shaking can be an expression as visceral as a scream – maybe even more effective because it does not obey any habit or any code. It becomes, in a way, the expression of that which has no symbolization or affects potentially attached to words. The spectators cannot but be sensitive to the performers' melancholy and to their radical rejection of these kinds of discourses. The body of the performer functions as a sounding board for questions with existential dimensions, raising awareness of what constitutes people: most of all these emotions, desires and needs that belong to the individual but maybe not to the subject. Moreover, if rhythm is linked to the movement of thought or, in Jean-Luc Nancy's words, the movement towards oneself,[25] here it is a rhythm that tends to cancel itself out, to annul the subject. Body and rhythm are a reminder of the non-subjectivized part of the individual (the "constitutive outside") that, for Butler, helps to make subjects out of people. (Fig. 2)

Poetic recognition and sense-making?

Not expecting anything in particular from the performer or the performance, the spectator can participate in his/her own way in the performance. In the absence of any expectation, another form of recognition emerges: the other may be recognized as a non-subject, situating him/herself beyond the social game wherein, according to Butler, people are subjects in relation to the recognition they receive. The spectator may recognize another form of identity, another performative identity as it is performed for the audience, an identity starting from the implosion of subjectivization. The body's shouts and partly unintelligible words might open breaches that allow the spectators

25 "The subject feels […] he thinks himself […] approaches himself and strays from himself and thus always feels himself feeling a 'self' that escapes or hides as long as it resounds elsewhere as it does in itself, in a world or in the other." (Jean-Luc Nancy: *Listening*, transl. from the French by Charlotte Mandell. New York: Fordham UP 2007, p. 9.)

Fig. 2
Angels of Disobedience
in *Rhythm Conference Feat. Inner Splits*, 2014.

to experience other thoughts, perhaps bringing him/her back to his/her psyche and to his/her own outside; in this way, the performance could become a place of encounter between non-subjects. The encounter would relieve the obligation to see the other first as a subject, but also even as an individual in his/her singularity.[26] This is exactly "a sharing of community between singular existences that are not subjects."[27] And this sharing is possible for Nancy because

26 Butler distinguishes between the individual and the subject, the latter being the intelligible and performative part of ourselves. None of the elements of the show are presented as autobiographical and none of the reactions as psychological, so that the person of the performer does not matter in itself.

27 Nancy writes for instance: "Community is what takes place always through others and for others. It is not the space of the egos – subjects and substances [...] – but of the *I*'s, who are always other." (Nancy: *The Inoperative Community*, pp. 14, 25.)

> community necessarily takes place in that which Blanchot calls "unworking" referring to that which withdraws from the work and which, no longer having to do either with production or with completion encounters interruption, fragmentation, suspension.[28]

Thus, the performance opens up holes for the spectator concerning the self and the others, with ethical consequences.

Furthermore, the anonymity of the words and the abstraction of the evoked discourses, joined to the rhythm of unprecedented bodies and emotions, are close to constituting a sort of common, Deleuzian plane of thought that is accompanied by dance and that could permanently capsize to give rise to another plane of thought.[29] These actions are not only a way of reflecting upon words and on the pressure notions exert but also a way to think or rather to feel the outside, which resists the discourses or their sense-making.[30]

This reflection culminates at the end of the performance. The performers, and maybe the spectators, are ready for the conclusion and the drastic rejection. As "there will be no revolution" and "it will only get worse", the only solution is to leave the earth. Announcing the departure from earth and of what constitutes them may nourish the melancholy of the spectators. But the performance goes on. The moment of farewell is as simple as it is striking: Anneke Bonnema simply says goodbye to all the things she leaves. "Bye butterflies, bye dreams. Bye tables and chairs. Bye bye flowers and meadows. Bye grass, bye dew. Goodbye my watch, goodbye time. Bye bye cats, bye bye birds. Bye tears, bye rain. Bye aunts and uncles. Bye autumn sky, bye sea at dawn. Bye bye bye ..." The list is long, but it is not a litany: each word is turned back upon itself or to the ideas of the spectators, each word reflects

28 Nancy: *The Inoperative Community*, p. 31.

29 I did not mention another long passage of the show with a similar construction, both semi-logical and chaotic. The performers try in turn to foil their own potential authority: Hans Petter as a father who does not wait for anything from his children, Anneke as a person lost in the woods (of discourses) and thrown back to her loneliness. Both take care not to emit any norm themselves and to prove being human in their resistance to obedience without conscience, but they play with the limits of foolishness.

30 Jan Lauwers and Elke Janssens both mentioned at the end of the rehearsal on June 21, 2014 a way to get physically and mentally upside-down, an overwhelming effect.

an experience, an atmosphere or a person, each word jumps out from any sentence, any discourse, lives from the absurdity and relevance of this saying. The future evades any representation and often does not answer to any will but neglects no loss. The loss extends, as wide as the earth, anchored to the backbone of words. And these words are all the more vested with life, with ideas, because they threaten to become skeletons.

By telling what is not told (too many words are told) and what people are afraid to think of (by living as they do, humans will eradicate themselves), the performance may appeal to resistance and to humanity, which are nevertheless not perceived as principles and are not constituents of a normative discourse. It appeals to us, the spectators, with our 'access' to the world, our forms of being-with. The performance creates conditions for unconditioned recognition and for listening to the fringes of discourses: for a poetic listening, receiving the inconceivable, slipping into the interstices of language. In this non-ordered space that wants to liberate itself from duties of selection and of rational structures, in this upturned and almost disordered relation to the other, sense is in re-creation. The spectators catch a "sense in every sense"[31] that is likely to resonate with everybody, as it is a sense-making that is not completely articulated, that evokes the formation of sense.[32] Because the sense is open and open to everybody, it appeals to everybody. The void creates a space between the stage and the spectators and calls for it to be filled. Therefore the "being-with" on stage goes beyond personal movements and seems to prepare a larger being-with. Spectators may in fact feel disobedient as they participate in the performative indictment of our discursive constitution and in thinking what they do not want to think.

This kind of (potential) participation remains ambiguous: why would it not respond to an (implicit) "interpellation" of the spectator? Of

31 Mathilde Monnier / Jean-Luc Nancy: *Allitérations. Conversations sur la danse.* Paris: Galilée 2005, p. 78.

32 Nancy does not always refer to subjects, because sense making includes the senses, and all the ways persons and bodies interact. The senses need not to be related to a subject. This perception precedes in a certain way Karen Barad's considerations about intra-actions that are especially relevant for dancers and performers (as well as for spectators of dance and performance). Cf. for instance Karen Barad: Posthumanist Performativity: Towards an Understanding of How Matter Comes to Matter. In: *Journal of Women in Culture and Society* 28:3 (2003), pp. 801–831.

course, the self-technique exposed by Anneke Bonnema is in no way imperative: it is not an injunction to be or even to behave differently, and it is not a kind of model one could adopt: this self-technique in a body that seems not 'completely subjectivized' situates itself at the fringes of the social frame and is not self-centered but addressed to the others. Eventually it may open up the space for another kind of reflection, and maybe other ideas, prepared by a physiological and neuromimetic liberation, a reflection departing from an appeal of the words which may meet an unarticulated and repressed, melancholic thought. And this may also go hand in hand with emotion, as every existential thought is bound to emotions[33] (and something related to the subjection and to how someone's way of thinking is felt existentially by the subject). The reactions of Jan Lauwers, Elke Janssens and many journalists attest to such strong effects: they were shaken up.[34]

Emotions and thoughts of this kind go along with the responsivity and creative "diastase" of the spectators[35] which are partly liberated by the creation of another space of encounter. Normally this kind of response is due to "disorders (blinding, injuries), anomalies, confusion, catastrophes: In all these cases something emerges that hits us, hustles us, before it can be understood or rejected"[36]. *Pathos* comes here into play: "[S]omething that does not just appear *as* something", that evades "usual expectations of sense [*Sinnerwartung*] [and rises

33 See note 13.

34 See note 23 regarding the reactions of Jan Lauwers and Elke Janssens. One should also consider the fact that some passages were re-used in the next show of Jan Lauwers: *The Blind Poet* (Premiere: May 12, 2015, Kunstenfestivaldesarts, Kaaitheater, Brussels). Another review attests for instance "a crazy breakaway" and a "joyful apocalypse". (Hugues Le Tanneur: Bonnema et Dahl, joyeuse apocalypse. In: *Libération*, February 24, 2015. http://next.liberation.fr/theatre/2015/02/23/bonnema-et-dahl-joyeuse-apocalypse_1208463 (accessed March 10, 2017).)

35 "En réalité, la diastase désigne, comme le dit déjà Waldenfels dans *Antwortregister,* 'un processus de différenciation dans lequel naît [*entsteht*] pour la première fois cela-même qui est en train de se scinder'. À côté de la différence significative, la diastase s'exprime aussi comme événement fondamental en tant que différence représentative, appétitive et responsive." (Marc Rölli: Phénoménologie et empirisme s'excluent-ils mutuellement? In: *Revue germanique internationale* 13 (2011), pp. 109–123. http://rgi.revues.org/1128 (accessed March 10, 2017). The quotation comes from Bernhard Waldenfels: *Antwortregister*. Frankfurt am Main: Suhrkamp 1994, p. 335. This book has not been translated into English.)

36 Bernhard Waldenfels: *Bruchlinien der Erfahrung*. Frankfurt am Main: Suhrkamp 2002, p. 33, quoted from Rölli: Phénoménologie et empirisme, p. 118.

above] apprehension until a point where the world collapses for us."[37] Here the space allows for the encounter of somebody or something "that [is] accessible by being not identical with itself and not representable"[38]. Maybe this experience results in self-transformation as one may behave differently vis-à-vis oneself and vis-à-vis one's existence – which, according to Michel Foucault, constitutes human beings as ethical subjects.[39] The performance somehow suggests the idea of another space, another mode of thinking together … through the void, the absence of discussion, the being-shaken-up. Text and gestures may indicate a way of being-with as regards the performers beyond identities, appealing to ethical concerns, so that the spectators could constitute themselves as ethical subjects in an experience as Walter Benjamin conceives it: where events can give rise to "experiences because they are related significantly with the personal as well as collective future and past"[40]. The movement of sense and of sense-making for oneself is made in common here, thanks to the performers and perhaps to the feelings of the group of spectators. It confronts them with an urgency and may open to another movement that exceeds each of them.

37 Ibid.

38 Natascha Adamowsky: Dies ist (k)ein Spiel. In: Marianne Bäcker / Verena Freytag (eds): *Tanz Spiel Kreativität*. Osnabrück: Henschel 2013, pp. 19–34, here p. 33.

39 This is Judith Butler's interpretation of Foucault. She joins self-transformation, virtue and critic. Cf. Judith Butler: What is Critic? An Essay on Foucault's Virtue. In: *Transversal Texts* 5 (2001). http://eipcp.net/transversal/0806/butler/en (accessed January 08, 2018).

40 Hartmut Rosa: *Social Acceleration: A New Theory of Modernity*, transl. from the German by Jonathan Trejo-Mathys. New York: Columbia UP 2013, pp. 144–145; original: *Beschleunigung: Die Veränderung der Zeitstrukturen in der Moderne*. Frankfurt am Main: Suhrkamp 2005, p. 235.

Marie Vandenbussche-Cont

Nature Theater of Oklahoma

A Theater which Calls Us to Remake (the) World

Nature Theater of Oklahoma is a New York City company led by Pavol Liska and Kelly Copper. In *No Dice* and *Life and Times*, the two artists stage recorded phone conversations that evoke the perpetual conversations of daily life. *No Dice*[1] lasts 3 h 30 and compiles elements of ordinary conversations in which Pavol Liska talks about everyday life with some close friends. They talk about their jobs (annoying low-earning jobs or creative though not very artistic ones), about how they use their free time, about their addictions and their lack of motivation. *Life and Times*[2] consists of 9 episodes and would last 24 hours if it were integrally staged. The show is made of 9 phone conversations in which a musician and actor of the company, Kristin Worrall, tells her life in detail, from her birth to the age of 34.

Episode 1, on which I will focus here, lasts 3 h 30 (break included) and is made of the first of those conversations, in which the young woman tells her very first moments of life as they were told to her as well as her earliest personal memories and all her childhood discoveries …

I will examine how, in each show, Kelly Copper and Pavol Liska have invented a specific way of staging the verbal score which renders

1 Nature Theater of Oklahoma: *No Dice* (Premiere: December 6, 2007, Soho Rep, New York) was presented in 2010 in Théâtre de Gennevilliers (France).

2 Nature Theater of Oklahoma: *Life and Times – Episode 1* (Premiere: September 5, 2009, Burgtheater Vienna); Nature Theater of Oklahoma: *Life and Times – Episode 2* (Premiere: November 5, 2010, Burgtheater Vienna). Both shows were programmed in Festival d'Avignon 2011.

perceptible the speakers' singularity as well as their existence in the conversation via the relationship to an interlocutor. They have sought to expose the being-with, which unfolds itself in ordinary conversations as a praxis through which the speakers' existence forms itself and makes sense. By saying that, I assume, following Jean-Luc Nancy's perspective, that "we don't exist first and then relate to others"[3]. I assume that "existence forms itself in and through the relations to others"[4] and that meaning occurs by passing from one interlocutor to another.[5]

In *No Dice*, the verbal score is randomly combined with a multiplicity of elements. In particular and most effectively, it is combined with arbitrary gestures (arbitrary in so far as they are not linked to the content of the conversations but juxtaposed upon them). There are 3 pre-established sequences of gestures: 3 sequences of 13 hand gestures linked to street magic techniques, to disco dances or to gestures used by Pavol's mother to make herself understood in the United States. At the beginning of each scene, the actors choose to perform one of those sequences. Their gestures look all the more arbitrary since their speech is rhythmically spaced by the real-time earphone delivery of the conversations to them. So the verbal flux (whose tempo is fixed) is randomly combined with these entirely arbitrary gestures which, because they are arbitrary, shed light on some bits of the conversation, enabling us to catch such or such singular phrasing. The gestures are revealing in the midst of the show's banal conversations to which we would not pay attention for very long otherwise. They enable us to realize what the conversations are in the author's perspective, namely creations. Attempts to exist, one could say. Attempts to singularly relate to others[6]:

3 Cf. Frédéric Neyrat: *Le Communisme existentiel de Jean-Luc Nancy*. Fécamp: Lignes 2013, p. 32.

4 Ibid.

5 Cf. Jean-Luc Nancy: *La Pensée dérobée*. Paris: Galilée 2001, p. 36: "[...] le sens ne se donne qu'en passant de l'un à l'autre."

6 Cf. John Cage according to whom music or theater is something continuous, which "only stops when we turn away and stop paying attention" (Jean-Yves Bosseur: *John Cage* [1993]. Paris: Minerve 2000, p. 29). Ordinary sounds or words are singular as soon as we pay attention to them. They are art. And art, considered as an introduction to daily life, can reveal music or theater in its continuity.

Bobby
[...]
Just imagine if ... !
If – you could then hear
the cosmic murmur ...
Be able to HEAR ... !
(pause)
Because you don't hear yourself right now, right?
And I don't hear myself.
We don't hear ourselves.
We just talk, and – and things ...
things go unrecorded.
The – the creativity ... that we –
that we ... uh ... USE ! – to –
(pause)
To – let's say to talk right now
or to ... LATER or ... !
Or the conversation that we have ...
[...]
We take it for granted!
We don't – we don't make anything out of it.
And then ... how can we transform this ...
universal cosmic murmur ... ?!
This – this uh – *(pause)*
STREAM of constant –
Into – into – so that we can notice it ... !?[7]

In *No Dice*, thanks to a pure *gestus* – a purely revealing *gestus*[8], never-ending conversations are 'transformed' so that we can notice the being-with which unfolds in them.

7 Kelly Copper (transcription and arrangement): *No Dice*. New York: 53rd State Press 2007, p. 28.

8 According to Patrice Pavis, Bertolt Brecht's fundamental *gestus* is close to what is called today "the staging discourse". It is a set of signs, which makes that discourse readable. Cf. Patrice Pavis: *Vers une théorie de la pratique théâtrale*. Lille: Presses Universitaires du Septentrion 2007, p. 56. As to me, when I say "pure *gestus*", I am referring to a set of signs, which is not signifying and serves only to shed light on some phrases.

Fig. 1: Nature Theater of Oklahoma: *No Dice*, 2007.

In *Life and Times 1*, that pure *gestus* is essentially musical. The textual score has been put to music before the beginning of the rehearsals: the creators wanted to use music "as a way to formalize the material"[9]. The textual score has therefore been combined with pop opera, and this formalization of the text makes it more perceptible. Music plays the role of a *gestus* because of its constant modulations, either successive or simultaneous: stylistic, melodic, vocal, choral or instrumental ones. To say it briefly, the irruption of a gospel sequence into a heroic one, that of a melodic line (very lyrical and dynamic) into a homogeneous part, or the irruption of a half-sung, half-spoken moment, that of polyphony or that of instrumental tutti, make some narrator's phrases stand out, shedding light on their singularity. It makes us perceive in the banal story she tells a sharing of singularity which makes sense.

No Dice and *Life and Times 1* do not only reveal the being-with in the conversations, they concretely expose actors and spectators to it,

9 Cf. http://www.fta.qc.ca/sites/fta.qc.ca/files/documents/ps_life-and-times_5.pdf (accessed June 06, 2012, not available anymore).

through a "general *gestus*"[10] which shows performance as address, as relationship. Indeed, these two shows gradually appear as being-with performances in which we take part. The actors progressively appear as mere existents engaged in a pure address. That general *gestus* derives, in the first place, from the multiple constraints which make the actors initially look like transmitters who laboriously work to make us perceive singularity: "As long as [our demands] are impossible", says Kelly Copper, "there are always going to be holes that allow for you to see [the actors]."[11] In *No Dice*, in addition to the sequences of gestures, the actors have to make stage pictures[12] and melodramatic mimics. And in the first part, they also have to speak with the foreign accent they master the least (French, Irish or Jamaican accent).

In *Life and Times 1*, the main constraint or struggle for the actors consists in singing hesitant, awkward speeches that are not meant to be sung.[13] On top of that, they also have to execute some choreographies inspired by *spartakiads* in a random order they discover in real time

10 In *A Short Organum for the Theater*, Brecht says each shown *gestus* must be accompanied by a general one, which consists in showing the showing. Cf. Bertolt Brecht: A Short Organum for the Theater. In: *Brecht on Theatre: The Development of an Aesthetic*, ed. and trans. from the German by John Willett. London: Methuen 1964, pp. 179–208, here p. 203. What I call here general *gestus* to go on with the parallel I made with Brechtian terminology, shows performance not only as monstration but as address, as relation.

11 Cf. Kelly Copper / Amber Reed: Getting Cosmic with Kelly Copper. In: *The Brooklyn Rail*, December 8, 2006. http://brooklynrail.org/2006/12/theater/getting-cosmic-with-kelly-copper (accessed January 8, 2018).

12 13 paired positions on the stage, based on melodramatic possibilities. (One such position can be one person standing as if to walk off the stage and leave, and another in the far upstage, standing as if he would stop the person from leaving. It can be one person leaning with his head down against a wall and the other person with his hand on the person's shoulder as if to console.) If there are just two people on stage, one person goes to one spot and the other goes to the complimentary spot and forms this picture. If there are two persons and one more walks in and stands in a different spot, it opens up another possible paired image, and therefore opens the possibility that someone can move.

13 "The speech of the telephone monologue is itself restrictive, has its own rules, and resists being put into the theatrical frames Copper and Liska invent for it. No filler removed, no rhythm smoothed out, the signifying elements stay in conflict, they don't agree on a common syntax. And the performers are always in the midst of this struggle." (Florian Malzacher: Previously on Nature Theater of Oklahoma. In: *Life and Times, episode V*. New York: Nature Theater of Oklahoma 2012, pp. 125–126.)

(*spartakiads* were mass gymnastic events which took place in several Communist countries including Czechoslovakia and worked on melting individuals into a group). Here is what Kelly Copper says about those choreographic constraints:

> In *Episode 1* there is [...] a prompter in the pit who is prompting the dances live. 90 % of the dance in this show is unscripted and chance generated. Every night before the performance, the prompter shuffles a deck of cards consisting of 34 separate 4-count dance phrases. The actors are shown cards during the performance and choose when to insert a dance phrase before moving on to the next card.[14]

All the constraints in *Life and Times 1* are deliberately conceived to go against everyone's competences, so that virtuosity does not reduce the general *gestus*. Florian Malzacher (the company's dramaturge at the time) stresses that point:

> Julie La Mendola, a singer, also acts and dances. Musician Kristin Worrall is pressed into service as an actor as well – as are the actors, as singers and musicians and dancers (which only few of them really are). Robert M. Johanson, a performer with the company for many years, is given [...] his first commission as composer, and composes the entire work on ukulele, an instrument he is, at the time, just learning.[15]

It should be noted that by showing the actors' addresses and the revealing work they make for us, the performance constraints also show the singularity of those addresses – they show the actors' singular way of singing, moving or being. The visibility of the actor's singularity is made even stronger by the effects of duplicating the executions of the same stylistic exercise. Since the *gestus* in these shows is composed of a limited number of sequences (gestural sequences or choreographic and musical ones), the spectators can see different actors executing the same sequence and therefore perceive singularities in the execution.[16]

14 Kelly Copper / Pavol Liska: Application to the Alpert Award in the Arts. http://www.alpertawards.org/artist/about-pavol-kelly (accessed July 21, 2013).

15 Malzacher: Previously on Nature Theater of Oklahoma, p. 126.

16 "[Le double est] un *révélateur*, dans le sens photographique du terme [...], qui suggère l'invisible unicité [du réel]." (the double is a revealer, in the photographic

Fig. 2
Nature Theater of Oklahoma:
Life and Times Episode 1,
2009.

Progressively, the 'general *gestus'* dissociates itself from what is represented and shows the actors not only as (singular) transmitters but also as real persons who address their story to us. In *No Dice*, the fact that the actors drop their accent at one point contributes to that evolution. In scene 12, while he's talking about existential vocation, Bobby loses his Jamaican accent, as if the actor were suddenly speaking for himself. Further on, in scene 13, it is Anne who drops her French accent for a while, to evoke addiction problems, as if they were really hers. Both Anne and Bobby resume their accents in scene 14. As for Zack, he drops his accent during scene 19, as if he were speaking of a personal ill-being at work … In the second part of the show, the actors progressively all drop their accents to speak the way they do in real life.

sense of the term […], which suggests the invisible unicity of the real) (Clément Rosset: *L'École du réel*. Paris: Minuit 2008, p. 104).

In the same way, the actors of *Life and Times 1* also seem to speak of their own lives, to the point of personalizing the names appearing in Kristin Worrall's story:

> It begins with a single voice at the top of the show, says Kelly Copper, and then another joins and another, finally there is not just a woman's voice, but a man's, and the story expands to include finally a cast of 10. The actors – though they all still employ Kristin's original firstperson perspective – speak of themselves, even down to changing the name to their own in performance.[17]

In *No Dice* as in *Life and Times 1*, the actors' singular addresses to us eventually overcome what is addressed. The actors simply appear then as singular existents who address us on behalf of telling stories. In *No Dice*, this results from an erosion of representation, an erosion of the conversational material, which is deliberately produced through repetition. The same lines start to circulate from one actor to the other and up to us. The writing principle of the show ("I don't know any goddamn stories!") circulates, for example, up to us, from Anne to Bobby (in scene 14), then from Bobby to Zack (in scene 20), and eventually, in the second part, in a slower and sadder way (as the text requires), from Zack to Bobby (in scene 33). As repetition develops and erodes representation, the spectators' focus moves from the singularity of what is addressed to the singularity of the addresses themselves. When the verbal score of *No Dice* is finally eroded, Anne Gridley throws herself, completely out of context, into a demonstration of her acting skills, as if to extend by any means the being-with induced by the show. It is obvious then that the text in *No Dice* is first and foremost a way to open up a circulation in various directions between the existents who are gathered in the theater: the actors open themselves and open us to those relationships through which existence forms itself. The show makes it explicit in the end:

17 Kelly Copper / Pavol Liska (conceived from a telephone conversation with Kristin Worrall): *Life and times, Episode 1*. New York: 53rd State Press 2013, p. 5.

Kristin
We don't want to say where do we come in or where do we go out, because we would like – I think –
to stay – uh ...
To NOT LEAVE, hm?
[...]
-- the question is more ... uh ...
How do we, uh – how do we spend our TIME ... ? [...]
We don't just want to enjoy ourselves ALONE ... but we want to enjoy ourselves in SOCIETY, right?
... with other people.
(pause)
Our conversations, for instance here ... uh, had we – been having them, say 50 years ago – we would probably been talking about ... *(breath)*

Pavol
They would have been much shorter -- and had more
QUALITY! Ha ha!

Kristin
[...] So, it's no longer ... um ... um ...
(pause) It's a form of
ENJOYMENT! – actually ...
To converse! *(pause)*
I would say on ANY subject[18] ...

After this manifesto, the separation between stage and audience is abolished, and the actors leave the stage to go and speak directly to the spectators. They give them words of encouragement to persevere in life, replicating those which have already circulated from Bobby to Anne (in scene 15) and from Bobby to Zack (in scene 17):

18 Copper: *No Dice*, p. 145.

Scene 15
Words of encouragements

[...]
BOBBY
[...] I feel good things are ... *(pause)*
you know ... if you ...

ANNE
Well, they're definitely out there – it's just a matter of ...

BOBBY
Yeah.

ANNE
-- how you work your way towards them.

BOBBY
Yeah. *(pause)*
Well -- I think --
I think we're -- we're workin'–
our way towards each other[19].

Scene 37
Words of encouragements *(reprise, all)*

(Each performer speaks directly to someone in the audience, in a normal, quiet, reassuring manner.)[20]

In *Life and Times 1*, the primacy of address is not as explicitly put forward but at the end of the show, the actors also appear as singular existents who address themselves to us on behalf of autobiographical stories. Here again, it is the result of the erosion of representation, which is produced however in a less proactive way than in the previous show. Here that erosion results partly from the duration of the show: after

19 Copper: *No Dice*, p. 73.
20 Ibid., p. 146.

3 hours of attention to the actors' revealing work, it becomes difficult for the spectators to play the game and keep on focusing on such a rotten text! It is also the result of an erosion of representation, which occurs in Kristin Worrall's story itself. As time goes by, the young woman loses more and more often her thread of thought, minimizing the importance of what is told: "Wait. What was I gonna say?"[21]; "What was I talking about?"[22] At the same time, her story emphasizes more and more the relation to others in conversation:

> Rob
> Oh my god! I could –
> I could seriously –
> Talk ON and ON about the games that Cindy
> And I would play.
> Um.
> [...]
> So um.
> You know,
> I have to go ...
> But um ...
> But I could seriously talk about
> Cindy Legrand and what we would do –
> All the time![23]

In any case, at the end of these shows, there are, in the theater, only actors and spectators who are in relation with each other and share their singularities. As a spectator, I feel that I exist through those relations and that those relations make sense. Such a concrete experience of existence as coexistence invites us to put ourselves in relation with each other. It makes me feel that, this way, we can satisfy our desire to remake (the) world. For if we have accepted the loss of the world considered as a whole-structure, if we don't expect to find a place in such an organized whole anymore, we have the desire, nevertheless, to inscribe ourselves in the deworlded world in which we are living,

21 Copper / Liska: *Life and Times, Episode 1*, p. 7.
22 Ibid., p. 97.
23 Ibid., pp. 120–121, 124.

we desire to remake (the) world in another way. *No Dice* and *Life and Times 1* make me feel that by relating to others, by exposing ourselves to others, it is possible to inhabit this world – in the perspective of Jean-Luc Nancy, for whom to inhabit means to be in a certain *habitus*,[24] that is to say, in an active disposition towards what exists. They make me feel that it is possible to make (the) world – world referring here, not to a closed system anymore, but to an open totality, which is created within the existents. By creating an experience that we exist by being in relation to others, *No Dice* and *Life and Times 1* can therefore make us believe in the possibility of a world founded on the praxis of the being-with. However, such an experience is only possible if the spectators are as much engaged in the process of the show as are the actors. Only if they make the effort to remain active all throughout the show can they eventually feel emptiness in the theater space and experience "a more than the work, which is the relation itself between the one and the other"[25].

24 Jean-Luc Nancy / Pierre-Philippe Jandin: *La Possibilité d'un monde*. Paris: Petits Platons 2013, p. 31.

25 Entretien avec Jean-Luc Nancy: Pour un communisme existentiel. In: *Philosophie magazine* hors-série 21 (2014): Les philosophes et le communisme, p. 88.

Chloé Déchery

The Guest Performer

Neo-Liberal Agency and Conflicted Authorship in Contemporary British Theater

In today's Britain, instead of resorting to traditional casting, a growing number of contemporary playwrights and performance-makers are choosing to work with professional guest performers. Within this task-based performance genre, the participant is conducted, step by step, by the author who walks them through a script that is being shared in real time with the audience. The author is either present on stage as a co-performer or absent from the stage and directing the performer through various means of remote communication.

This trend belongs to what Claire Bishop describes as "delegated" or "outsourced" performance.[1] Identifying the mechanics of delegated performance, Bishop defines guest performers as "specialists or non-professionals, paid or unpaid, [who] undertake the job of being present and performing at a particular time in a particular place *on behalf of the artist, and following their instructions*"[2]. While Bishop's work deals with artistic practices that take part in curatorial contexts associated with public museums and art galleries within the world of contemporary art, I will be focusing on the role of the guest performer in contemporary performance, looking at three particular examples in British theater and performance: *An Oak Tree,* written by Tim

1 Claire Bishop: *Artificial Hells. Participatory Art and the Politics of Spectatorship.* London / New York: Verso 2012 (my emphasis).

2 Ibid., p. 219.

Crouch,[3] *The Man Who Flew Into Space from His Apartment,* written by Michael Pinchbeck,[4] and the two-handler performance *RomCom, or the Distance Love Can Be Maintained Between Any Two Divergent Points* co-created by Ant Hampton and Glen Neath.[5]

According to Bishop, the guest performer is invited to insert themselves within an *apparatus*[6] that is already conceived and formed by its author. In itself, this is nothing new within the theatrical realm. What is more surprising is that the guest performer must familiarize and interpret the playtext without any preparation or rehearsal time with the author-director, thus taking their cues directly in front of a live audience. Furthermore, when the author is absent from the stage, the guest performer often *stands in* for them and effectively acts as both the performer of the text and the representative of the author. This relates to the nature of the performer's role in theater. When the performer utters the words of the playwright, he also immediately authenticates those words. With the author of the work explicitly absent from the work, the performer not only gives the artistic work the weight of their bodily presence but also their emotional intelligence, empathy, and other discreet hints of liveness. In exchange for a symbolic reward and (often moderate) economic gratification, the guest performer lends their presence to an author who has made the deliberate choice of absenting themselves from the work. This is even more striking when the author also happens to be a performer who

3 Tim Crouch: *An Oak Tree* (Preview: April 29, 2005, Nationaltheater Mannheim; Premiere: August 5, 2005, Traverse Theatre, Edinburgh). Text published in: T. C.: *Plays One.* London: Oberon 2011, pp. 49–106.

4 Michael Pinchbeck: *The Man Who Flew Into Space from His Apartment* (Premiere: November 28, 2014, Zion Arts Centre, Manchester). The performance, inspired by the work of Russian artist Ilya Kabakov, was created by Michael Pinchbeck in 2014. The show is to be performed for an intimate audience of twenty spectators at a time. It was commissioned by hÅb Arts, Manchester, and Lincoln Performing Arts Centre, Lincoln University.

5 Glen Neath: *RomCom, or the Distance Love Can Be Maintained Between Any Two Divergent Points* (Premiere: March 2003, 291 Gallery, London, Director: Ant Hampton). The performance was later revised, rewritten and re-edited in 2011.

6 I use the concept of "apparatus" (or "*dispositif*") as developed by Giorgio Agamben: What Is an Apparatus? In: G. A.: *What Is an Apparatus? And Other Essays.* Stanford: Stanford UP 2009, pp. 1–24, here p. 14: "I shall call an apparatus literally anything that has in some way the capacity to capture, orient, determine, intercept, model, control, or secure the gestures, behaviors, opinions, or discourses of living beings."

would normally be performing in their own work.[7] Therefore, the guest performer plays a complex role via delegated performance, operating simultaneously as the interpreter of the playtext, as the author's representative and as the member of a spectating community who discovers and deciphers a performance for the first time. However, if the guest performer can often be described as the representative of the author, the nature, extent and range of their agency when it comes to making creative decisions on stage are limited by the boundaries of a strict performance "apparatus", itself reinforced by constraining technologies and time limitations.

When examining the role of the guest performer, what strikes me as particularly interesting is the way delegated performance seems to both highlight and question a fundamental principle of theater-making: someone (the author) writes words which someone else (a performer) will repeat out somewhere else (on a stage) some other time. But delegated performance does not only reproduce the process of transfer and delegation inherent to theater writing; it also highlights the limited creative agency of the performer. Analyzing the role of the guest performer can then help provide a political critique of the dynamics of neo-liberal labor as it occurs today within and beyond the art world. As a few sociological studies dedicated to the contemporary transformation of cultural labor have recently demonstrated, cultural workers in the current neo-liberal moment have to prove themselves more and more flexible, adaptable and entrepreneurial while, paradoxically, having their agency and creative freedom increasingly challenged and undermined.[8] In that sense, the guest performer becomes the exemplary figure of the neo-liberal artist. While at the forefront of recent developments in contemporary British theater and possibly benefiting from exposure and visibility, the artist who works as a guest performer has limited creative

7 It is no coincidence that most of the British authors currently experimenting with delegated performance are themselves professional performers, often within their own work (such as with Tim Crouch, Michael Pinchbeck and Ant Hampton).

8 Cf. Jean-Michel Menger: *Portrait de l'artiste en travailleur. Métamorphoses du capitalisme*. Paris: Seuil 2006; J.-M. M.: *Le travail créateur. S'accomplir dans l'incertain*. Paris: Seuil 2009; J.-M. M.: *Être artiste. Œuvrer dans l'incertitude*. Brussels: Al Dante & Aka 2012; J.-M. M.: *The Economics of Creativity. Art and Achievement under Uncertainty*. Cambridge: Harvard UP 2014. See also Luc Boltanski / Ève Chiapello: *The New Spirit of Capitalism*. London: Verso 2007.

control over the artwork in which they take part while their authorship, if not denied, is undeniably restricted.

With this essay, I would like to further examine how the role of the guest performer can exist in relation to the function of the author through shared and delegated, and sometimes contested, authorship. For this, I will be considering three different systems of authorship delegation and will consequently examine how authorship circulates and proliferates; how it is transferred and contained, rebuked and undermined. Finally, I will be considering what forms of community – what images of "coming-together" and "coming-apart" – the model of delegated performance can construct and how the role of the guest performer can, on the one hand, support and partly coincide with that of the spectators and, on the other hand, contradict and remain separated from both the spectator and the author. From this perspective, the guest performer becomes the typified figure of an overly-connected but ultimately isolated being, increasingly constrained within the differentiated and dehumanized realm of the neo-liberal ideology.

Delegation of authorship

Three systems of delegation

The three theatrical performances I wish to discuss within this essay provide idiosyncratic models of delegation while resorting to unrehearsed professional performers rather than amateur performers or volunteer audience members.

In *RomCom*, which follows the story of a heterosexual couple falling in and out of love, the co-creators of the piece are not only absent from their artistic work but display a distant and casual attitude with their handling and management of the performers. According to one of the guest performers involved in the show in 2013, only one of the co-creators came to see the show at the venue.[9] The co-creators communicated the performance guidelines to their guest performers

9 Two interviews were conducted with UK-based performers Neil Callaghan and Karen Christopher to discuss their involvement as guest performers in *RomCom, or the Distance Love Can Be Maintained Between Any Two Divergent Points*, which was performed at the Gate Theatre in London as part of a Forest Fringe festival on April 22–27, 2013. A first interview with Karen Christopher was conducted

through email a few days before the show,[10] and the casting of the guest performers was delegated to the curator of the venue.[11] By contrast, the multimedia *dispositif* of the performance appears surprisingly constraining. In the piece, the two performers are standing in front of a large video-screen on which images and texts are being projected throughout the performance, but the performers cannot look at the screen as they are specifically not allowed to turn their backs to the audience. Both performers carry a set of headphones through which lines and instructions are fed to them in real time. The timing of the video-projection is matched to the one of the pre-recorded audio instructions, which means that neither performer can step out from this set timeframe.

through Skype on November 29, 2015, followed by a second Skype interview with Neil Callaghan on December 5, 2015. During the run of the show, Glenn Neath was present for the six performances while Ant Hampton was away, travelling for work.

10 "This is just a quick e-mail to say hello and tell you a few things about ROMCOM, which you're performing at The Gate on April 22nd. First of all, thanks for agreeing to perform. We hope you enjoy the experience. [...] On the night you will turn up at the venue an hour or so before the show. You will need to know a few things before you start. You will be given these instructions when you arrive. For the show you will wear headphones, which will feed you your lines and any instructions for actions. You will follow the instructions. You will not be asked to do or say anything compromising. That is the basic premise of the show. You'll be given words to say, but it's up to you how you say them: you don't need to copy the intonation, which is deliberately 'flat', allowing you to give it your own colour. As far as costume goes. A skirt and a shirt/blouse is ideal, so that you look slightly formal, maybe what you might wear if you worked in an office. Flat shoes, plain. You need to have a safe and empty pocket in which to carry the mp3 player – so don't wear anything too baggy (we don't want the mp3 player to fall out.) If you don't have a skirt then trousers are fine. The pocket can also be in your shirt as the mp3 player is very thin and light. It can't be a back pocket as you need to sit. It's all very relaxed and the most important thing is that you feel comfortable. You'll be given a lipstick to use during the show. If you don't feel comfortable with this you might want to bring your own. You throw it on the floor. You might want to use the one provided! Could I just ask that you acknowledge having received this. And if you have any questions feel free to ask. Thanks, Glen & Ant." (This introductory email was sent by Glen Neath to Karen Christopher in early April 2013.)

11 With the example of Andy Field selecting the guest performer in *RomCom*, the delegation of curation was not necessarily intended from the start but mostly happened for "practical reasons". Neither creator of the piece could curate the piece at the time, as one was absent from the country and the other one "wasn't familiar enough with the London experimental theater and performance scene at the time". However, this was made possible because of the "close working relationship" that already existed between Andy Field and the co-creator Ant Hampton, meaning that there was a "level of trust that enabled for [their] relationship to work". (Unpublished interview with Andy Field, January 13, 2017.)

Communicating instructions by email prior to the show seems to be part of a recurring protocol in delegated performance. Before the guest is about to perform *The Man Who Flew Into Space from His Apartment*, the author communicates with them by email before meeting them at the venue for an hour prior to the show. In his introductory email, the author justifies the principle of delegated performance: "The idea is that you are travelling on a journey into the unknown so I am not sending you the script for the show in advance of the performance"[12]. When meeting the guest performer in person, he communicates a set of instructions for the course of the evening but issues a reassuring guiding principle: "There is no right or wrong way of performing it, only your way of performing it."[13] The fact that the guest performer is the delegated and unrehearsed stand-in of the author is made known to the audience at the very beginning of the piece as the performer says: "I have been invited to perform a piece of text I have never seen – travelling into the unknown, like the man who flew into space". Here, the risk and uncertainty experienced by the guest performer are not only explicitly shared with the audience but also cleverly incorporated within the fictional narrative of a character who leaves their comfort zone to fly into space – never to return.

An Oak Tree operates slightly differently as Tim Crouch is both the author and co-performer of the piece. As the author, he is present and accompanies the guest performer at all times: before the show, to meet and greet them, and during the show in which he plays the role of a hypnotist. The guest performer plays the role of Andy, a recently bereaved father. The spectators later discover within the performance that the hypnotist is responsible for the death of Andy's daughter. In this show, the lines and the task-based instructions are given to the guest performer via a wide range of technologies, including notes written on cards or pre-recorded audio instructions communicated through a set of headphones. There are also oral instructions that very clearly manifest the power relation between the guest performer and the author who literally puts his words into the performer's mouth while both are on stage:

12 This introductory email was sent to the author by Michael Pinchbeck on November 9, 2016.

13 This quote is an extract from an unpublished interview conducted with Michael Pinchbeck on Skype on December 7, 2015.

Fig. 1: Tim Crouch: *An Oak Tree* with Amy Griffiths, National Theatre London, 2015.

> Hypnotist: Let's face out of front. Ask who they are, say 'And them?' (i.e. the audience)
> Father: And them?
> Hypnotist: They're upstairs in a pub near Oxford Road. It's this time next year, say. Let's say they're all a bit pissed. But don't worry, they're on your side. It's me they're after.
> [...]
> Are you okay?
> Say 'yes'.
> Father: Yes.[14]

In this particular instance, the text highlights the circulation of words being transferred from one person to another and articulates the complexity of authorship within the realm of delegated performance.
The mechanics of delegated performance and the role of the guest performer are also communicated to the audience at the very beginning of the show when the hypnotist greets and introduces his guest as they come on stage:

14 Crouch: *An Oak Tree*, pp. 59–60.

The HYPNOTIST invites the second actor out of their seat in the audience and into the stage. Ladies and gentlemen. This is X (the name of the second actor). X will be performing in the play this evening. X has neither seen nor read it. X and I met up about an hour ago. I have given him/her a number of suggestions. I've suggested that they enjoy themselves! But the story is as new to X as it is to you.[15]

An Oak Tree highlights and playfully demonstrates the potentially contested control and agency of the author, who takes on the role of the "hypnotist", a person endowed with the capacity to suggest to others what to say and how to behave. The choice of this fictional construction is the reason why Crouch chose to explore the form of delegated performance in the first place. For him and his artistic collaborators, Andy Smith and Karl James, the delegated performance format ought to interrogate and mirror the fictional set-up in a performative way, allowing them to "explore deeper ways to tell a story"[16]. Thus, the grieving figure of the father who loses agency in life through the accidental death of his daughter is interpreted by a guest performer who loses agency "by being in a play that they never read or discovered"[17] before.

Although the three performances provide reasonably similar models of delegation, the way authorship is distributed between the author and the guest performer varies widely from one piece to the next.

With *RomCom*, which provides the most controlling and restrictive set-up, the limited authorship and agency of the guest performers aim to reproduce the limited agency of the fictional characters falling in love with each other. The fact that the two guest performers are being given words to say on cue provides an ironical comment, if not a bleak vision, on the limited range of vocabulary that exists in love discourses, exemplified by the use of stilted figures of speech and clichéd metaphors. The guest performers, struggling to keep up the pace of the instructions that are being fed to them and unable to properly communicate with each other, embody an experience of incommunicability and isolation within a romantic relationship.

15 Crouch: *An Oak Tree*, p. 57.

16 This is based on an interview conducted with Tim Crouch on Skype on December 5, 2015.

17 Ibid.

In *The Man Who Flew Into Space from His Apartment*, the guest performer takes on the persona of a man who leaves his home for a voyage into the unknown. But if the format of the delegated performance and the role of the guest performer are incorporated within the fiction of the performance, for Pinchbeck, the role of the guest performer is closer to that of the author. According to the theater-maker, only the performance with the guest performer constitutes a formal rehearsal.[18] More importantly, after every new performance, Pinchbeck asks the guest performer for feedback so as to revisit and rewrite parts of the script. The fact that the guest performer is invited to influence the performance text also signifies that the piece always remains unfinished. Pinchbeck thus recognizes the open-ended nature of the show despite its pre-arranged set of constraints:

> What is interesting is how different performers bring different qualities to the work. Some make it more melancholy. Some make it more comic. Some make it more like a poem. Others make it more like a Tarkovsky film. I am always surprised and amazed by how many different performers have made it something I didn't know it was.[19]

Consequently, for him "[t]he guest performer is [the] representative of the author and of Ylia Kabakov as the author of the installation."[20] However, the expression "representative of the author" hints towards a lesser role than the one expressed with the wording "co-author" and implies a role akin to the one of a "spokesperson" for which creative freedom and agency might be less important than an ability to understand the author's intentions and interpret and follow their instructions. Interestingly, Tim Crouch also chooses another word than the one of "co-author" and rather speaks of his guest performer as a "nominate"[21]. Here, the word choice is particularly telling as "nominate" both designates the one who is named, chosen and elected, and the one who is being shown off, pointed at, differentiated.

18 "When I do rehearse I have a stand in performer, or perform it myself, but this is more to rehearse the timings and to make sure the recordings work. This is more of a technical rehearsal. The performance itself is the actual rehearsal." (Interview with Michael Pinchbeck.)

19 Ibid.

20 Ibid.

21 Ibid.

Control *versus* failure; authorship as a force of contestation

Whether they choose to be physically absent from their work or not, the authors always manage to maintain their presence within the play-text. In that sense, each example of delegated theatrical performance is restrictive in its own way, either because of the technologies involved or the weighty presence of the author on stage or on the page. Directing the performer live or *in absentia* seems to be at stake for all the artists. And since the guest performers involved in the three case studies are professional performers, I would like to try and uncover the reasons why Crouch, Pinchbeck and Hampton/Neal have decided to work with them rather than with amateurs or specialists from other disciplinary fields.

Although guest performers discover their lines within the temporality of the performance event itself, their training, practical knowledge and professional experience unquestionably enable them to quickly grasp and often playfully interpret the instructions given to them. Therefore, it is worth wondering if the skills and expertise of professional guest performers are necessary conditions for the delegated performance to come together. With this in mind, it is worth remembering that it is precisely the unrehearsed nature of the event that gives the audience the impression of a more labile, versatile, open-ended form of performance. How can organized delegation coexist with a performance whose unfolding seems to borrow its flow from a more improvised and spontaneous type of event?

Even when imposing hefty technological and time-based constraints, the dynamics of delegated performance make room, call out and prompt failure. For Bishop, while the overall objective of outsourcing in a globalized economy is to decrease risk (and to increase the worker's performance, therefore profit and capital), in the performing arts, the objective intended by the artists is rather to increase risk and unpredictability "even if this means that a work might risk failing altogether."[22] Pinchbeck recognizes that resorting to a different performer every night enables him to reflect upon the journey of his character into the unknown more thoroughly:

> Someone who mirrors that man's sense of not knowing. Not knowing what would happen. Not knowing whether they would live or die. Fly or fall.

22 Bishop: *Artificial Hells*, p. 231.

Fig. 2 Michael Pinchbeck: *The Man who Flew Into Space from His Apartment*, 2014.

> Succeed or fail. Because I wanted them to represent the audience in a way too and go on a journey of discovery into the unknown together.[23]

While the agency of the guest performer can be limited by the framework of the performance, nothing prevents them from misinterpreting or consciously disobeying the rules set by the author. The guest performer can choose to 'fail', which can then be translated into various actions: to mishear instructions, to overact, to replace a word by another, to partially improvise, to take more time than instructed to deliver (or fluff) a line, to interrupt themselves, or to exit the stage. Those interpretative micro-accidents are enough to shift and displace the meaning of the artwork itself. But while it is important to understand what 'failure' might mean from the author's point of view, it is also important to understand what it might mean for the performers. When reflecting upon her role as a guest performer in *RomCom*, Karen Christopher notices that creativity and interpretative freedom manifested themselves to her within a singular option, which

23 Interview with Michael Pinchbeck.

consisted in deliberately choosing to *not* position herself as the author of the performance text:

> My only margin was in the delivery of the speech (if I was going to decide to undercut or to undermine it or to give an ironic delivery). I could only have been the author of the delivery but I was never going to be the author of the sum total of it.[24]

If the original author of the artwork maintains authorship in the form of 'authority' over the artwork by organizing the process of delegation, the performer has the possibility to assert their authorship 'by default' or in negation, that is by refusing to fully own and 'authenticate' the performance text. However, if most models of delegated performance won't allow the guest performers to embrace a large range of interpretative choices, an interesting process of transfer and circulation of power dynamics remains between the author and their guest performer. It is precisely within the circulation of the instructions delivered by the author and the consequent response of the guest performer that lies the possibility for failure. Failure occurs when linearity and causality are undercut by the refusal of authorship: a decision to not take responsibility for someone else's intentions.

"Coming-together" or "coming-apart": imagining the contrasting figures of the guest performer

The guest performer as a co-spectator

The experience of the guest performer closely mirrors the activity that the spectator undertakes each night. Both the guest performer and the spectator work towards a common act of deciphering and interpreting, reading and making sense – albeit for different purposes. While the guest performer tackles lines and performing instructions, the spectator can enjoy watching them negotiate and sometimes struggle with their own interpretative activity. Pinchbeck articulates the nature of the pleasure derived from spectating real-time problem-solving:

24 Interview with Karen Christopher.

> I am interested in seeing the performer think as they perform. So often, acted work is done without thinking and we don't really believe in or commit to the world the actor is creating. With this piece, the performer is always thinking, listening and speaking at the same time and performing something for the first time that they haven't seen before.[25]

In that sense, the interpretative act becomes a shared territory in which the guest performer and the spectators collide and work towards a collective outcome. The pleasure that the spectators collectively draw from watching the guest performer also comes from the experience of watching them struggle, and, sometimes, break free from their assigned role. As Andy Field observes, in delegated theatrical performance, there is often a "collective camaraderie, a mischief" that is shared amongst the audience who empathizes with the guest performer precisely because of the existence of a shared "relation to that absent authoritarian structure that you want to resist in small ways."[26] The spectators actively seek out "the heroic battle of the performer, aiming for some sort of agency despite the piece", looking for "small decisions", "moments when someone has managed to find a space for themselves to do something different."[27] In those instances, there is a community of co-interpreters that comes together at the expense of the artwork's author, this deliberately "absent authoritarian structure"[28].

The solitude of the guest performer

Although the experience of the guest performer can mirror the interpretive activity inherent to spectatorship, there is an unequal distribution of competences between the audience members and the guest performer. The fact that no amateur performer or member of the general public can take on the guest performer's role is testament to the set distribution of roles and skills that exists between these categories of participants. Paradoxically, it is because the author doesn't want to draw attention to the contrived nature of delegated performance that the author chooses to enroll a professional performer, so as to make

25 Interview with Michael Pinchbeck.
26 Interview with Andy Field.
27 Ibid.
28 Ibid.

the rigid structure of delegated performance less apparent. As Crouch acknowledges, the struggles of the guest performer should not prevent the spectator from following and enjoying the plot: "As the play is not about the formal device, I don't want someone struggling so that the formal device becomes too apparent, obvious, manifest."[29]
However, because of the unequal distribution between guest performer and spectators, the guest performer can also experience a form of isolation and disenfranchisement. For starters, the audience is often in possession of more contextual elements, which enable them to have a better understanding of the overall narrative and overarching structure. This is what the testimony of Karen Christopher, a guest performer on *RomCom*, confirms:

> I only understood half of the performance and I did not know what it was about in the end; I felt it was disempowering and isolating. I did not have enough time to think about what it was about; I was not able to establish the liaison between the sequences, nor understand its logic. I could not hear nor see the audience (as we were being lit by the video-projectors only). I had lost all my "sensing mechanisms", and I felt disconnected with the audience, visually and orally. I did not feel that my decisions were made as freely as usual. I did not have time to engage in a real thought-process and presence, akin to any you would have from a conversation (because of the mediation that occurred through technical technologies). It's like a train-wreck, except that you're not going to die.[30]

The interpretative act inherent to the creative labor of the guest performer can thus lead to a sense of discomfort or alienation for the performer. Although this experience might be defended by the authors of the artwork as a way to exemplify the commodification and mechanization of the creative worker's labor in the neo-liberal ideology, it remains problematic especially when examined in relation to an economical context in which the guest performer is not or lowly paid, and whose artistic credits can remain minimal.[31]

29 Interview with Tim Crouch.
30 Interview with Karen Christopher.
31 To give additional elements on artist's wage and economic conditions of creative labour, Forest Fringe's co-curator, Andy Field offered a "symbolic" (his words) fee of £50 as well as traveling expenses to the guest performers involved in *RomCom*

The guest spectator, at once singular and interchangeable

Finally, it is worth insisting upon the fact that the experience of the guest performer can mirror the experience of a cohesive community as well as that of a heterogeneous community, set apart by different skills, with, on the one side, a performer defined by a know-how of which members of the audience are deprived and, on the other side, an assembly of spectators able to grasp a bigger picture than the one the guest performer is allowed to embrace.

When delegated performances are extended over a long run of dates, the repeatability of the guest performance's role marks out both the individuation of the guest performer and the fact that this guest performer is eminently replaceable, therefore constantly going through a process of de-individuation. Every night, the role that the guest performer takes on is highlighted and embodied in a unique way while also being duplicated and neutralized through sheer repetition.[32] However, because of the rolling cast of guest performers, the authors of the artworks cannot help but compare the performances and express certain preferences. Crouch, for instance, observes that "the show is at its most successful, it works at its best with a woman. This allows to dispel obsession on appearances."[33] Differentiation, comparison and competitiveness also happen to be key characteristics of the labor market in the neo-liberal era. On stage and beyond, the neoliberal worker is condemned to relentlessly demonstrate their uniqueness while being irremediably compared to other similarly-gifted creative workers.

While the role of the guest performer emphasizes the unequal dynamics and problematic organization of creative labor, making particularly clear the power relationship and conflicted distribution of authorship that can exist between the author and the performer, the overvalued 'authenticity' of the guest performer (who is singled out while

at the Gate Theatre in April 2013, while Michael Pinchbeck wasn't in a position to provide a performance fee when *The Man Who Flew Into Space from His Apartment* was performed at Forest Fringe in Edinburgh in August 2016 or at InDialogue2016 at Nottingham Contemporary in December 2016.

32 This is what Andy Field observes about the run of *RomCom* at The Gate Theatre when stating that "it is less different than what you would expect." (Interview with Andy Field.)

33 Interview with Tim Crouch.

remaining a replaceable representative of the author) is also the sign of an increasingly mechanized and dehumanized labor within the neoliberal ideology.[34] While the authors I have examined in this essay can use delegated performance to critically comment upon the logics and procedures of outsourcing and externalization, it is notable that when the guest performers involved in the creative outcome experience a lack of pleasure, dissatisfaction and disempowerment, they embody, despite themselves, an experience of disenfranchisement and alienation that, while being the thematic of the artwork, can set apart the ones who authorize *versus* the ones who authenticate within the realm of the theatrical performance. Delegated performance provides both a way of emphasizing liveness (the actor we are watching is discovering and saying these lines for the first time) and a way of undoing and commodifying liveness with each night's performance being repeated, night after night, over an extended run of performances carefully planned and of which the casting is an important component of an overall marketing strategy. In that sense, it is useful to conjure Christian Boltanski and Ève Chiapello for whom the extraction of profit from the intangible uniqueness of a given person in the labor market can be identified as the "commodification of the authentic".[35] Similarly, the role of the guest performer can highlight the contrived nature of the 'authentic' in the theater world and beyond, within the creative industries. Paradoxically perhaps it is precisely the theatrical apparatus which requires the intervention of guest performers that can best emphasize and bring to our attention the way theatrical performance can so easily be turned into a commodified product.

34 Bojana Kunst notes that while in the origins of the history of performance art, performers used to linked their own bodies and voices with the production of their own text or autobiographical experience so as to produce their own subjectivity, the opposite is true today, specially within the realm of delegated performance and performance re-enactment: "This is why the greatest part of the artists' work was not delegated; their lives and presence were not to serve celebrities – in other words, it was not work for someone else, as for example is the case of the spectacular reconstructions of performance art pieces in recent years." (Bojana Kunst: *Artist at Work. Proximity of Art and Capitalism*. Winchester / Washington: Zero 2015, p. 43.)
35 Boltanski / Chiapello: *The New Spirit of Capitalism*, p. 444.

Artist Talk

Interview with Ivana Müller

A *Pas de Deux* You Cannot Dance Alone

Eliane Beaufils: I hesitated because it is so heavy-handed, but I think I should introduce Jean-Luc Nancy's concept of being-with. I think you know it partly. His departure point is that we are co-existent. What is first, is not the individual, but his/her being-with others. We are always and first together. Nothing makes sense without others, and we know that our perceptions, our feelings are matrixed by the social, by our experiences with others. So Nancy does not reflect the person as a subject in the Hegelian sense, as conscious and transparent of him/herself, but as a person who is always in relation to, and in a process of becoming. The philosopher does not call our world completely immanent because of the permanent transcendence of sense by or in relation to others. Art is a privileged realm for him because art wants to leave the sense open and to give an impetus to think, a thinking in common that is not (necessarily) thinking together nor thinking the same thing. It creates a relation but leaves it open. It enables us to think differently, and it thwarts our criteria of judgment, as Juliane Rebentisch puts it, it makes it impossible for us to judge as we normally do. This brings me to my first question: Last time we met you underlined the role imagination could have. I would be interested to know what you meant by this and if this is related to a being-with for you.

Ivana Müller: I think that, indeed, in any form of creation, even in any form of communication, the space between one and the other is the space where the imaginary really happens. I give you an 'impulse' with a certain expression or a certain situation, you relate to it and the imagination gets created in the space between you and me, and then it is very simple, it is like the basics of language. If I say "a spoon", you will imagine a kind of a spoon and I will imagine another kind of a spoon. For me this is almost magical; we are sharing something, but this something is not entirely fixed, it is nearly an approximation and yet, it creates a possibility for us to be in touch, to be possible, to be in a situation of exchange. So for me the imagination is a very strong vehicle that allows us to have these individual existences but at the same time to relate to each other. Being together does not mean to be the same. Being together is accepting the possibility of the other, or enhancing the presence of the other, sharing the frame we are in. And we are never only in one frame, we are always in many different frames at the same time. For example, at this moment you are interviewing me, so you are an interviewer, but at the same time, you are also someone I've known for a long time , you are practically a friend, you are also a researcher, you are a French researcher that speaks German very well, etc. ... you see what I mean. And for me, imagination is a very very powerful tool because it allows us to explore the realms of 'possibilities', with the other, it allows us to make the other possible by being next to him/her. That's why imagination can be very political, because it recreates the relationships with others, without necessarily needing to manipulate the other or to impose, let's say, one dominant idea. Because, if we imagine something together, we are both in a way engaged in the act of imagining. It is like a dance, like a *pas de deux* that you cannot dance alone. When you dance alone, you can clearly feel your own sense of gravity, your sense of center. When you dance with someone else, the center is not inside you any more, it is in between you and your partner. If you lean too much, if you give too much of your weight, the other one will fall, and you will not be able to dance together. If you don't lean enough, you will fall apart in the other direction. So you have to find a good center, a good balance together. This is also something that can be translated in the experience of theater. The relation between the spectator and the performer is this kind of dance, where we find the right middle, in order to be able to imagine together. Imagination is like an invitation for that dance. That means that it will not be only me who will give the rhythm. The music will be created together. For me the best theater experiences are when I, as a spectator, am invited to watch, but in this sense also to imagine and in this sense, also to co-create. When we imagine together, we co-create this new possibility. And that is every time a new thing, it is every time a new experience. And that is what makes this whole idea of theater very interesting and very engaging for me.

Yes, and we feel that there is a free space left for this engaging and imagining.

Yes, this idea of engagement as a spectator functions very differently in theater and in cinema, for example. We are not affected in the same place, if we are physically present or not. In theater the event is possible only in the here and now with all of us being there. If I am not there as a spectator or as a performer, the whole thing falls apart. It is like dancing together. For it to happen you cannot be remote. In theater, as a spectator, if I am not there I'm going to be missed, and I am going to miss it. If, as a spectator, I'm not in a cinema during the projection of a movie I am not going to be missed as the projection will happen with or without me. And the fact that I missed that projection is not a big problem because there will be another one, with exactly the same film, which I can even watch at home. And the television, that is even less engaging, as it functions like a tap that is always open; so you come in and out, it does not matter if you are there or not, the tap will always run. In that sense, television is not very ecological, it is just running and running, spilling all over.

But you have to modulate the space somehow to make the people feel that it is a space of encounter. If you have a fourth wall, or if you have loads of videos, you can suggest a space that is quite the same as television.

Of course there are degrees. I know that in my work I am always making that fact clear because, for me, it is a crucial part of the theatrical experience. But even on a subconscious level, if you are sitting in a theater and the person next to you is coughing, you will be affected in the way you are looking, understanding, and feeling. That will change your gaze and your gaze will affect the performance that happens on stage. In fact, all the elements present in the space we share affect us and affect the performance as well. For example, the temperature of the air in the venue that we share will affect the perception. If somebody starts laughing, it will affect everybody, because it is a kind of open invitation that says something like: "It is OK to laugh, what we are watching now is potentially funny!"

And it is spontaneous, I mean, you do not control it.

But you notice it. Sometimes a spectator wonders, is this really funny? Can I laugh? And then if the impulse comes from others, it is like an open road for everybody to join in. There are a lot of suggestions, voices, and impulses that happen from the side of the spectators during a show, and that will, in a way, recreate the piece every time again. How they behave will change the piece because it will change the way they are looking at the piece. And then, going back to this idea of imagination or imagining, I think it is a very creative force, it is something that allows a lot of space for the other. For the work I do, it is extremely important that whatever is being presented on stage, can be interpreted in as many ways as there are spectators in the room. If you have 100 people watching it, you will have 100 versions of the same performance. Of course, there is a structure, there are many things that people will notice and understand in the same way, but the final idea will really be the one of the spectator. So I never think of the spectators as a mass, they are always individuals being together. This means there is not one story but different stories written by the spectators. Then you have the idea of the collective writing I worked on during my last project *Notes.*[1] And that is also echoing in different processes I proposed while working on my other pieces. There is a lot of imagination in the work, of course, that is not necessarily coming only from me. The way the final structure is composed is decided by me, but it is inspired by all the persons I worked with during the process. There are kind of reminiscences of all the 'dances', to use the same

1 All the participants in the project chose a book together: Daniel Heller-Roazen: *Echolalias. On the Forgetting of Language*. New York: Zone 2008. They read the same copy of the book one after the other, during a five months period, and while reading they wrote their notes in the margin. See the description of the project on the site of the artist: http://www.ivanamuller.com/works/notes.

Fig. 1: Spectators read the text of *We Are Still Watching* and enact the show themselves: a doing by reading and imagining. Ivana Müller: *We are Still Watching*, 2012.

metaphor, that we danced throughout the processes. So the multiplicities of views, of possibilities, are already inherent in the texture.

And also a condensation.

Yes, of course. I just kind of give the form to it, which allows access to it, which enables others to join. It is a perpetual process of dancing, so to say. I completely assume my responsibility. But there is never this kind of mastermind. Whatever I do, I do with the others. It was always like this. Maybe I create a frame, and then I ask people to contribute.

For me it is a strength because it is difficult to leave things open for others. How did you learn it, or how did you feel that your way of working would be collaborative?

I think that is something that has been evolving, or that has been created from the moment I started working, but I was not aware of it. It is a sum of experiences I had, a sum of meetings, of working processes, etc.

Maybe this is easier in dance?

Maybe, but in theater you always work with a lot of people, with collectivities. I remember at school,[2] when you start creating your own choreographic work, you often start doing solos, because it is the easiest way to work in terms of organizing the rehearsal place, rehearsal time, also organizing ideas. But, while doing solos, I simply noticed that I was often very bored with myself. I wanted to dialogue. I realized that my thinking got more precise when in dialogue. It felt good, I guess. And once I became aware of it, I tried to create conditions for that kind of processes. But it took me a very long time to learn how I should work in a way that would really be interesting for me. I think the first process where I really figured it out was *How Heavy Are My Thoughts*[3] in 2003, where we worked together with Bill Aitchison and Nils De Coster for this lecture-performance. In the piece there is this idea of 'Ivana Müller', unable to be present on stage, she gets replaced by a lecture given by a British man that refers to her as to IM. She became a fictional construction represented by another person.

So I think that was very interesting for me, to play with something that is potentially real or fictional, the idea of representation, how thoughts are represented, how people are represented, how they are represented by themselves and by others, all this came into play. But I could not name any moment where I decided: I should work like this or like that. It is a question of experience. I work a lot with intuition, I think this is an important part of artistic practice. And sometimes people are surprised when I say that, because often the forms of my pieces are very clear, recognizable, they seem like 'perfectly composed and decided scenarios' … And they are, but they became that through processes powered by a lot of intuition.

They seem very conceptual…

2 Academy of Theater and Dance, Amsterdam University of Arts. http://www.ahk.nl/en/atd.

3 *How Heavy Are My Thoughts* (Premiere: October 24, 2003, Plateau Festival, Künstlerhaus Mousonturm, Frankfurt am Main) was created in 2003 and co-produced by Künstlerhaus Mousonturm Frankfurt am Main and Theater Gasthuis Amsterdam.

Maybe. But, again, working with intuitive ways of grasping ideas was always extremely important to me. It is the same with scientific research, if you do not work with intuition, you will never find new things. You will always repeat the ideas that somebody else thought of, or embellish them, or glorify them ...

But we still have to work a bit more on togetherness, in France at least (laughs).

But also in the performing arts world, it is not that everybody recognizes this collective way in creation and writing, which is strange. A couple of months ago I was in the Prado in Madrid, and you see that even in the 17th century paintings people were collaborating, different painters would paint the same image together. One would paint the figures, the other one the landscapes. Very famous painters, like the collaboration of Pieter Breughel and Peter Paul Rubens, for example, on *The Five Senses*, where Breughel painted the settings and Rubens painted the figures. It is something that has been part of the process of making things. But it is very interesting, because it comes to this question of authorship and therefore there were periods with "prodigies", geniousness, but I think this geniousness happens in between, it is interstitial, it happens in spaces around the artist and art pieces, not always only within them. You know, theater is not 'about', it is always 'between'.

Yes, you mentioned it at the round table,[4] *I found it very nice and wanted to ask you to deepen this.*

I already talked a bit about it in relation with imagination. Theater does not happen on stage, it does not happen in the seats, it happens in between. Interstitial space is created between proposition and expectation, previous knowledge and discovery, it is the way we can offer our gaze as spectators and gestures as performers towards each other. Theater also happens between stage and backstage, because there is

4 Round table during the conference at theater de La Commune, in the Parisian suburb Aubervilliers, on December 9, 2015.

no stage without backstage, there is no representation without process, and they are always present side by side when you make a work in the context of theater. You think about the representation when you make a show, but you can make it happen only if you think very thoroughly about how you bring people on stage, how you write your text, how you light them, who is coming in and out, what you make visible. Because the most important gesture when you are an artist is exactly this: how to make the invisible visible or leave it invisible for the sake of your piece. And so this happens between stage and backstage. The third relationship that, for me, is a lot about in-between is the relation between the sound and the image, which took quite a long time for me to realize. Jean-Luc Godard already said we have two fronts to fight on, the sound and the vision. I learned a lot from his movies. If you separate the sound and the image, you can create a space in between, where you can suggest a lot of new relations. When they are not parallel, when you do not hear and see the same thing, then you also dismantle this whole mechanism of how they can co-exist. So that becomes another *pas de deux*.

Could you just come back to this notion of pas de deux?

It is a term from dance that sounds a bit romantic, but for me it relates to the basic idea of sharing the same movement … and again all those questions of giving your weight, and taking the weight of the other, giving your trust, and taking the trust of the other. You cannot decide alone in any kind of dance that engages two or more people. This also produces another awareness of the space and another awareness of time. You have to give and take all the time, it is a kind of a negotiation. It is a nice metaphor for the relation between the spectator and the performer, this kind of give and take. We need each other. What is very interesting in theater is that you can never be alone. Even if you make your own movements, your own text, your own music, even if you are alone on stage, you are still there with the spectator.

This brings me to another point, because you mentioned imagination in relation to poetry. This was surprising but very interesting for me.

Maybe we were talking about *Edges*[5]?

Yes, maybe.

What is interesting about the exploration of poetic language, and why I think it is political today, is that it allows you to see things radically differently. Poetic language(s) operate(s) very differently from everyday language or language that comes through the media or even through a political discourse. And I think we are very much affected by media language and political discourses, that our minds and our vocabulary are very polluted with them, or dominated by them. I often do an exercise when I am teaching, it is a kind of instantaneous collective writing, where I ask a group of people to create sentences together. Each person gives one word and they accumulate into sentences. And very often the sentences that come out sound like publicity slogans because they want the thing to work, to be efficient. Because we are trained to do so, even if we are not paying attention to it. Publicity slogans are everywhere, in any kind of public space, we don't notice them any more but they start to shape the way we speak, and eventually think about ourselves and others. And it is important to say that by poetic language or poetic structures I do not mean only poetry in a kind of alexandrine verse or whatever – but different sorts of languages that are proposing different relations to the way we look at things or understand them.

It is another language…

Yes. Poetry operates very much like the "other" language or a new language, it becomes this possible grid to imagine the world, to imagine each other, and I think that it is what we need now. We are in such a deep crisis, a crisis of collective imagination. We are really formed with this constant media presence and even through different kinds of narrations, different kinds of fictions that became a kind of normative

5 *Edges* (Premiere: January 20, 2016, Performing New Europe Festival, Salzburg) was developed during residencies in La Villette (Paris), Ménagerie de verre (Paris), Musée de la danse (Rennes) and BUDA (Kortrijk).

way. Like, all these disaster-scenario movies. To imagine oneself differently, one's relation to the other differently, gives a way to reconstitute ourselves.
For example, when you do this kind of body scan that comes from different dance and somatic practices but also from meditation, you imagine your body not with bones, etc., but you imagine it as a garden … (*laugh*) you have a different relationship to yourself, and you have different entrances to the idea of yourself. This is changing how you feel, it can really change your body, how your blood is streaming, how it functions, because it becomes something else. I think it is very necessary to offer these new languages, it is almost essential to any artistic practice. And I think poetry is very interesting because it goes very deep in this personal tissue. The problem is that people are maybe not always available to go into that new language, to let themselves go. But I feel that it is important to propose it. It is never possible to make a piece that everybody is available to look at anyway.

Yes, but maybe, when it does not belong to their expectations somehow, they become more available?

Possibly. Look for example, the work of Pier Paolo Pasolini – because for me it is the clearest and very well known example to see how poetry and politics can really function. His first published poems were in this language from Friuli, which is a dialect from the North of Italy. He was first a poet and then slowly he started writing in prose and then he made movies that for me are still kind of poems. But it is interesting to see that writing poetry was his way of entering artistic practice, and it remained a very important vehicle for his work. And I see different kinds of poetic structures now: slam for example, that are …

… that are not sentimental … ?

By poetic I definitely do not mean anything romantic or sentimental; on the contrary, it is a language that proposes a new order of an experience of looking, of engaging.

The problem could be that poetry is often thought of as quite solipsistic. But if you 'put' it in a common space, this changes the activity maybe.

When put in a place of "collective", it echoes in a very different way. What also is important, is that these poetic structures often propose different kinds of temporalities. For me it is interesting to think about how to use this language today. The fact that "poetic language" is not totally natural can provoke a different kind of relation to it. And when I say 'language' I don't mean only text, poetry is not only in the text. That is only one part of textuality of a work: you have the visual part of it, and you have also the visceral side. For me there are always three dimensions that I work with in the theater. In a work you have what you hear, what you see, and what you feel. By 'feel' I do not mean emotional reactions, but more physical ones …

… how you are affected?

Yes, for example, in *While We Were Holding It Together*, where people stand in the same position for seventy minutes,[6] the limitation creates a lot of affect and people are very empathic to the fact that those on stage cannot move. You have two reactions: either people in the audience stay in the same position and they don't want to move, as a way of being in solidarity with the performers; or you have the opposite situation where people move a lot during the piece, or much more than usual, to compensate for the fact that those on stage cannot move, or because they are afraid of being stuck like this, I don't know, but it is very interesting. This is, for me, also part of the texture of a theatrical experience. Or for instance when you have a piece like *Playing Ensemble Again and Again*, which is entirely performed in slow motion. After seeing this for more than an hour, when you go out of the space, you feel that something has fundamentally changed in the way you see or experience time and movement. So I mean, going back to poetry, this slow motion is a poetic gesture, because it proposes another language, another physical frame, another way to see, hear, and feel others.

6 *While We Were Holding It Together* (Premiere: October 19, 2006, Sophiensaele, Berlin) was produced by LISA and I'M'COMPANY, in co-production with Sophiensaele Berlin (DE), Productiehuis Rotterdam / Rotterdamse Schouwburg (NL), Dubbelspel (30CC and STUK Kunstencentrum Leuven, BE).

So you see gestures as language?

Absolutely, but this is a larger gesture, a dramaturgical gesture, a choreographic gesture, which is spread over the whole piece: the fact that you are very slow, or the fact that you put people in a state of immobility or the fact that in *Edges* for instance, nobody on stage spoke, all of those decisions can be seen as gestures. Going back to *Edges*, in this piece performers were never speaking on stage they were only opening their mouths but the voice was coming from back-stage. This decision was made because in *Edges* we were working on the idea of extras and when you are an extra, you don't have a voice, even by contract. When you get a sentence, you are not an extra any more, in French you become a "silhouette". So there are different degrees in which poetic gestures can be proposed, seen, shared. And in general I could maybe define a poetic gesture as going out of the known structures of languages or understanding and not responding to something that is entirely established, or entirely expected. Therefore, the poetic gesture is always an artistic gesture, and never a cultural gesture. It is never possible to have culture in poetry for me, because culture never really innovates, it always confirms. And here I am referring to a notion of culture and art a bit in an Artaudian way. The culture is basically establishing and repeating something that art has invented.

Do you work with the word 'critical' because your poetic gestures could also be called critical gestures?

Maybe.

But in 'critical' you have something more negative than in poetic?

Oh no, critical can be positive. Maybe I was more inspired by this word when I was starting, when I was younger. Now I am not so interested in that, it doesn't bring me to an interesting place. But it is funny, you remember when you invited me to this symposium, on poetry in stage work? I was thinking: "Why is she inviting me, my work has nothing to do with poetry!?" I was not thinking through those grids. The world has changed a lot, me as well, and I think it is very healthy to reinvent or reestablish the words that can bring us into some inspiring contexts. I think that poetry could be one of them.

Fig. 2: People go for a walk and spend hours, months in a forest conversing without endings ... The spectators accompany their reflections. Ivana Müller: *Conversations Out of Place*, 2018.

I am happy with that. I just want to come back to this word 'critical', because it is also important in my work, how I can use it or not. What did it mean for you before, and why don't you need it anymore?

This word could be interesting in creating a certain distance from what you are looking at, what you are observing: relationships between us, and the world around. Maybe this distance in criticism also found a form in a certain type of irony that I used a lot. It is still a little bit present but much less than in the beginning. And I found this distance very important because it gave me another place from which I could look, that you were not immersed into the problem but that you could be a part of it and at the same time – again that binary thing – be outside of it. To have this picture that is multi-layered, that is tri-dimensional. And I used it in this way. An interesting thing about being critical is that it is always very personal. You cannot be 'impersonal' when being critical because you propose 'your' point of view. That makes you vulnerable as well.
And then there is an interesting place of humor in all this, irony produces humor ... Humor was for me a way, on the one hand, to stay at a distance but simultaneously to create something that is very engaging.

When you laugh, you are very much engaging, you are somehow part of the thing, even physically … laughing produces shaking.

I noticed this a lot in Positions,[7] *and I found it nice to hear the people laugh.*

Laughing also depends a lot on the context. The first time I performed my work in the States, I got so scared, because people reacted much more than in Europe: they were laughing, and really showing openly "yeah, yeah, we got it and we like it", and it was very frightening, because I thought it would very much flatten the work, it would only rise superficial ways of reading the work. And then you have other places with no reactions during the show, like in Belgium sometimes for example, but afterwards you realize that people appreciated it a lot. It is a bit of a cultural thing. And of course it depends if it is a festival where you know half of the audience, or in a place where you just come as a guest.

I just wondered if these adjectives 'critical', 'political' were at stake in your work.

I would say they are. I am about to make a new piece that is a bit inspired by a *conte philosophique* and in itself this form wants to be critical towards the world. But I think that it is so important for me to be critical nowadays, because everything can be criticized, there are very few things that you cannot be critical of. So I think this refers to what I already said about immersing oneself in the thing and not staying at a distance. Today it makes more sense.

Lately the dominant or mainstream attitude in contemporary theater and performing arts is to be, so called "openly, visibly, directly political". There is this jargon: Let's change the world, let's take positions … I don't believe that big gestures like "let's change the world" work really today. They sound suspicious, and work like publicity slogans, which today sound like political slogans from the 1960s. These days I think it is more interesting to work in smaller gestures, step by step, like

7 At the first presentation of *Positions*, at the "Festival de danse" of the Théâtre de Vanves, February 10, 2013.

somebody that walks and takes time to look where she walks, whom she walks with, what she walks by. Some months ago, while trying to answer to a question: how can I continue living in a healthy way in this world, where everything is so global and interconnected and when we can't change the large structures in a simple way, I realized that the only way is to keep my immediate ecosystem healthy. When applied to my work it concretely means: how I work with my collaborators, where I work, which resources am I using, etc. It makes more sense to work locally now for example, to construct working places and working relationships from close. Maybe I don't have time to be critical now. Maybe I have to immerse myself into this and to immerse others too.

This is maybe true activity and some adjectives came into mind like constructive or concrete utopia, as Ernst Bloch puts it. I mean there is no utopia you want or you are looking for but there is some utopian dimension in this, I think.

In any utopia there is this idea of a collective: because it is an organization that is shared by many, and I am very concerned and sensitive to the ways I work with others, how I organize or propose the process of working. Because these ideas of how to work will for sure have immediate repercussion on the artwork you see at the end. So I always have to think what the kind of frame is that I propose for others to contribute to. And maybe that has to do with creating those mini utopias again and again. You work with people and every time you work on a new piece you work differently... because if you would work the same all the time it would always be the same work. I am very busy with that reflection. You can talk about utopias, but they are realizable because they have an outcome, which is the work itself. So the piece is always in some way, a representation of that utopia or of that specific way of working. It is very concrete as you said, also bound to many external factors, the places where we work, how we are paid, the world outside the studio, all these elements are important and will affect the hierarchies or organization. So yes, I think we can speak about mini utopias but not about these big systems. It is funny, the 20th century really was the age of utopias, but these were kind of gigantic social utopias like Communism or Nazism, and then there was capitalism – which survived into the 21st century. But when they began to be practical, they were very soon starting to fail; they created a sort of deceiving violence. This idea of realizable utopia is based on the idea of desire: on what you want to share, what you want to give, what you want to take. Here we are going back to this idea of *pas de deux*, except that here the idea is based on a larger amount of 'participants'. There is this nice metaphor of the *jardin passager* (temporary garden[8]), this is a type of a garden where you actually have the whole shape of the garden that changes according to where different plants want to continue growing. And the gardener is there to notice where they want to go and to change the garden according to that. It is a beautiful metaphor for a possible society where we actually follow the desires of the citizens and not try to impose boxes or try to follow predetermined concepts and shapes.

Do you think your work can also make desires arise in the spectators?

Yes, I hope so. I mean you will never want to dance with somebody who does not want to, you have to have a desire to dance. Of course. What happens on stage is really an invitation for a dance. I am honestly and thoroughly inspired by certain things, I just want to share them in a certain form, in a certain type of writing, etc. There are a lot of choreographers who want to share their personal physical movements. They are first dancers and then they teach their choreographies to other people and then they all dance like the choreographer himself. I am not interested in these movements. But maybe I am interested in certain movements of the mind, of ideas, that I want to share. But I never ask others to think like me. I am just proposing those thoughts almost like questions. The ideas you get from my pieces are a bit suspended in the air, they are never the "one kind of truth". There are merely suggestions.

There we are in the being-with, as a movement of sense made together.

8 The adjective '*passager*' is a play on words and signifies both 'temporary' and 'passenger', relating to the movements of the plants as well as those of the people going through the gardens.

Fig. 3: The unseen and the unheard become the people in the center of the stage in *Edges*. Ivana Müller: *Edges*, 2016.

Yes, absolutely. My suggestions are not fixed, not stuck, they are like clouds. You can relate to them or grasp them if you make an effort to look at them. But they can also simply pass by without you even noticing them. I try never to push things onto ...

... So that you engage in suspension. Yes, this is nice and it already answered a few questions I prepared. And it reminds me of a quotation from Gerald Siegmund I wanted to discuss with you. Siegmund comes back to the king's body, embodying the relation between power, legislation and knowledge: "Since there are no more stable embodied relations between power, legislation and knowledge, choreography and its bodies become a testing ground for relations of the body to the empty and incomplete symbolic orders of societies. Dance becomes a rehearsal space for possible ways of entering the social and of positioning oneself with others within its sphere."[9] *How do you think about dance as such a rehearsal space?*

9 Gerald Siegmund / Stefan Hölscher: Introduction. In: G. S. / S. H. (eds): *Dance, Politics and Co-Immunity*. Zurich: Diaphanes 2013, pp. 7–18, here pp. 9–10.

What is interesting in what happens with dance actually was this movement that started in the 1960s. There were some germs in the 1930s but I think it was not yet developed that much. Working on dances, creating dances together became a certain way of creating societies. What was great was that it allowed all 'the backstage' to go into what you see, what you are offered to look at. And the idea of movement, or of dance, is very important for that. The fact that you have to create movement all the time, something that is ephemeral, that is not fixed, generates a possibility to create all sorts of movements, not only physical movements and gestures. And I think that is quite important. Of course, it is also very important that the dancing groups became communities. When making dances, it is very possible to move quickly from one context to another because there is no language barrier, so dance became even more international. It was also a community because it was not belonging to a national context, it could reinvent the way that we relate to different questions of identity, to issues of gender for example, it became a community that started to be increasingly more tolerant. This whole movement is based on the fact that there is movement. And this is very beautiful.

And you, if you are more theatrical or performance oriented, has it something to do with sense, with more different ways of sense making, with language?

I am not more theatrical, I was often called "theatrical", but I am not so happy with that word. It is very interesting, I got interested in dance through the studies of literature. I started to be interested in dance as a language, as a non-verbal language, which brought all these layers that I talked about previously. In the beginning, I didn't start being involved in choreography by dancing, I started to be interested in dance not by dancing but by watching. First I watched dance before I started to do it, which is quite rare. Most of my colleagues began dancing when they were children, and then there is a break-up as teenager, and then they pick it up again as young adults. For me dancing was not at all part of my 'identity' during my formative years. It started as an analytical practice almost. And I always made dances as a spectator. I still do, I am more so making dance by imagining myself on stage than being on stage. But this experience is very strong because, as I already explained, imagination can be visceral. And that makes a strong physical experience for a spectator. For me the experience of being a spectator is always very physical.

Maybe this is a way to leave it open to the spectator, to stay open. If you want to affect or to speak to the spectators, it's impossible if you are only on stage.

I don't know. There are people who are very egocentric and show the narcissism of their position and people are very fascinated by that. (*laugh*) But I always prefer watching things from the side. I like the marginal position. The place of the margin was always very inspiring for me. In all sorts of ways: being a foreigner, being a spectator, being a woman. A lot of those denominators can be seen as slightly marginal. I also like the margin on the stage, the space where there is just a little bit of light, where the visible ends and the invisible starts unraveling.

Thank you very much for this very nice conversation!

III

On and Beyond Partage: Theatrical (De-)Communification

Stéphane Hervé

Testing Spectatorship at the Limits of Collective Experiencing

"What the hell are we doing here?", Sara Manente and Marcos Simões asked the audience attending their performance *Lava* in the foyer of the Kortrijk Budacentrum in June 2016, before entering the theater. In response, this surprising introduction was followed by a tarot session involving a professional tarot reader (Reynald Halloy) and voluntary spectators. Spectators were encouraged to question their expectations about what would be seen (an eccentric and enigmatic blending of choreographies, texts and screened drawings inside a moving textile installation), and incited to interpret mysterious associations of objects and gestures. Moreover, spectatorship was questioned at both individual (What do I have to do? What am I expecting?) and collective (What explains this gathering of individuals?) levels. Consequently, the opening question reflects the radical contingency of the performance: since the markers of identity and the usual emotions generated by a performance did not sufficiently account for the gathering, the performative being-together was problematized. The paradoxical *captatio benevolentiae* reveals the tendency of contemporary theater to test spectatorship. This approach is not particularly recent (let's think of Peter Handke's *Publikumsbeschimpfung* from 1966), but it is not the spectator's capacities to give up their passivity prescribed by the theatrical apparatus – like in all the ritual or participatory experimentations in the sixties – nor his perceptual patterns – like in the later postmodern performances – which are tested, but his/her presence inside a "transitory" community, whose "composition is arbitrary" because its members "have little or nothing to say to one another; they lack a shared identity, a common prehistory that could have produced common memories they could share".[1] The perception of the theatrical audience is changed: it is no longer composed of a homogeneous group, it is not a community but a random gathering not significantly different from other groupings typical of mass culture. Yet, testing spectatorship precisely allows the theatrical audience to avoid the seriality of a transitory community. Beyond these ethical and political aspects, it seems relevant to consider the test first of all as a supplement to the heterotopic assemblage that has been popular on the performative scenes for half a century. Indeed, testing spectatorship fills the gaps in the heterotopic scene, including the utopian or exemplary communitarian image.

Philippe Quesne's *Next Day*: a theatrical heterotopia

Heterotopia is a central item in Philippe Quesne's recent works: in *Swamp Club*[2], the art centre lost in the marsh is a kind of artistic heterotopia, while the cave of *La Nuit des taupes*[3] presents an ecological and animal one. But, in addition to these two renowned performances, *Next Day*[4] commissioned by the Ghent structure Campo, coalesces the values, patterns and functions of a scenic heterotopic community, owing to its fragmented dramaturgy as well as to the succession and superposition of its numerous forms of being-together.

Heterotopia as microcosm

The performers in *Next Day* are thirteen children or teenagers who playfully embody apprentice superheroes trying to save the world. This fiction is used as a pretext for the observation of a microcosm composed of young people. Their relations to the group, their interpersonal relations and their ways of being-together are indeed the main subjects of the performance. Therefore, the community issue arises not

1 Boris Groys: *Art Power*. Cambridge: MIT Press 2008, p. 181.

2 Philippe Quesne: *Swamp Club* (Premiere: June 04, 2013, Wiener Festwochen, Vienna).

3 Philippe Quesne: *La Nuit des taupes* (Premiere: May 06, 2016, Kunstenfestivaldesarts, Brussels).

4 Philippe Quesne: *Next Day* (Premiere: November 07, 2014, Théâtre Nanterre-Amandiers, Nanterre).

in terms of representation (with the performers representing a political, national or class-based community) but in a literal way: what do (often non-professional) performers do together on stage? Moreover, as the fantasy fiction of *Next Day* suggests, the formation of a scenic microcosm includes a prospective intention: the performers put forward potentialities of communities which are impossible to find in the extra-theatrical sphere. Hence, microcosm is the condition of possibility for the existence of scenic heterotopias.

Respect of singularities

Far from striving for communion, scenic heterotopias attempt to think community by respecting the singularity of each performer. Contemporary theoretical thought is haunted by the possibility of a renewed linkage between singularity and community.[5] Current performances adopt the same way of thinking: we could, for instance, mention how the idea of chorality has gradually replaced the chorus[6] or the reluctance of some choreographers to create dance sequences in unison.[7] In a different manner, in the first segment of *Next Day*, all the young teenagers introduce themselves to the audience by stating their name, their age, the musical instrument they play in the performance and the part of the show they prefer: the performers are not only members of a community, they exist by themselves. Furthermore, the preference they express at the beginning of the show is not a concession to the nowadays propagation of personal opinions, but a way of dissociating themselves from a possible global discourse. In other words, such statements reflect a subjective irreducibility: the singularity of the performer does not vanish in the performance.

5 Cf. Jean-Luc Nancy: *The Inoperative Community*, transl. from the French by Peter Connor / Lisa Garbus / Michael Holland / Simon Sawhney. Minneapolis: University of Minnesota Press 1991; J.-L. N.: *Being Singular Plural*, transl. from the French by Robert Richardson / Anne O'Byrne. Stanford: Stanford UP 2000; Roberto Esposito: *Communitas: The Origin and Destiny of Community*, transl. from the Italian by Timothy Campbell. Stanford: Stanford UP 2004.

6 See, for example, Christophe Triau: Choralités diffractées: la communauté en creux. In: *Alternatives théâtrales* 76–77 (2003), pp. 5–11.

7 In that way, Christian Rizzo, in a meeting after a performance of his piece *D'après une histoire vraie* held in the Lille Opéra in June 2014, explained that he has attempted to break the inaugural unison in order to obtain a collective composed of singular gestures which move from one body to the other and would be appropriated each time differently.

Resorts to extra-theatrical collective forms

We find two collective forms in *Next Day*, borrowed from other arts. First, the young performers compose an expanded pop band, as in the musical overture of the production. All thirteen teenagers manage to tune themselves and offer, perhaps basically but nonetheless consistently, a musical pattern, in spite of the number of instruments. As a result, the pop band provides a perfect model for being-together, in the sense that the gathering of singular voices generates a common discourse.[8] The agency of this model, besides its performative efficiency, derives from its respect of the singularities, since it is based on a division of tasks according to subjective capacities. Moreover, the ranking of functions typical of pop bands is often thwarted: the lead singer disappears or splits into multiple voices. Yet such borrowing concomitantly indicates a certain weakness of the theater which has become a concert, as if the scenic collective and the cooperation during the creative process turns out to be insufficient for producing common experiences.[9]

The second collective form proceeds from the cooperative work in which a work laid down as a shared aim is produced thanks to an equal division of tasks. The cooperation appears in *Next Day* during the construction of various buildings (a wall to protect the performers from the audience, a kind of castle, a tunnel) out of parallelepiped-shaped pieces of foam.[10]

8 Beyond pop band pattern, all the musical collectives should be mentioned, like the brass band in Alain Platel, Frank Van Laecke et Steven Prengels' *En Avant, marche!* (2015).

9 A pop band appears as an achieved collective form in Needcompany's works which include more and more live pop songs. More significantly, Maguy Marin's *Turba* (2007) ended with a sequence that followed the noisy explosions, the visual chaos, the blasting encounters of theatrical simulacra and allowed for the recovery of harmony in musical collaboration.

10 This way of cooperation could be compared to the staging of a movie shooting in many productions (Katie Mitchell, Hotel Modern, Liquid Loft among others): the spectators wonder at the virtuosity of the cooperative work, the solidarity between the performers, which foreshadow an achieved community, thanks precisely to the cooperation.

Funny and convivial reactivations of participatory processes from the sixties

The foam-cubes fight could be considered (the performers throw them into the audience, who send them back with pleasure), presented as training for the event of an extra-terrestrial invasion, as an entertaining reactivation of some aggressive performances from the sixties. The fight is not provocation but child's play. Later on, the sharing of crepes could evoke the bread sharing in the Bread and Puppet Theater's performances. There is no Eucharistic dimension here, just the pleasure of sharing food in a friendly atmosphere.[11]

Undermining the author's power

According to the German theorist Boris Groys, we must point back to the Wagnerian theories in order to trace the condition of possibility for a collective work or a work made for a community, meaning the undermining of the author's power that allows for the participation of all members and the collective appropriation of a work. That is why Groys quotes the essay *Das Kunstwerk der Zukunft* in which Wagner insists that a collective work requires the author's sacrifice:

> The last, completest renunciation of his personal egoism, the demonstration of his full ascension into universalism, a man can only show us by his Death; and that not by his accidental, but by his necessary death, the logical sequel to his actions, the last fulfilment of his being. The celebration of such a Death is the noblest thing that men can enter on.[12]

In *Next Day*, authorship is undermined during moments of latency, in which the performers seem to escape the authority of the director who precisely governs acts and movements. Incidentally, Philippe Quesne admits to having provided only an "elementary thread of actions to be

11 Sharing food is not rare in contemporary performances. To give just one example, Needcompany's *Needlab*, held in the Brussels Kaaitheater (December 2014), included the distribution of a delicious cocktail, which instituted a relaxed ambiance.

12 Richard Wagner: Das Kunstwerk der Zukunft, 1850, quoted from Boris Groys: A Genealogy of Participatory Art. In: Rudolf Frieling (ed.): *The Art of Participation from 1950 to Now*. New York / London: Thames & Hudson 2009, pp. 18–31, here p. 23.

accomplished" and to having delegated its realization to the performers.[13] Yet, as Groys stresses, undermining in such a case is never complete. In fact, undermining authorship is also paradoxically a way of heightening it, because it always depends upon the author's decision. Community is haunted by the author's ghost who willed it.[14]

Exteriority as the spectator's place

Spectators can feel empathy for the teenagers' energy and innocence. Yet, they remain in the position of observers, examining the scenic being-together from the "standpoint of death", as Groys says.[15] Such a funereal image was already used in the early seventies by the eminent Italian critic Giuseppe Bartolucci, who wrote about a corpse-spectator.[16] However, in this much politicized period, he applied it to denounce the consumption pattern in spectatorship. Nowadays, Groys neither calls for more participation nor criticizes spectators' passivity but wishes to evoke their withdrawal: "I look at the living drama from outside, I'm put, owing to the theatrical conventions, in the situation of a non-existing observer, of a non-existing god"[17].

This last item prompts us to consider the failings of the scenic exposition of a fictional and autonomous microcosm, as Quesne and many other artists present it. Despite the participatory sequences, the heterotopic community remains a model to examine or to follow, but not an experience shared by the singularities in the audience. How can a collective experience replace a picture of the collective? Why is testing more suitable to that purpose than participation?

13 Programme of the performances in Kortrijk Budacentrum, NEXT Festival, November 2014.

14 Moreover, in *Next Day,* credited officially to Philippe Quesne, some signature effects, such as fog generators, are present.

15 Sekte Bayreuth. Ein Gespräch zwischen Boris Groys and Carl Hegemann. In: Clemens Risi / Bettina Brandl-Risi / Anna Papenburg / Robert Sollich (eds): *Tannhäuser – Werkstatt der Gefühle*. Freiburg: Rombach 2014, pp. 233–241, here p. 237.

16 See Giuseppe Bartolucci: *Il Vuoto teatrale*. Padua: Marsilio 1972, pp. 47–58.

17 Sekte Bayreuth, p. 237.

From picture to sharing

In Brussels' La Monnaie, Romeo Castellucci imagined a powerful picture for the end of the third act of *Parsifal*[18]: two hundred extras walking without moving, as a community of anonymous voices "without end and without goal"[19]: a wonderful embodiment of a transitory community. How to think the transformation of this picture in experience, without betraying its attributes?

It seems that participation, as it was performed in the sixties and is still performed nowadays, does not fit this purpose for two reasons. On one hand, participation is like a delegated performance: spectators' actions stem from the author's decision. In other words, the spectator remains under the author's control. Therefore, it is difficult to talk about singularities because of the distribution of tasks in an apparatus originally designed by an author. For instance, the "free theater" experimentations in Living Theater's *Paradise Now* (1968) resulted in failure, since free theater led to the stopping of the performance dramaturgy, and spectators' improvisations came into conflict with the irenic and collective ideals of the American theater company. Singularities' apparition then meant collective disintegration, as if the collective can only be achieved in a frame, under supervision. On the other hand, participation implies a purpose to the being-together, which must be called a making-together. Singularities are assigned tasks to accomplish and are exceeded by the labor of creating.

According to Nicolas Bourriaud, theater cannot be considered as a relational art or as relational aesthetics because of its specific temporality and its apparatus in which the stage prevails:

> Art (practices stemming from painting and sculpture which come across in the form of an exhibition) turns out to be particularly suitable when it comes to expressing this hands-on civilisation, because it tightens the space of relations, unlike TV and literature which refer each individual person to his or her space of private consumption, and also unlike theater and cinema which bring small groups together before specific, unmistakable images.

18 Richard Wagner: *Parsifal* (Premiere: January 27, 2011, Théâtre Royal de la Monnaie, Brussels, D: Romeo Castellucci).

19 Joe Kelleher: Les hommes marchent sans fin. Entretien avec Romeo Castellucci. In: *Alternatives théâtrales* 113–114 (2012), pp. 16–19, here p. 17.

> Actually, there is no live comment made about what is seen (the discussion time is put off until after the show).[20]

However, this quotation seems to be unaware of numerous contemporary productions which undermine the stage's prevalence by building multidirectional relations through collective debate. The importance of debate for theater is nothing new – let us think about political theater in the sixties and early seventies. For instance, Pier Paolo Pasolini, in his *Manifesto per un nuovo teatro*, asserted that the most important thing in his theater were the debates after the performances, as if the performances were only pretexts for discussions.[21] In the same way, Peter Stein, then the undeclared leader of the Schaubühne collective, affirmed that theater's purpose was to offer:

> A kind of theater, where spectators will be fundamentally those who make theater – not by a more or less mythical participation, but insofar as what is represented concerns directly them and leads them to discuss, or even to question the way of discussing.[22]

Nowadays, novelty lies more in the integration of the debates within the performance, even to the point of changing the performance into discussion. We could evoke the debate moment inside the plot of *Ein Volksfeind*[23] directed by Thomas Ostermeier where spectators were incited to contribute to the discussion about democracy, but this fictional break was recovered by the dramaturgy, and the pronounced words had no effect on the plot. More significantly, a relatively unknown Italian production, Compagnia della Fortezza's *Il Libro*

20 Nicolas Bourriaud: *Relational Aesthetics*. Dijon: Presses du Réel 2002, pp. 15–16.

21 Pier Paolo Pasolini: Manifesto per un nuovo teatro. In: P. P. P.: *Saggi sulla letteratura e sull'arte,* vol. 2, ed. by Walter Siti / Silvia De Laude. Milan: Mondadori 1999, pp. 2481–2500.

22 Bernard Dort: La Schaubühne am Halleschen Ufer: Entretien avec Peter Stein. In: *Travail théâtral* 9 (1972), pp. 16–36, here p. 24.

23 Henrik Ibsen: *Ein Volksfeind* (Premiere: July 18, 2012, Festival d'Avignon, D: Thomas Ostermeier).

della vita[24], encouraged singularities to share by calling into question the polarization of the theatrical apparatus. This autobiographical performance followed the difficult life trajectory of a Moroccan illegal immigrant up until the Volterra prison, where he had met the director Armando Punzo. The sharing of singularities seemed to acquire an essential dimension at the performance's end, when discussion began. Debate was not postponed but belonged to the performance itself: the exemplary exposition resulted in dialogue, in voices sharing. This discussion did not look like the usual meetings after performances, which typically deal with the genesis and the meanings of the production, but built relations between the spectators, who witnessed their own experiences. The multidirectional relations undercut the theatrical apparatus's polarization, since the scene became a position among others.

Xavier Le Roy's *Low Pieces*[25] includes debate in performance in a more obvious way. This choreographic piece begins with a discussion, with nothing preceding it. The discussion proves to be abstract: how can we discuss nothing in particular, without any goal? After several slow and living tableaus by totally nude performers, the performance ends with a further discussion in total darkness. When I saw the performance, most of the spectators talked about the artistic value of the project, denounced its minimalism and its unintelligibility and questioned the meaning of the nudity. The darkness allows for resentment to be expressed vehemently. Yet a dialogue between spectators quickly established itself. The darkness caused a depolarization of the theatrical space, creating an abstract place where the voices' sharing could occur. The opening speculative discussion and the closing abstract debate brought forward the problematization of the audience's being-together: what unites in a same place spectators and performers in casual clothes? What can they talk about? How can a common space emerge, beyond the contingency of co-presence? How could a common experience arise from dissensions and the irreducibility of singularities?

24 Mimoun El Barouni, Armando Punzo, *Il Libro della vita* (Premiere: July 25, 2005, Sotterranei della Pinacoteca, Volterra, D: Armando Punzo).

25 Xavier Le Roy: *Low pieces* (Premiere: July 19, 2011, Festival d'Avignon).

From sharing to testing spectatorship: collective as experience

Xavier Le Roy's performance contributes to a relatively notable tendency: the problematization of the theatrical being-together in contemporary scenic experimentations, which substitute it for the participatory making-together. Through this problematization, we must understand the spectator's testing as a collective experimentation that takes into account the singularities' irreducibility. The theatrical event then consists of testing the relations between spectators without excluding any singular desire, probably contrary to the collective. This experimental tendency originates in the same dynamics that Claire Bishop brought to light concerning performance art: questioning the connection between the individual and the collective is relevant, she declared, when it considers the individualistic pleasure and asocial affects that hinder the collective composition, rather than by expecting only moral and social communion or cooperation.[26] Spectators then become the performance object: they are questioned, not as passive consumers, but in their rapports to the collective.

Three recent performances apply this experimental tendency, i. e. the testing of the spectator. The first is La Ribot, Juan Dominguez and Juan Lorente's *El triunfo de la libertad*[27] Its dramaturgy is very simple: four hanging electronic banners (normally used for surtitles) broadcast, in total silence, quotations from the pre-revolutionary period to the Indignados revolt or the Arab Spring, parts of absurd discourses and a very long joke on the exploits of a Scandinavian dwarf's penis. Consequently, the performance deceives all visual expectations. Furthermore, it employs the normally solitary practice of reading, transformed by the theatrical apparatus into a collective activity. The minimalism raises a series of questions, as each spectator simultaneous feels lonely and encircled by other isolated readers: what do others think in front of the enigmatic text? How can solitary reading connect with the others' reading? Is forming a collective even thinkable from such a lonely practice? Moreover, the complete refusal of visual spectacle in this performance can cause other thoughts: Are others as

26 See Claire Bishop: *Artificial Hells*. London / New York: Verso 2012, p. 39.

27 La Ribot / Juan Dominguez / Juan Lorente: *El triunfo de la libertad* (Premiere: August 29, 2014, La Bâtie Festival, Geneva).

embarrassed as I am at the scenic emptiness? What do the other spectators think of this performance that I find disappointing? Why did numerous spectators walk out during the performance, what is it that they couldn't stand? In other words, experiencing community happens paradoxically by increasing the sense of solitude inside a collective.

If lack and deception can lead to troubling the collective, it could be the same with an affective excess. For instance, Jan Fabre and Romeo Castellucci have declared several times that they do not address the audience, but individuals.[28] They want them to face their own traumas or fantasies. But this invocation of fantasy occurs inside a collective of other individuals. It seems that the spectator, who copes with inner drives during the performance, is not enclosed within him/herself but is also concerned with the possibility of a common fantasy, due to the co-presence. Therefore, these kinds of performances should not be regarded only as updated cathartic or ritual practices, as revivals of tragic theater, but also as the problematization of the possibility of a collective composed by what is normally the most singular.

The title of the second performance, *Audience*[29] by the Flemish company Ontroerend Goed, explicitly implies that spectatorship is at its core. It seems to belong to that kind of performance which seeks to provoke or upset the spectators. Performers greet spectators at the doors of the theater hall and invite them to take off their coats and to leave their bags, which are put on a rail. Spectators then sit down in front of a giant screen. After listening to some welcoming words like those on a TV show, spectators see a camera beginning to shoot them, one by one, and observe the filmed pictures broadcast live on the screen, at first in silence. After a while, the performers interpret the footage by inventing the spectators' thoughts, as a schoolboy joke. Later, images of the spectators' arrivals are broadcast, having been filmed without notice. Then the performers don the spectators' coats and comment on the contents of their bags, which they empty on stage. During all these sequences, the spectator finds himself exposed,

28 For example, Jan Fabre said during the controversial edition of the Festival d'Avignon in 2005: "We convey another relation to art, which aims to establish a secret strong link between an individual and a piece, beyond all socialisation, even antinomic to socialisation." (Quoted in Georges Banu / Bruno Tackels (eds): *Le Cas Avignon 2005*. Vic-La-Gardiole: L'Entretemps 2005, p. 257.)

29 Ontroerend Goed: *Audience* (Premiere: March 16, 2011, Voruuit, Ghent).

isolated from the group, his appearance and his intimacy are examined, as if the performance's purpose was to embarrass him/her through exposing him/her to the others' gaze. But the middle sequence goes a step further. One of the performers resumes a cheerful tone and thanks everyone for his/her collaboration. Suddenly, he breaks off and insults, vehemently and for a long time, one spectator chosen in the audience. Then, he promises to stop if the spectator agrees to show some intimate part of his/her body. After several minutes, he offers the audience a solution to break the embarrassment: another spectator should replace the victim. This sequence is intolerable. Ashamed spectators do not intercede, because they know it is only a game, but they nevertheless suffer an unbearable situation[30]. This last game becomes disturbing, since each spectator feels ashamed of being-there. In other words, the collective consciousness seems to appear through shame, through the impossibility of an effective solidarity, through the powerlessness of spectatorship. Shame stems, in that case, from the experience of asociality. In short, community proceeds from its contrary, from its impossibility, revealed by the testing of spectatorship.

My last example is Rimini Protokoll's *Remote*, which was created in several cities all around the world. Here, I will examine the Avignon version[31], but there is no doubt that the questions raised in this version are relatively independent from the location. It offers another way of testing spectatorship that has nothing to do with participation, despite the company's statement. Indeed, in the alphabet book dedicated to their recent work, members of the German collective claim that participative theater is "the only good one"[32]. However, regarding these productions, this affirmation should be tempered. Participation, collaboration and interaction are limited to some sequences inside a very controlled apparatus, varying from theatrical configuration to installation, where spectators are more supervised than free, for example: a few minutes of free questions in the various versions of *100 %*[33], some

30 In April 2014, at the Valenciennes Phénix, some spectators did intercede, but without effect, since it was not a real situation.

31 Rimini Protokoll: *Remote Avignon* (Premiere: July 08, 2013, Festival d'Avignon).

32 Helgard Haug / Stefan Kaegi / Daniel Wetzel: *Rimini Protokoll-ABCD*, ed. by Johannes Birgfeld. Berlin: Theater der Zeit 2012, p. 61.

33 Rimini Protokoll, *100 % City* (Premiere: February 01, 2008, HAU 1, Berlin).

contacts and physical exchanges in *Situations Rooms*[34], discussions in *Lagos Business Angels*[35], the conversation while drinking vodka at the end of *Cargo Sofia*[36].

Although one of the principal issues of *Remote* is community, this performance is not any more participative than the others. Interactions between the spectators are negligible. The work invites the audience to stroll in the city's streets with headphones and a player, like tourists listening to a guided tour or participants of an artistic soundwalk. The work can be considered in different ways: it questions the comprehension of the city, the omnipresence of technology or the manipulation by a synthetic voice, symbol of the contemporary technical orders. But its importance lies primarily in the problematization of the transitory community, through the script as well as through the technical apparatus.

At first, it seems odd to talk about community while each participant is confined within his own soundscape. We could even say that the community is composed only paradoxically by asocial singularity, since, according to Stefan Kaegi, using a walkman leads to the individual's decontextualization, to the suspension of the social environment. However, a collective is developing through a common walk, a common course, and above all in the puzzled look of the passer-by. Community exists then by behavioral difference in the public space. Moreover, the speech heard via the headphones increases the technical asociality. The participant is constantly invited to look at others, to think about his/her physical preferences, the gaits and the gestures s/he likes, and about the repelling individuals, about the member who may act as a scapegoat. In an auditorium of Avignon University, each participant had to write a confidential sentence and utter it at the same time as the others. This can crystallize what *Remote*'s community is: a group of singularities walking in the streets of a city, faced with its impossible identity through the display of asocial affects and singularity's irreducibility. While walking, participants share experiences

34 Rimini Protokoll: *Situations Rooms* (Premiere: August 23, 2013, Ruhrtriennale, Bochum).

35 Rimini Protokoll: *Lagos Business Angels* (Premiere: March 25, 2012, HAU 1, Berlin).

36 Rimini Protokoll: *Cargo Sofia-X* (Premiere: March 04, 2008, Balto Scandal, Tallinn).

of resistance to the collective. Testing spectatorship here means the exposition of the impossibility of group identity, because of the singularity of the desires.
Testing spectatorship appears, in these three productions, as a way of making community a uniting experience, much more than the exemplary image offered by the heterotopic scene or the irenics of the sharing of singularities. It questions the transitory community: can we think the collective on the basis of the contingency, indifference and anonymity that characterize mass society, without referring to former definitions? How can this social grouping be made to shift from obvious to problematical? Far from invoking glorious models, testing spectatorship takes the new status of the audience into account, i. e. an audience composed of "spectators-consumers", longing for individual aesthetical relations and "temporary sociability".[37] Furthermore, testing spectatorship includes the modification of the scene. As the theatrical site, it is abandoned (*El triunfo del la libertad*), disseminated in social space (*Remote*) or becomes the gaze's site (*Audience*). But the test cannot avoid authority, power, or at least control, since it is always decided by the author(s), even though this is undermined by its scenic absence or by its negative characterization. In sum, the production does not lead to the erasure of what exceeds the collective (a text, an apparatus, a disembodied speaker). So, can we conceive of a test that unites spectators and performers at the same time? It seems that an excess is needed to think an egalitarian collective, as in Site-Specific Theater, which, according to Hans-Thies Lehmann, establishes a "commonality" between performers and spectators because they are all "guests" of a same place.[38] Collective experiencing cannot be understood literally, for it requires a supplement to the aesthetic relation, but not the former ones (citizenship, nationality, class, etc.). The political task would then be to undermine this supplement and, consequently, the testing authority, to challenge the collective's identity until it resembles the de-identification of the disparate world.

37 Piergiorgio Giacchè: Le public est mort. Vive le public! In: *Alternatives théâtrales* 116 (2013), pp. 16–19, here p. 17.

38 Hans-Thies Lehmann: *Postdramatisches Theater*. Frankfurt am Main: Verlag der Autoren 1999, p. 306.

Isabelle Barbéris

Conviviality, Parasitism and the Common Meal

Toward a Dramaturgy of "Preparation"

My research on parasitic operations and characters can be located inside the frame of a larger reflection crossing postdramatic theater with *posthuman studies*.[1] The interplay between these issues brings to light a theater that plays on different processes: biological, economic and social. The question of the parasite allows the focus to be taken off the theatrical framing and given to mimesis, freeing the figurative and humanistic assumptions that inform the restrictive hypothesis that considers theater as built on the human scale. Parasitic figures are inalienable, can operate in a range of scales, and resist appropriation in their dramaturgic derivations (beginning with the *alazon* character[2]

1 Isabelle Barbéris / Françoise Dubor (eds): Après l'anthropo(s)cène: la création scénique à l'ère du posthumain. In: *Degrés* 163–164 (2015). See also I. B. / Florence Fix (eds): *Le Parasite au théâtre*. Paris: Orizons 2014.

2 *Alazon* belongs to the pool of Greek theatrical characters. Under various masks, the *alazon* possesses stable qualities: imposture and charlatanism; swaggering and boasting; greed and voracity; also vagrancy (linguistic root *alé-*). The non-fixity is a fundamental characteristic as we can find it in the picaresque figure. One of the most complex and accomplished characters, he appears in Aristophanes' comedy centered on the democratic process: *The Acharnians*. Dikaiopolis is at the same time above and below the common law. Uncaring of moral rules, he is like *Natura naturans*, and his energy is a vector of transformation. Pascal Thiercy contests a straight categorization of the Aristophanian parasite. Each figure appears as "the result of a complex mixing of […] three notions" (*alazon*, buffoon, ironist, by the classification of Cornford). (Pascal Thiercy: Introduction. In: Aristophane: *Théâtre complet*, Paris: Gallimard / La Pléiade 1997, pp. IX–XXVI, here p. XI (transl. I. B.).)

in Greek classical comedy). As shown by the Socratic[3] "seed of leaven"[4], parasitic figures have a heuristic capacity and evoke the imperceptible, the porous and the featureless. The parasite offers the possibility of deepening reflections on interactive and convivialist dramaturgies aided by Suzan Guerlac's Bergsonian idea of "*livingness*"[5].

From Lucian of Samosata to Jacques Derrida, the art of the parasite shares many consonances with historical reality and its contradictions: emancipation *vs.* interdependency; nature *vs.* artificial organicities; hospitality *vs.* the implosion of identities; productivity *vs.* waste, etc. The etymology of "*para-sitos*" contains a neutral spatial meaning: parasitism involves a process of con-junction or co-existence (entropic or not) between two agencies. By the end of his largely sarcastic *Eulogy for a parasite*, Lucian underlines this coordinating function with a genuine commendation of the simple process of "being-with". The parasite can be understood as a metaphor as much as a performative model for living together. Dramaturgies of the parasite reciprocally lead to considering theatrical plots and schemes as sort of "bioturgies" and to contemplating the extent to which theater could function as a parasite of the real environment and interfere with it. To such ends, infiltration, occupation, puncture, and recycling can be read as components and gestures of parasitic dramaturgies. From Latin comedy, the *allochthon* figure is omnipresent in the comic tradition and plays a key role in articulating the relationship between theater and the invention of democracy. Permitting the representation of the invisible, the parasite implies an extension of the democratic sphere. As can be observed in the works of Aristophanes, Suidas, Diphilos, and the Comical Alexis, the subversive power of the parasite also embodies the intrinsic contingency of the democratic government. From the beginning, a semantic conflict emerges between pejorative acceptation and

3 *The Symposium* dramatizes philosophic and parasitic operations simultaneously and in an exemplary way. Plato's Dialogue is built on an interference system, taking the form of an amorous play. Socrates embodies the parasitic figure by "donner le change" (as a change interface).

4 I anachronistically recycle the chemical and nutritional metaphor ("grain de levain") used by Denis Diderot to characterize Rameau's Nephew. "*Para-sitos*" literally signifies "beside the wheat".

5 The "art of the parasite" or "parasitique" in reference to Lucian. Cf. Lucien de Samosate: *Eloge du parasite*. Paris: Sillage 2014.

transformative subversion. This capacity of reversal draws one beneath the manifold skins and subtexts of the parasite, where additional buried, metabolic and pre-human meanings can subsist. The metabolic operation is fundamentally liminal as is all food intake, and this mode of cannibalism involves the absence of distinction or con-fusion between the same and the other.

I would like to cross the concept of parasitic mimicry with a very present notion in the field of contemporaneous cultural studies: "conviviality"[6], a term that sounds like a literal reformulation of Roland Barthes' "vivre ensemble" ("*con-vivere*": vivre ensemble)[7]. Convivialist thinking largely makes use of the image of food-sharing ("commensality") and the aesthetical device of the meal ("*convivium*"). Through this nutritional and participative metaphor, being-together reflects a more pragmatic and procedural significance. This prompts the consideration of being-together from the perspective of sharing, distributing and consuming common food.

In an age obsessed with food and its multiple stagings, parasitism has a new role to play. This obsession is amplified by the entertainment industry and broadcasted through an infinite range of television programs and games. The rotation axis of this new imaginary is related to the anthropology of survival and emphasizes the question of preparation before the old capitalistic issue of production. The change of direction is anything but anecdotal. It leads to a new pragmatic approach where the notion of "preparation" reflects multiple meanings: to make food edible; to compose a medicine or a plaster; to get ready in order to confront a disaster and make provisions for the future (see, for example, the prepper communities in the USA)[8]. The food obsession has also affected many "Nouveaux Philosophes" (we also speak about "Nouvelle cuisine") who have recently signed the

6 The philosophical concept of conviviality was popularized by Ivan Illitch – meaning a counter-power inside the industrial society. More recently, Shannon Jackson used it to state a new aesthetic category: "aesthetic conviviality". (Shannon Jackson: *Social Works. Performing Arts, Supporting Publics*. New York: Routledge 2011, p. 6.)

7 Roland Barthes: *Comment vivre ensemble. Cours et séminaires au Collège de France (1976–1977)*. Paris: Seuil 2002.

8 See, for example, the very popular TV Show *Doomsday Preppers* (National Geographic Channel, 2011–2014).

Convivialist Manifesto (2013), calling themselves "convivialist philosophers"[9]. The explicit objective of this new brigade is to reach an agreement between thinking and action – to 'stir things up'. This trivial metaphor helps us to understand the convivialist object of desire: the overcoming of the opposition between two intellectual postures, the French intellectual *vs.* the Men of action. François Cusset[10] has already analyzed the ingredients of this recipe also present in the *Convivialist Manifesto*, available in open source, underlining the limitation of resources and the urgency of this question:

> Never has humanity disposed of so many material resources and of so much technical and scientific expertise. [...] However, on the downside, one can no longer believe that this accumulation of power can continue on indefinitely, such as it has, in a logic of unaltered technological progress, without turning against itself and threatening the physical and moral survival of humanity. [...] Threats and urgencies that we must always keep in mind.[11]

Subtitled "Interdependency Manifesto", this collective text does not openly display nutritional connotations. But it nonetheless establishes a convergence between two figures, the major one being the citizen figure who arises from politics' great narrative; the minor other being affiliated with the figure of the guest. Through this convergence, the discourse about the parasite unfolds in two distinct spaces: the city and the table. This congruence depends on a context in which the question of *resources* supersedes the question of *production*. The typical 20th-century production-oriented paradigm of unlimited growth

9 The Convivialists, anonymous group of authors: Convivialist Manifesto. http://www.lesconvivialistes.org (accessed February 19, 2018).

10 François Cusset: *La Décennie. Le Grand cauchemar des années 1980.* Paris: La Découverte 2008.

11 "Jamais l'humanité n'a disposé d'autant de ressources matérielles et de compétences techniques et scientifiques. [...] Pourtant à l'inverse, personne non plus ne peut croire que cette accumulation de puissance puisse se poursuivre indéfiniment, telle quelle, dans une logique de progrès technique inchangée, sans se retourner contre elle-même et sans menacer la survie physique et morale de l'humanité. [...] Menaces et urgences qu'il est indispensable d'avoir constamment présentes à l'esprit." (Convivialist Manifesto. http://www.lesconvivialistes.org (accessed February 19, 2018; transl. from the French by Margaret Clarke).)

has given way to the alternative model of resources that points out the fundamental aporia between *pleonexia* and ecological limitations. Only dangerous *illuminati* of the 'Invisible Hand' (as transhumanists) persist in the belief of the endless ... Interdependency is the new categorical imperative of contemporary practical judgment. The faith in growth includes a concept of participation that begins with the productive individual force and then grows into collective fulfillment. Individual performance was the center of this prosperity and its dream of abundance. The new ecological anthropology stresses the importance of the collective way in which we deal with limited and extinguishable start-up capital.

These questions are present in the following analyses of two performances, underlining and dramatizing the limitation and the consumption of common resources while questioning the initial contract of "being-together" through the theatrical paradigm (also limited in time and space). The convivialist situation (spectator-guest in El Meddeb's performance, or guest-and-cooker in Meierhans') is geared each time towards the collective consumption of a meal that brings performers and audience members together at the end of the session. The public becomes the co-worker of the performance, the agent of food circulation and transformation. Neither of these performances exploit the meal as the utopic model of a fusional and festive being-together. On the contrary, the communal experience happens thanks to the interference of parasitisms: misunderstandings, captures, mismatches, communication traps, etc. In reverse order, parasitisms are what permit communication or reflexivity on the collective *potlatch*,[12] thereby facilitating the possibility of community. The contractual dimension brings to light points of reversibility and instability in the process of collective subjectification.

12 I am taking the liberty of referring to the *potlatch* in this common sense, though the notion relates to a much more complex reality. As the *potlatch* was banned in North America, like other crucial spiritual practices and regalia, many nations and communities are doing the work of reclaiming and relearning practices like the *potlach*, and so its use within western philosophy may be bound to the violence of colonizing cultural appropriation.

1. From Jacques Derrida to Radhouane El Meddeb: towards a dramaturgy of misunderstanding?

Founder of the Compagnie de soi ('The Self Company'), the Tunisian choreographer Rhadouane El Meddeb has produced his culinary solo *Je danse et je vous en donne à bouffer*[13] ('I dance and I feed you with it') for almost ten years. It can be described as a danced couscous for 50 people. The performance draws from the traditional ritual in Tunisian society and in the north-African countries more broadly where preparing couscous takes place in each rite of passage. As the artist states on his website,

> In my family I have always carefully observed my mother and my aunts preparing couscous. Our national dish, served at every occasion: marriages, circumcisions, mourning... One same dish for the different events which punctuate the same existence.[14]

On a quadrifrontal white stage stands a well-stocked table with all the ingredients and kitchen utensils needed. Saucepan, stew-pot, big pitchers, couscous grain, vegetables, meats, seasonings and spices shape a scenic, temporarily peaceful, and apollonian picture – all ready and waiting for the choreographer's frenzy. Then El Meddeb switches on the music through his iPod.

From the first dance steps, the spectators understand the dimension of "appris par corps"[15]. The agility of the grinning dancer's lips tells us a lot about his cultural familiarity with these traditional songs. In Tunisia, it is the men who dance to these songs while the women prepare food in a separate room. Alternating dance with culinary gestures, El Meddeb blurs the gender boundaries of the separation of duties. He multiplies the back-and-forth movements between the dance floor and the kitchen space, here brought together in a single area: the place of the "kinesthetic" performance (according to El Meddeb). The *mixis*

13 Cf. Rhadouane El Meddeb: *Je danse et je vous en donne à bouffer* (Premiere: 2008, Centre national de la danse, Pantin). See http://www.lacompagniedesoi.com (accessed April 19, 2017).

14 http://www.lacompagniedesoi.com/spectacles/je-danse-et-je-vous-en-donne-a-bouffer (accessed April 19, 2017).

15 "learnt-by-body". This expression was coined by Pierre Bourdieu: *Méditations pascaliennes*. Paris: Seuil 1997, pp. 168–169.

allows El Meddeb to "open the catachresis" of the traditional "danse du ventre" (belly dancing); extracting it from its gendered frame of reference with snide and sensual grace. "Between tomato purée, zucchinis, carrots, cinnamon, a leap, a gaze, a suspension or a rupture, between the semolina and a two-way crossover, the dish is simmering."[16] Codes of dance mixed with a kitchen recipe form a hybrid: for instance when the dancer, nearly in trance, does serial laps mimicking the thurifer. El Meddeb really "incenses" the public, but with cinnamon powder! Sometimes he throws a spray of couscous grain, or the jet of plastic cutlery at the end of the session, before the collective meal. The simulacrum of a fusional rite produces effects quite divergent from the traditional one – divergent in terms of cultural and sexual codes. In March 2016, the rework of the performance at Houdremont Center in La Courneuve (a very popular place in a Parisian suburb with a majority of immigrants) was held with an audience from the "Cité des 4000" neighborhood. Many of the scenes I saw on this occasion shaped a micro-theater of cultural negotiation. Some veiled women supported the queer dancer by clapping their hands or with ululations. Other spectators covered their mouths with a flap of veil to guffaw furtively. Still others were very embarrassed in front of the queer entranced body and hid their eyes with their palms. The spectator in front of me across the stage was a North-African man around 25 years old who was evidently very disturbed to see this exhibit. The Tunisian tradition, paradoxically, not only allows, but even incites men to dance! In other contexts (a white, French audience for instance), the culinary performance generates a quite different repertory of identity chiasmus. But in any case, spectators are referred back to their own gazes. The performance, above all, causes prejudice, cultural projections, and conditioned behaviors to simmer. El Meddeb makes the audience salivate during the two-hour performance before setting the table, serving the dish, and disappearing with a last negligent and graceful, but also contemptuous gesture. He doesn't share the meal with the public. This disappearance seems like a final verdict: the ex-colonized dancer resists the metabolization and abandons his voracious spectators who are ready to pounce on the delicacies and

16 http://www.lacompagniedesoi.com/spectacles/je-danse-et-je-vous-en-donne-a-bouffer (accessed April 19, 2017).

consume the work. Assuming the position of the host, the Tunisian performer leaves the place of the parasite to the spectator, reduced to the function of profit and destruction of the ingested work. Instead of unifying, the dramatization of parasitism as a conjunctive and unproductive process (literally being next-to-the-food) sets up a conflictual and agonistic situation involving production and waste (of calories and signs). The work – and the dancer as well – stay ineluctably un-digestible (in French, the term of "assimilation" is used to speak about immigrants who have succeeded in their social integration, but "assimilation" is also a biological term denoting a digestive process!). Significantly, the only non-Tunisian musical song of the performance is Nina Simone's hit *Don't Let Me Be Misunderstood*. The Derridean notion of "parasitage" as "communication malheureuse"[17] (unfortunate communication) is helpful in understanding *Je danse et je vous en donne à bouffer* as an attempt to communicate by way of losses and frictions.

2. Parasitocracy or democracy?

Christophe Meierhans' performance *Verein zur Aufhebung des Notwendigen* (English Title: *A Hundred Wars to World Peace*, 2014)[18] invites spectators to participate in the preparation of a meal for a hundred people (the entire audience). The script reuses the ancestral art of the random draw in Athenian democracy: at the entrance to the theater, each member of the audience picks a ping-pong ball with an attributed number between 1 and 100, each one referring to a specific task. Instructions cross the codes of the cooking recipe and the tradition of the script in performance art. Although quite coercive, each task conserves a margin of interpretation that provides the outcome of the performance. For instance: "remove an ingredient if you're

17 About Derridean parasitism and Derrida/Searle's controversy on speech acts, see Kevin Halion's thesis: *La Déconstruction et la théorie des actes de langage*, 2002. https://www.e-anglais.com/thesis_fr.html#3.2.1 (accessed January 03, 2017), ch. 3.2.1.

18 Christophe Meierhans: *Verein zur Aufhebung des Notwendigen* (Premiere: September 25, 2015, Kunstencentrum Vooruit, Ghent, Production: Hiros, Coproduction: Kaaitheater, Vooruit, BIT Teatergarasjen, Kunstencentrum BUDA, Nouveau Théâtre de Montreuil, Vaba Lava).

allergic"; "fry something in oil"; "do something with a little saucepan" or "clean 50 portions of something", etc. The ludic aspect of this experience consists in the play of scale between the detailed ("put ten seed of something in a coffee filter") and the quantitative ("sieve 5 kilos of manioc flour in a big basin"; "peel 100 lobster tails") tasks.

As the performance moves along, the tasks become longer and harder. The theatrical shape risks disappearing into the live meal preparation. But interludes (glug-glugs and throaty sounds; texts delivering enigmatic morals of the story) remind the audience of the performance's artificial dimensions. The participation doesn't cancel the representation, and the frame is always recalled by effects that disturb the immersive aspect of the experience. The random draw underlines its metademocratic meaning. According to Meierhans, it spurs us to reflect on "democracy as a practice of individual and collective responsibility"[19], on the successes and the failures. The collective meal served at the end of the session can be catastrophic, disgusting and inedible, as well as satisfying or even enjoyable for the taste buds. *Verein* makes sense at a time when "having lunch together" becomes more and more of a challenge due to nutritional taboos, pathologies, and flexible job schedules. Jonathan Crary wrote in *24/7: Late Capitalism and the Ends of Sleep*[20] that capitalism is also assaulting our dishes. *Verein* tries to assert the responsibility of each participant inside the convivial process. Many dysfunctions might bring the performance to ruin and waste: the temptation of narcissism, mistrust, racial prejudice or machismo, authoritarianism or submission, etc. The performance works to expose these dysfunctions. But *Verein* generates a more global meaning that I would like to compare with another performance that deals with the topic of democracy in a similar way: Joël Pommerat's *Ça ira (1): La Fin de Louis*[21] whose political imaginary, in contrast to Meierhans' attempt, is also participative but very romantic.

Pommerat depicts democracy as a juxtaposition of enthusiastic voices which are captured in the historical moment of the French Revolution.

19 Cf. brochure of the performance, Nouveau Théâtre de Montreuil, February 3–13, 2016.

20 Jonathan Crary: *24/7. Late Capitalism and the Ends of Sleep*. Brooklyn: Verso 2014.

21 Joël Pommerat: *Ça ira (1): La Fin de Louis* (Premiere: September 15, 2015, Théâtre du Manège, Mons).

By way of spirited orators standing and speaking, raised hands and bodies haranguing the audience, etc., Pommerat stages the *vox populi*'s mythology. In contrast, the Swiss artist Meierhans develops a pragmatic and methodological vision of a democracy conceived as judicial structure (the recipe, the instructions, the laws). To implement the law isn't sufficient for peacekeeping any more than the simple conjunction of voices and egos. The meal can only be edible if each individual decision is negotiated with collective criteria. In other words, democracy isn't idealized inside of a romantic conception of being-together. Democracy is only what we make of it, and the way we perform a system of rules. It can be conclusive or it can be catastrophic and dystopic. Democracy reproduces its own system of interferences and parasitizations. This is very far from the enthusiastic and romantic storytelling of Joël Pommerat. Meierhans sees the issue on the empiric side in order to criticize the "egocitizen" and to promote the "ecocitizen".[22]

3. Conclusion: from parabola to metabolic process

Both performances reproduce democratic tensions on a theatrical scale. Using the parasite as mode of operation as well as metaphor, the performances look like social experimentation, anthropological laboratories of the democratic process and collective *mana*. Mining limited culinary resources, *Verein* tries to operate a fair and efficient sharing. But the convivial topos harbors a well-known dystopic side-effect (present from Trimalchio to *La Grande Bouffe*): the laboratory can veer towards catastrophe, orgy, destructive fusion, oblivion of the external reality, and the bulimic process (as in *Manger seul* (2014), a performance by Fabrice Gorgerat inspired by Thyestes' anthropophagy[23]).

The *convives* represent the positive and reassuring face of the profiteer parasite and freeloader whose goals depend on a survival logic.

22 Joël de Rosnay: *The Macroscope. A New World Scientific System*, trans. from the French by Robert Edwards. New York: Harper & Row 1979.

23 Fabrice Gorgerat: *Manger seul* (Premiere: November 11, 2014, Arsenic, Lausanne). After *Médée/Fukushima*, *Manger seul* deals with "the new catastrophe" of obesity. For the anthropologist and dramaturge Yoann Moreau, Thyestes doesn't know what he eats, nor does the contemporary overeater. The alimentation is seen as a process of solitary alienation.

However, parasitism is a vitalizing ingredient of both performances by infiltrating interferences and noises that resist 'eradication' and assimilation, and that look towards an overall balance – a chemist symbiosis. The fear of the parasite, in its contemporary hysterized threat, goes together with the hygienist target of eradication and the anxiety caused by its liminal status. At present, the parasite is always the antithesis of the responsible citizen. After the Holocaust, Hans Jonas described the modern subject as a destructive parasite, turning the disgusting metaphor against the whole of humanity.[24] But the metaphor is not exhausted; the parasite still resists consumption and metabolization, as the residue of a meal. *Eulogy of a Parasite* highlights the parasite Simon as the paradoxical allegory of a stateless liberty.[25] The parasite stays out of the production circuit. To the life cycle of the product, he prefers the cycle of the seasons. Its ends and means are the same thing. As a supplement grafting itself onto a situation, like Socrates, he plays the negative function inside the dialectic process.

In conclusion, it bears reminding that the inventor of "*vivre-ensemble*" was interested in food and cooking, as illustrated in the famous *Mythologies*.[2] Barthes' remarks in "The Wine and the Milk" or "Steak and Fries" settle for a symbolic interpretation. We find the same approach in his analysis when he calls "Ornamental Cuisine" a modern myth, notably concerning the "toppings" and "sides": Barthes doesn't deal with processes but settles for understanding food as a marker of social status. But today *alimentation* as a process generates new signs of civilization: the preparation, the participation, the sharing, the emulsion – that help us to think being-together in metabolic terms. Both of these performances go beyond the symbolic meaning of culinary topoi. To some extent, they participate in a new ritual investigation of food and conviviality: one as a model of democratic coproduction; the other as a situation generating cathartic and dynamic misunderstandings.

24 Cf. Hans Jonas: *The Imperative of Responsibility: In Search of an Ethics for the Technological Age,* trans. from the German by Hans Jonas with the collaboration of David Herr. Chicago: University of Chicago Press 1985.

25 Cf. Lucien de Samosate: *Eloge du parasite.*

Leon Gabriel

Scenes of Plural Constellations

Partage, Community and *Struction*

1. Introduction: being-with and the globalized conditions

Our world is one of an enclosed space organized by a ubiquitous economy: We live in an era of huge accumulations and of totalized equivalences – equivalences of values, goods and humans. This condition is part of what we call the 'globalized' world, but without doubt, this world offers new problems and even a crisis of the sense itself: New conflicts emerge inside this world; people are being excluded without a place inside this unified neoliberal economy; and human resources are being exploited at the same time as natural ones. How to think the being-with and its sense under these conditions? How to observe them still from a critical standpoint? We witness a homogenization and a dissemination that both take place at the same time. In this article, I will outline and problematize two different reactions towards that crisis: the move backwards to communities isolated from the outside and the indifference towards the interchangeability of everything with everything.

The being-with or being-together is bound to a thinking of the world. The world is traditionally the image for what concerns everyone, for the global, the universal history and values. Since his early writings about *La communauté desoeuvrée*[1] and the following development of

1 Jean-Luc Nancy: *La Communauté Désœuvrée*. Paris: Bourgois 1986, esp. pp. 220–234.

the being-with, the philosopher Jean-Luc Nancy has related the thinking of the common with the notions of the world and the sense.[2] In 2011, Nancy and Aurélien Barrau wrote: "[The world] has become the crucial point where all of the aspects and stakes of 'sense' in general become tied together."[3] The world and the alteration of the world are forming the secret background of my research. Nancy and Barrau continue:

> At a time when we say that every day the world is more "globalized" [globalisé] or "world-formed" [mondialisé] – and thus unified – and simultaneously that our worlds and our ways of life and culture are constantly more diffracted, scattered, heterogeneous, and even unidentifiable, the question of the world must be reconsidered: the question of the idea of "world," of the "reality" of the where in which we live, of its "unity" and "unicity", texture, or dissociation.[4]

But it is no coincidence that the two authors mention in the French original of this passage also the expression "il faut remettre *en chantier* la question du monde" (one must put the question of world back into work) instead of writing about a mere 'reconsidering' as in the English translation.[5] They re-open a terminology of labor that is structurally linked with the common, the being-with and the world. And at the same time, the 'globalized' world sets the task to think again the sense between the two poles of a closed space and complete disintegration. How to approach this task?

I have started with an introduction of the being-with under the globalized conditions (1). I will now strengthen the thinking of the community and its relation to work/labor, contrasted with the idea of the "partage" (2). This will be followed by an analysis of the project of an isolated community in the staging of Romeo Castellucci's *FOLK* (3). Then I will introduce the concept of the *struction* (4) and a way to

2 Jean-Luc Nancy: *Le Sens du Monde*. Paris: Galilée 1993.

3 Aurélien Barrau / Jean-Luc Nancy: *What's These Worlds Coming to?* New York: Fordham UP 2015, p. 1.

4 Ibid., p. 3.

5 Aurélien Barrau / Jean-Luc Nancy: *Dans quels mondes vivons-nous?* Paris: Galilée 2011, p. 11.

negotiate the *struction* will be presented by the choreography *Untried Untested* by Kate McIntosh (5). Finally, I will resume with a claim for a thinking of the being-with according to its shifting political and historical conditions (6).

2. The community as work and the *partage*

Instead of proclaiming unified communities, Jean-Luc Nancy insists in many texts on what he calls the being-with (derived from Martin Heidegger's *Da-Sein* and Hannah Arendt's "World as in-between"[6]): "The with is the most basic feature of Being, the mark [trait] of the singular plurality of the origin or origins in it."[7] It is a being together-with-others but at the same time not-being-one-whole-with-the-others. He also describes this being-with as "partage": "Partage" itself is language and is the world, as that what we share but what comes between us. Thus, the practice of "partage" is our only sense within our being-with according to Nancy. For

> [the] sense cannot be subsumized under the unity of a whole, may it be a collective or an individual one (this is one of the consequences of 'the death of god' which itself is insofar the life of sense), the sense is in the partage / sharing and in the passage between us.[8]

Whereas "community" in its simple and traditional sense means a homogeneous whole, this hope for unity was nothing more than the phantasm of nearly any political agenda in modernism (be it the fascist, the socialist or the liberal one) functioning as a catalyst for work/production. Modernity seeks to overcome the economic and social differences within itself by its promise of equality within a harmonic community that can be achieved by work or rather by labor:

6 Cf. Hannah Arendt: *The Human Condition*. Chicago: University of Chicago Press 1998.

7 Jean-Luc Nancy: *Being Singular Plural*. Stanford: Stanford UP 2000, p. 61.

8 Jean-Luc Nancy: Entretien. In: *Le Philosophoire* 1:7 (1999), pp. 11–22, here p. 13 (transl. L. G.): "[L]e sens n'est pas assignable dans l'unité d'un tout, que celui-ci soit collectif ou individuel (c'est une des conséquences de la 'mort de Dieu', laquelle est donc la vie du sens), le sens est dans le partage et dans le passage entre nous."

community is thought as the self-fulfilling promise of the shared work.[9] It is its own product and in Aristotelian terms, a *poiesis*. Here lays the main difference with Nancy's concept: The being-with isn't a *poiesis* at all, but must be understood as a *praxis* – this would go along with Marx' theories.[10] If the modernist communities were the attempt to assemble the many under one closed notion of togetherness, the being-with is the togetherness of the undeniable plurality or dissemination of plural-singularities: "[I]t is necessary to refigure fundamental ontology (as well as the existential analytic, the history of Being, and the thinking of *Ereignis* that goes along with it) with a thorough resolve that *starts from the plural singular of origins,* from *being-with.*"[11] But what does the community and the work have to do with the globalized world? During the so-called 'Globalization' since the 1990s, a "totalitarisme inédit" or "immanentisme" became reality:[12] The western market logic finally established itself as new and ubiquitous order which created the world as one closed and immanent space of the rationalized polity of the productive sphere, which excludes anything that does not function according to its own logic.[13] So, globalization projected itself like the modernist utopias as a world, whose sense lies in its work to become the fulfillment of this community as

9 Martin Jörg Schäfer: *Die Gewalt der Muße. Wechselverhältnisse von Arbeit, Nichtarbeit, Ästhetik*. Zurich / Berlin: Diaphanes 2013.

10 Jörn Etzold: Community and Practice. Nancy, Aristotle, Arendt, Marx. In: *Oncurating*: *Being-With* 7 (2011). http://www.on-curating.org/files/oc/dateiverwaltung/old%20Issues/ONCURATING_Issue7.pdf (accessed February 29, 2016).

11 Nancy: *Being Singular Plural*, p. 26 (emphasis in the original).

12 Philippe Lacoue-Labarthe / Jean-Luc Nancy: Le 'Retrait' du politique. In: P. L.-L. / J.-L. N. (eds): *Le Retrait du politique*. Paris: Galilée 1983, pp. 183–198, here pp. 191–192. Both philosophers stress that the political is in retreat from what they call "the modern city state" (*cité moderne*) or even "civité de la cité".

13 The "totalitarisme inédit" means: the dissolution of transcendence or the retreat in the Heideggerian sense as the *Entzug* of what is supposed to be present. This corresponds with the movement of the Heideggerian *alètheia*. Philippe Lacoue-Labarthe / Jean-Luc Nancy: Annexe. Circulaire de preparations de la discussion du 15 mars 1982. In: P. L.-L. / J.-L. N. (eds): *Le Retrait du politique*, pp. 201–203, here p. 202. Instead of such transcendence or alterity, the authors stress the installation of a mere immanence, which Nancy will later elaborate on as "immanentism": A homogeneous closed space of the absolute inside. What is at stake is nothing less than alterity itself. See Jean-Luc Nancy: *The Creation of the World or Globalization*. Albany: SUNY Press 2007.

its own end.[14] But as we all know and witnessed in recent years: Globalization did not imply the 'end of history', instead, new conflicts broke out.

3. The formation of a community and its failure – Romeo Castellucci's *FOLK*

In 2012 Romeo Castellucci created in direct reference to Nancy's writings on community the staging *FOLK*[15] exclusively for a former steel-production site at the Festival Ruhrtriennale.[16] The setting links the industrial production with the production of a community: Within a huge former industrial hall, the spectators gather around a large inflatable swimming pool. Meanwhile, an ongoing ritual takes place: A person is standing inside the water, another person approaches. Both embrace each other, the first drowns or 'baptizes' the second. The second repeats this ritual with a third person and so it goes on for more than half an hour. It seems, as if some people from the audience decide to take part. But actually, it is completely unclear if the more and more people who pass on this community ritual of absorption and immunization have been instructed before or if they are audience members.

Suddenly, a harsh and increasing knocking of dark bodies against the milky windows high above the heads of the audience starts: Something, somebody, a strange other *crowd*. As they can't enter, they produce a sound of raptor birds: The dark crowd inserts via voice, what they can't bring in with their bodies – an outer threat. The dark bodies

14 And one might add here that this problem was already foreseen by Hannah Arendt on the question of stateless people who are literally expelled from a world that only accepts human rights as civil rights, i.e. rights bound to the citizenship of a state. See Hannah Arendt: *The Origins of Totalitarianism*. New York: Schocken 2004, pp. 376–377; also Werner Hamacher: On the Right to Have Rights – Human Rights; Marx and Arendt. In: *The New Centennial Review* 14:2 (2014), pp. 169–214. I thank Jörn Etzold for bringing this article to my attention.

15 Romeo Castellucci: *FOLK* (Premiere: August 25, 2012, Ruhrtriennale, Duisburg). For my analysis, I make reference to my notes of the performance as well as to the video recording.

16 This place links the production directly to the industrial and political projects of modernity mentioned before, as well as their discontents: The whole Ruhr-area was the main production site for steel and thus, for warfare in Germany.

Fig. 1: Romeo Castellucci: *FOLK*, 2012.

Fig. 2: Jacques-Louis David: *Le Serment du Jeu de paume*, 1791. Musée national du Château de Versailles.

disappear at the windows, the bird sound will stay while the ritual continues. But it is also not the foreign sound that will split up this phantasmatically united community:
An old man appears, but he is not baptized. The man positions himself in the middle and erects his finger in an unreadable gesture. (Fig. 1) While the man is moving his finger like cutting the space into two halves, stage workers cut the huge inflatable swimming pool into two parts and the water floods everywhere. Loud pipe organ chords are heard. The two huge plastic parts of the swimming pool are being hung up high in the air – like dead meat. Underneath, the old man sits now down at a small table and tries to do a children's game of symbolic recognition – which he fails. He desperately starts crying and walks off, alone.
FOLK shows two 'outsides' that come inside: The sounds, but also the inner 'outside-within'. And it is the latter that lets the unified community collide. The excluded is already inside: Within the same world, a gap and before negated otherness violently pops up. The non-identical that lies *within* any phantasmatic community opens up like a wound (see the reference of the hanging dead bodies). Associations to actual geo-politics might emerge: The excluded refugees, the inner tensions and expulsions upon those who cannot perform up to standard (i. e. the old or challenged by health reasons). *FOLK* plays with the hopeless claim of a unified community that is not endangered by what it tries to keep out, but by its own included exclusions.
At the same time, Castellucci is playing with the position of the spectators who are part of this game between inside and outside. *FOLK* walks on the small line between two different modes of staging: the community as a spatial and unstable movement by the immersive, installative setting with the assembled crowd, but then also the logic of the symbolic image or tableau especially with the figures of the literal outsiders and the old man. It's precisely the moment of the cut, the *partage* as a rupture which shows this thinking in images of the staging. One could easily forget the gesture of the old man, but it seems to me that with this moment, Castellucci is directly citing the painting *Le Serment du Jeu de Paume* by Jacques-Louis David. (Fig. 2) This is *the* emblematic image of the foundational myth of the modern and democratic state. By this, *FOLK* links the being-with to a ritual but also to the foundation of modernity.

From a critical perspective, *FOLK* somehow mystifies the being-with as a religious assumption and doesn't take the important notion of the *partage* seriously: The *partage* of the being-with means that there would always be an otherness in *any* togetherness, and not that there are only some people ('the others') that don't fit. And the *partage* doesn't necessarily mean *per se* a harsh conflict. But *FOLK* shows how the modernist projects of the closed unities such as the factory or the nation-state can't immunize themselves against an outside. Even if *FOLK* is not explicitly dealing with globalization, we find here a way of thinking about the construction of a community by its presumed coherence. It is precisely this construction that is challenged by globalization, but that is also reproduced by the fact of being in connection with others on a shared and single globe.[17]

4. The movements of the sense – the *struction* and the equivalence

From here, I want to focus on the other problematic reaction towards globalization: The mere indifference.

We are today facing other modes of assemblies. Instead of being disciplined by foundational institutions (factory, state, church), we are more often self-willingly guided by open structures like e.g. networks and feedback-based interfaces. The assumption of the world as a globalized *closed* space is incomplete, if we don't see the *technical interweaving and structuration* of this closed space. This technicity makes our globalized world not a single, unitarian space that we can be either inside or outside. Rather, the techno-globalized world are *worlds*: it creates connections inside itself. Governance, business, leisure time are shaped by feedback-loops, big data mining and comparability within a networked structure. Further, contemporary work and labor themselves function by technological networks and through processuality and less and less through the production of objects. Hasn't the actual

17 In the small program-book, Castellucci is citing a large passage from Nancy about the globalized condition where wars and conflicts between identitarian unities reappear. See also Jean-Luc Nancy: The Confronted Community. In: *Postcolonial Studies* 6:1 (2003), pp. 23–36.

condition of the world already overcome by itself the paradigm of the oeuvre, of production and construction?
This brings me to a neologism that Nancy recently invented in order to describe our being in a globalized world where everything is technically connected: *La Struction*, a mode of being connected and together, but only as a mass in an indifferent and changeable way under the increasingly technologically shaped *kybernetic* infrastructures.

> "*Struo*" signifies "to amass," "to heap." It is truly not a question of order or organization that is implied by *con-* and in-struction. It is the heap, the non-assembled ensemble. Surely, it is contiguity and copresence, but without a principle of coordination.[18]

Struction is what lays behind the dualism of construction and destruction. It is a paradigm of "that is labile, disordered, aggregated, or amalgamated rather than conjoined, reunited, paired with, or associated"[19]. Mankind doesn't produce any longer techniques or institutions as its extension.[20] And technical inventions or planned structures don't deform nature. Instead human techniques/projects and nature are intertwined and insofar indistinguishable, as the modernist division of both spheres turns out to be inappropriate as a tool for rendering out a definition of what is 'given' by essence and what is human production/creation.[21]

18 Jean-Luc Nancy: Of Struction. In: Barrau / Nancy: *What's These Worlds Coming to?*, pp. 42–58, here pp. 48–49.
19 Ibid., p. 49.
20 See also Erich Hörl: Thousand Ecologies: The Process of Cyberneticization and General Ecology. In: Diedrich Diederichsen / Anselm Franke (eds): *The Whole Earth. California and the Disappearance of the Outside*. Berlin: Sternberg 2013, pp. 121–130.
21 "By speaking of 'nature,' we used to presuppose or rather superimpose a coordination that was proper and immanent to the profusion of beings (a spontaneous or rather divine construction). With 'technology,' we used to presuppose a coordination that was ruled or regulated by ends that were particular to 'humankind' (their needs, capacities, and expectations)." (Nancy: Of Struction, p. 49.) Thus, 'nature' was and is being used often as an ahistorical/prehistorical or even essentialized status – even if this status can also be described as lost by modernity. The state of *struction* that Nancy and others aim at also implies that 'nature' is understood as not being detachable from the notion of 'history'. See also Serge Moscovici: *Essai sur l'histoire humaine de la nature*. Paris: Flammarion 1968.

But also, *la struction* could help us to find possibilities to articulate an actual movement of sense.

According to Nancy, *struction* is the mode of being-together *after* the project of communities. The being-with seems to have become more than an ontological condition, but also an infrastructural and epistemic status[22] – but where a questioning of sense has completely vanished:

> What I am calling here "struction" would be the state of the "with" deprived of the value of sharing, bringing into play only simple contiguity and its contingency. It may be, to take back the terms that Heidegger wants to distinguish in his approach to the "with" (the *mit* in the *Mitdasein* as the ontological constitution of the existent), a "with" that is uniquely categorial and not existential: the pure and simple juxtaposition that does not make sense.[23]

Struction disables the question of sense at all[24] and instead of a new way of questioning the "partage" of the being-with, *struction* installs itself as *infra-struction*[25], but without being an infrastructure according to a centralized directive and not any longer something that can be classified with the old opposition between nature and culture. The paradigm of production might be overthrown, but the important point of *la struction* is its deeply capitalist logic of processes that accumulate, compare, value and exchange. Nancy describes *la struction* as a mode of technically assembling anything under the conditions of changeability and equivalence.

22 This – under other premises than mine – can even be described as a new geochronological era, although I am avoiding the all-too popular term *Anthropocene* as an equation for *la struction*. For a critic on the notion of the *Anthropocene* and thinking of togethernes as entanglements see Donna J. Haraway: *Staying with the Trouble. Making Kin in the Chthulucene*. Durham / London: Duke UP 2016, pp. 30–58.

23 Nancy: Of Struction, p. 49.

24 Nancy even writes that "[W]e are being exposed to a catastrophe of meaning." (Jean-Luc Nancy: *After Fukushima. The Equivalence of Catastrophes*. New York: Fordham UP 2015, p. 8.)

25 I thank Bernhard Siebert for this expression.

> Technology is not an assembly of functioning means; it is the mode of our existence. This mode exposes us to a condition of finality that had till now been unheard-of: Everything becomes the end and the means of everything. In one sense, there are no more ends or means.[26]

But „we must understand that equivalence is not equality"[27]. The mode of *struction* seems to be the fulfillment of a heterogeneous but still closed world without a *telos*. – Instead of a search for one or plural senses, a "*destinérrance*"[28] takes place. In short, *struction* is the mode of what seems to be equality, but instead means an *indifference*. Under the sign of equivalence goals constantly become means and means become goals, where the being-with is confounded with the non-assembled ensemble under the paradigm of equivalence.

5. Kate McIntosh: forming plural constellations

Is it nevertheless possible to bring up the question of *partage* as question of what lays between us and insofar as questioning of sense again? How to deal with the mere accumulation and equivalence? Can the ontological condition of the being-with as a *partage* come into question (again) in theater? And how to find a new sense?

The Brussels-based performance artist and choreographer Kate McIntosh has been implicitly working on questions similar to mine but often in a cheerful mode: Her works or rather scenic essays often create worlds populated by unusual beings, sometimes in contact with an audience, sometimes raising philosophical questions on life science, knowledge and cognition. In 2011, McIntosh started – without naming it so – to work more in the direction of the here mentioned being-with as it seems to me.

26 Nancy: *After Fukushima*, p. 36.

27 Ibid., p. 40.

28 Nancy: Of Struction, p. 57. This expression was introduced by Jacques Derrida. See for example: Jacques Derrida: The Spatial Arts. An Interview with Jacques Derrida by Peter Brunette and David Wills. In: P. B. / D. W. (eds): *Deconstruction and the Visual Arts: Art, Media, Architecture*. Cambridge: Cambridge UP 1994, pp. 9–32, here p. 12.

Fig. 3: Kate McIntosh: *Untried Untested*, 2011.

Fig. 4: Kate McIntosh: *Untried Untested*, 2011.

In her performance-research project *Untried Untested* from 2011,[29] McIntosh uses the stage as blank working paper to try out bodies, materials, shapes and positions in their interrelations. Without naming it *struction* or anything like that, McIntosh assembles various things together with humans. The staging experiments with the absolute equivalence of both humans and objects, and tries out new subject–object relations: The four female perfomers start to inflate balloons, but then leave them alone and let them be 'dancing', moved only by a machine, a fan. Whereas the performers then start to do what humans do best – i. e. destruction (of the balloons) – their relationship towards the balloons begins to change: They begin to examine their materiality and then start to imitate the objects: They fall down when the balloons explode. More and more things are brought on stage: a potato, books, a rope. Which size does it have? Which weight? What happens if I step on it? (Fig. 3 & 4)

The things are observed each in its singular way, played with, imitated. The performers always proudly show their new discoveries like children. Finally, their testing of everything takes even over the paper-material of their own stage: Their stage of experiment itself is brought into the testing field as it is being wrapped up and newly assembled together with the performers' bodies that already behave like objects. (Fig. 5 & 6)

It seems as if the performers are turning upside down the anthropocentrism of our thinking of a world where man uses equivalence as a tool of appropriation and start new alliances coming out of things. They do so, by using a mimetic play which resembles what Walter Benjamin has called "entstellte Ähnlichkeit"[30] (disfigured similarity). Benjamin describes with disfigured similarity our mimetic ability which should not be confounded with acting or imitating: Rather, this disfiguration does not imitate but is our affectivity to be transformed by what surrounds us: Things or other beings that change the coherent

29 Kate McIntosh: *Untried Untested* (Premiere: February 09, 2011, Campo, Ghent). For my analysis, I am referring to my notes from the performance as well as to the video recording.

30 Walter Benjamin: Berliner Kindheit um 1900. In: W. B.: *Gesammelte Werke*, Vol. 4.1, ed. by Rolf Tiedemann / Hermann Schweppenhäuser. Frankfurt am Main: Suhrkamp 1991, pp. 235–304, here p. 259.

Fig. 5: Kate McIntosh: *Untried Untested*, 2011.

Fig. 6: Kate McIntosh: *Untried Untested*, 2011.

self, as one could say in addition to Benjamin (who describes the experience of being he himself 'disfigured by similarity').
Untried, Untested reminds of children's plays, cheerful explorations of the world. *Untried Untested* alters the thinking of the world within the order of the *struction*:[31] New and other connections are possible between the singularities: connections and relations that exceed the existing thinking of comparable values, of the exchange of goods. Kate McIntosh builds scenic constellations of pluralities, where new entanglements can be observed and subject-object hierarchies come into reformulation. She develops settings that set free new movements of sense.

6. Conclusion

Both stagings presented here work as scenic constellations of a current reaction towards today's mode of being: Castellucci works on the implosion of a closed community. But this presentation remains itself inside the logic of the recognizable (readable) image – especially of the modern state which itself is based in Christian tradition. McIntosh on the other hands steps away from the order of the image and is searching together with the performers for new alliances between humans and objects – alliances which are not representational and maybe not even visible.
To come to an end: Facing globalization, our question is not to build new unified communities (whose aporias are shown in *FOLK*), but to find new entanglements (which is played with in *Untried Untested*). Neither do we need to negate the existence of a shared world (our planet), but with Jacques Derrida, one could say that there is always a singularity of any access to the world, which is always *incomparable*.[32] This marks the difference towards *la struction* and equivalence: The

31 As in *Untried Untested*, *struction* also means that the formerly homogenic world consists more and more of smaller 'worlds' but that connect together without a plan or clear sense (and are insofar indeed an ecological complex).
32 Timothy Clark: What on World Is the Earth? The Anthropocene and Fictions of the World. In: *The Oxford Literary Review* 35:1 (2013), pp. 5–24, here p. 19. See also Jacques Derrida: *The Beast and the Sovereign. Volume II (2002–2003).* Chicago: University of Chicago Press 2011, pp. 266–267 (Session 10).

incomparable negates the claim of equivalence as exchangeability and as comparison of values. Instead, the incomparable stresses the equality of that which is "absolute and irreducible particular". And indeed, maybe this brings up a new thought of the sense within the globalized world of *struction*: a "communism of unequivalence"[33].

Castellucci shows us a condition which organized modernity and which has not vanished but is still working within juridical, religious or political systems. But it is the second condition about which McIntosh is working which becomes more and more important today. Thinking the being-with in the age of a maybe already post-globalized world (that itself might have surpassed its own process of becoming-global and now turns into a status of new divisions as well as entanglements) sets us the task to search modes how to give credit to the plurality of the *partage*, of the "communism of unequivalence", but also to make new meaningful relations and connections. These scenic constellations are short interventions that question if there still is a meaning or even a new sense within our shared condition of being-together. If the struggles of a globalized world can also open our view on new relations, then it might be our critical task to find not one, but many other senses within them.

33 Nancy: *The Equivalence of Catastrophes*, p. 41.

Marie Preston

From Community-Based Art to the Art of Co-Creation

Jean-Luc Nancy proposes that we conceive of the world as populated by beings who are not so much connected by any "social bond" as they are *comparaissant* or co-appearing, a term that may be understood as the "appearance of the *between* as such".[1] Being-with, replacing the overused term "community," precedes our usage. In 2000, in *Revue Parachute*, Nancy remarked to Chantal Pontbriand: "I have tried to think not what is called 'a community', but being-with insofar as it is constitutive of being itself (or being-self, if you prefer): that is, insofar as one cannot conceive a subject, a 'self', preceding a relation with others."[2] Here, then, my aim is not to undertake a long discussion on the organization of our interdependencies, since being, ontologically, "is with." Rather, I aim to discuss how this philosophy forces us to invent the existence of this "with" other than as a purely theoretical vision, since it seems so simple to act as if one were alone in the world. The task is thus to explore the productive calibrations of our interdependencies and the different breadths of their gaps, the *betweens*, without denying dissent, agonism, and the exercise of democracy, i. e., imagining and carrying out something other than a cohesive

1 Jean-Luc Nancy: *The Inoperative Community*. Minneapolis: University of Minnesota Press 1991, p. 29.

2 Jean-Luc Nancy / Chantal Pontbriand: An Exchange. In: *Parachute, L'idée de communauté* 100 (2000), pp. 14–31, here p. 15.

community of beings gathered under a unified "us"[3]. Starting from the philosophy of being-with and the debates provoked among critics of "community-based practices" by the philosopher's thinking, I will share my experience with a group of women to which I belonged and whose gathering I instigated. I will develop the hypothesis that cooperative and co-creation artistic practices, through precise modalities that I shall explain, allow us to experience being-with, reveal it to us in our finitude and through the separation of each singularity, through what simultaneously links and separates us.[4]

My use of "art in cooperation" corresponds to what Pablo Helguera, who strove to define "socially engaged art," calls "collaborative participation," wherein an individual (who is neither *a priori* a visitor, nor a spectator, nor an artist in the sense of a professional belonging to different artistic realms as defined by the market and art institutions) "shares responsibility for developing the structure and content of a work in collaboration and in direct dialogue with the artist"[5]. What I call co-creation refers to situations, performances, or works of which each participant is equally an author. Therefore, it is not a question of "participation," in the sense of an action undertaken by an individual asked to "take part" in an artistic proposition whose framework has already been conceived by the artist or a group of artists.

These cooperative practices presuppose that future co-authors will constitute a group that can include one or more artists and one or more "amateurs." This division between statuses, current in artistic institutions, seems difficult to sustain when, for one, the question of technical mastery remains a matter of debate and, for another, co-creation practices rest on the presupposition that each person may, in an egalitarian manner, bring a constructive element to the collective work and that the amateurism and/or professionalism of each one is constantly

3 "It is not a community that fuses the ego into an *Ego* or a higher *We*. It is the community of *others*." (Nancy: *The Inoperative Community*, p. 15.)

4 "A singular being *appears*, as finitude itself: at the end (or at the beginning), with the contact of the skin (or of the heart) of another singular being, at the confines of the *same* singularity that is, as such, always *other*, always shared, always exposed." (Ibid., p. 28.)

5 Pablo Helguera: *Education for Socially Engaged Art*. New York: Pinto 2011, pp. 14–15.

shifting. These practices express the desire to reshuffle roles assigned by society and undertake the distribution of the sensible, as defined by Jacques Rancière. Thus (professional or amateur) artists and (professional or amateur) citizens, residents, neighbors, and friends strive to have a communal experience. All of them go beyond participation, and each contributes to the creation.

It seems necessary here to clarify that I do not evoke cooperative and co-creative practices because they help mimic the implementation of a fixed, essentialist community, or the creation of an ersatz being-with. On the contrary, I use them as a reference because, according to certain modalities, they seem to offer an experience, though they are no less reliant on being-with than any other activity.[6] The first modality and minimum condition is that the meeting of singularities must not take place within the perspective of creating community because, according to Nancy, such cannot belong to the realm of the *œuvre*. "One does not produce it; one experiences or one is constituted by it as the experience of finitude."[7]

Community-based art

In the 1990s, many critical texts attempted to grasp, analyze, and define the "New Genre Public Art," thus named and defined by the artist Suzanne Lacy in her work *Mapping the Terrain* (1995), and most particularly in her introductory article, first published in 1993. According to the artist, this form, spurred by, among other things, feminist movements and the art of Allan Kaprow, appeared in the 1970s:

> For the past three or so decades visual artists of varying backgrounds and perspectives have been working in a manner that resembles political and social activity but is distinguished by its aesthetic sensibility. Dealing with some of the most profound issues of our time [...] a group of visual artists has developed distinct models for an art whose public strategies of

6 It is, moreover, very revealing that each question asked by Chantal Pontbriand in her interview with Nancy, "An Exchange", was systematically taken up and deconstructed by Nancy: "Is a differentiated community conceivable?" – "No other community is conceivable", etc.

7 Nancy: *The Inoperative Community*, p. 31.

engagement are an important part of its aesthetic language. The source of these artworks' structure is not exclusively visual or political information, but rather an internal necessity perceived by the artist in collaboration with his or her audience.[8]

Taken as a starting point, this definition, which can encompass a very significant number of different practices, necessitated understanding who this 'public' was and how it could become a collaborator. Did it refer to those who visited artistic institutions, from which some of the artists distanced themselves? Other artists? Activist groups? Members of diverse associations? Students? As the realization of the importance of these orientations from a political and artistic point of view began to dawn, the idea of community and then that of being-with appeared very insistently throughout the debates that flared between critics and defenders of these practices.

I wish to re-examine an exchange between Grant Kester and Miwon Kwon, two American art critics and historians of cooperative practices. This debate occurred between 1995 and the early 2000s. It began with the observation that these practices were attracting increasing interest from private foundations and public institutions, also manifested in the organizations of large-scale exhibitions, of which *Culture in Action* by Mary Jane Jacob in Chicago in 1993 is the best-known and certainly one of the most discussed. In January 1995, in the review *Afterimage*, Grant Kester published an article entitled "Aesthetic Evangelists: Conversion and Empowerment in Contemporary Art." In this text, he attempted to define two distinct modes of cooperation, differentiated by whether or not the artist works with individuals belonging to the "communities" with which the artists themselves identify. He also warned artists to be careful of the ideological basis in which they were trafficking. At the start of his essay, he suggested renaming "New Genre Public Art" as "new community-based art" or "community-based art." He then observed that the definition of the word "community" in the art world could be articulated thus:

the term "community art" is often used to demarcate those works that are produced by, or address, subjects defined by their difference from a white,

8 Suzanne Lacy: Cultural Pilgrimages and Metaphoric Journeys. In: S. L. (ed.): *Mapping the Terrain. New Genre Public Art*. Seattle: Bay 1995, p. 19–30, here p. 19.

> upper-middle class norm. [...] The "community" in "community art" often, although clearly not always, refers to individuals marked as culturally, economically, or socially different either from the artist him or herself, or from that audience for the particular project.[9]

He then refined the definition that he would go on to use in the remainder of his text:

> Community can be defined in relation to spatial or institutional boundaries (e. g. urban neighborhoods, trade unions, prison population, etc.); in relation to specific issues (e. g. free speech, environmentalism, health-care reform, etc.); or in connection to specific identities (racial, national, ethnic, gender or class-based, etc.).[10]

The debate with Kwon was structured on the distinction established by Kester between "community-based" practices, wherein, on the one hand, the artist collaborates with people defined as the "inchoate aggregate" (or induces them to participate), in the paternalistic expectation that the artist "will take on the delegate's role and attempt to literally 'create' a community consciousness out of the atomized social detritus of late capitalism"[11]; and on the other hand, practices wherein the artist collaborates with a group seen as fighting "to define their political identity and interests" and whom Kester thus defines as "politically coherent".[12] For the critic, cooperation with this type of community makes "the process of mutual exchange and education more equitable"[13]. Finally, he warns, with particular emphasis concerning these two modes of cooperation, that these practices rechannel extremely problematic conservative Victorian ideology, according to which the artist as a social worker, philanthropist, "enlightened and generous" bourgeois, can replace the welfare state. This substitution derives from the belief that the "poor" person, if he strove to work and raised his morale, if he was able to testify

9 Grant Kester: Aesthetic Evangelists: Conversion and Empowerment in Contemporary Art. In: *Afterimage* 22 (1995), pp. 5–11, here p. 5.
10 Ibid.
11 Ibid., p. 6.
12 Ibid.
13 Ibid.

to his conversion, could succeed. "The particular aspect of Victorian reform [...] conceives of the working-class itself as a mass to be transformed through the implementation of a moral-pedagogical program."[14] Thus, for the critic, community art rests on a dialectical relationship between the artist and a person or group of people who are assumed to have need of what the artist can potentially supply: emancipation, creativity, etc.

In her book *One Place After Another: Site-Specific Art and Locational Identity*, published in 2002 and adapted from her thesis defended in 1998, Kwon examines Kester's analysis. In it, she questions the very existence of "coherent political groups"[15]. She contends that this belief revives the very essentialism denounced by Nancy, for whom "what this community has "lost" – the immanence and intimacy of a communion – is lost only in the sense that such a "loss" is constitutive of "community itself".[16]

Kwon defines these practices (without distinguishing between the typologies created by Kester) as "descriptive," within which communities inscribe a "social identity" and whose artistic success depends on the "affirmation of a coherent collective subject".[17] This is far from Nancy's thinking, according to which community ensures the "impossibility of a communitarian being in the form of a subject"[18]. This is Kwon's main criticism of Kester's analysis: the coherence of various groups and communities, the specificity of "community-based art," is an illusion, a theoretical pitfall. Furthermore, she adds that these supposedly unified groups, whose identity allows a particular relationship

14 Kester: Aesthetic Evangelists, p. 8.

15 Miwon Kwon: The (Un)Sitings of Community. In: M. K.: *One Place after Another. Site-Specific Art and Locational Identity.* Cambridge / London: MIT Press 2004, pp. 138–155, here p. 145.

16 Nancy: *The Inoperative Community*, p. 12.

17 "Community-based art, as we have seen, is typically understood as a descriptive practice in which the community functions as a referential social entity. It is an other to the artist and the art world, and its identity is understood to be immanent to itself, thus available to (self-)expression. The degree of success of an art project of this kind is measured in relation to the extent to which these (self-)expressions, as signifiers of community identity, affirm rather than question the notion of a coherent collective subject. The mirage of this coherence, fortified by the fact that the representation of the community is ostensibly produced with or by the same, is consumed as authenticity." (Kwon: The (Un)Sitings of Community, p. 154.)

18 Nancy: *The Inoperative Community*, p. 45.

to be linked to a social issue, are more easily rendered subject to claims that divert their initial aspirations.[19] These are the terms of cooperation, the type of "community art" that artistic institutions solicit more easily in order to supplement a real social policy.

In a book published in 2004, *Conversation Pieces: Community and Communication in Modern Art*, Kester responds to Kwon by analyzing Jean-Luc Nancy's thought as well as the elements that lacked in his 1995 essay.[20] To do so, he grounds himself in the Wochenklausur collective's practices and in the work of Suzanne Lacy and Stephen Willats. He does not deny the criticisms, responding:

> After developing my critique of community-based practice, I was confronted by the contradiction between the unrelenting purism that drives a certain kind of theatrical reflection (one that orients criticism around the postulation of ideal or hypothetical models of identity) and the pragmatic demands of artists working in social movement here and now.[21]

He thus exposes the gap he observed between theoretical thinking and its practical application: "Should the members of an African American community who establish some solidarity around a resistance to environmental racism be faulted for their reliance on a 'coherent' identity?"[22]

"Since the 'with' has nothing to do with what is called 'collective'"[23], taking Kwon's critique into account, the issue encountered by Kester

19 Kwon: *One Place after Another*, p. 146. See also Kester: "As a result, Kwon is highly skeptical of art projects that conceive of community members not as singularities-in-waiting but as members of an existing collective." (Grant Kester: *Conversation Pieces: Community and Communication in Modern Art*. Berkeley: University of California Press 2013, p. 159.)

20 In this book, he mentions that Nancy's thought is often evoked during the period in which he wrote. He refers to three issues of *Parachute* mentioned at the beginning of this text and to an article by Gillian Rose: Performing Inoperate Community: The Space and Resistance of Some Community Arts Projects. In: Steve Pile / Michael Keith (eds): *Geographies of Resistance*. New York: Routledge 1997, pp. 184–202.

21 Kester: *Conversation Pieces*, p. 161.

22 Ibid., p. 162.

23 "The co- of collectivism is a mere external 'side by side' which implies no relationship between the sides or between the parts of this '*partes extra partes*.'" (Jean-Luc Nancy: Communisme, le mot. In: Alain Badiou / Slavoj Žižek (eds): *L'idée du communisme*. Paris: Ligne 2010, pp. 197–214, here p. 204, quoted from

seems close to that described by Pierre Dardot and Christian Laval in their work *Commun, essai sur la révolution au XXI*^e *siècle:* "Is there a politics of being-with or of being-in-common?"[24] Their response is that this/the policy would have "the sole purpose of opening a space in which the affirmation of communal inequivalence can take place."[25] By taking this direction, Kwon posits that associating groups must include, in what is shown of their cooperation, the impossibility of creating community. Thus, she proposes a new terminology: "it is meant [...] to suggest that such an impossibility is a welcome premise upon which a collective artistic praxis, as opposed to 'community-based art,' might be theorized."[26] Contrary to *community-based practices*, this artistic and collective praxis is a projective undertaking. This supposes that

> a provisional group, produced as a function of specific circumstances instigated by an artist and/or a cultural institution, aware of the effects of these circumstances on the very conditions of the interaction, performing its own coming together and coming apart as a necessarily incomplete modeling or working-out of a collective social process.[27]

To the modalities described by Kwon, I would add that every cooperative and co-creative experience requires the invention of specific ways to assemble, which must endure over time through a communal activity. Duration and activity presuppose particular attention to the creation "process," which in turn presumes an accounting for and orientation of every stage of the experience. Yet orientation does not mean a mastery of what develops. The process necessitates indeterminacy. It implies the triggering and following of a process, which must be thought of in a collective, reflexive, and contextual fashion. Thus, it lets a communal space form and engaged relationships

Pierre Dardot / Christian Laval: *Commun, essai sur la révolution au XXIe siècle.* Paris: La Découverte 2015, p. 278. English translation: J.-L. N.: Communism, the Word. Notes for the London Conference, Birbeck College. In: *Lacan Dot Com*, no date. http://www.lacan.com/essays/?page_id=126 (accessed May 21, 2017).

24 Dardot / Laval: *Commun*, p. 280.

25 Ibid.

26 Kwon: The (Un)Sitings of Community, p. 154.

27 Ibid.

be maintained by encouraging the development of new subjectivities. For Félix Guattari,

> the mechanisms of the production of subjectivity vary. In traditional systems, for example, subjectivity is produced by more territorialized mechanisms, on the scale of ethnicity, professional body, or cast. However, in the capitalistic system, production is industrial and takes place on an international scale.[28]

Therefore, according to the psychoanalyst, some spaces and practices allow the emergence of new agencies. He refers to social workers, people engaged in pedagogical or cultural work, "all those whose profession consists in paying attention to the discourses of another."[29]
This directly concerns those collectively involved in creation processes and who, thus, work towards a micropolitics. But does the reflexive work toward a group/collective's development and its dispersal? Does the come-and-go between desire and impossibility, idleness, "interruption, [...] fragmentation [...] suspense"[30], all combine in communal activity and a conscientiously observed, influenced process? Does the time spent together suffice to create the experience of this being-with which is going "beyond oneself"? To create an "experience-we" which entails a relationship with the "non-self"? By evoking a personal experience, I will attempt a response.

Commérages, multiple voices

If the group operates while remaining conscious that it is composed of singularities with mobile identities, and that this makes the group identity, itself, prone to fluctuation, if heterogeneity and heterophony are fostered, if the group's activity is not pre-planned toward an end but involved in an open process, then perhaps the experience of being-with, of an us-together can emerge. It was in this sense that I – and then "we" – envisaged the collective experiment *Commérages*. This

28 Félix Guattari / Suely Rolnik: *Micropolitiques*. Paris: Les Empêcheurs de penser en rond 2007, p. 37.

29 Ibid., p. 43.

30 Nancy: *The Inoperative Community*, p. 79.

project, which assembled a group of six to eight women – Stéphanie Airaud, Aïcha Akremi, Françoise Alexandre, Arminda Alves, Carine Faribol, Alejandra Montalvo, and Nelly Zeitlin – began in May 2013 and finished two years later, in March 2015. The experiment began on the initiative of Stéphanie Airaud and the Musée d'art contemporain de Vitry, or MAC VAL. The group was formed through the mediation of the museum and two town social centers. However, attentive to Kwon's critique and the instrumentalization of participative practices by public policies and cultural action, we meant to counteract the idea of community or any kind of group belonging. These reflections appeared in the two publications presented in the final installations. These books included my work journal (reports from sessions), transcriptions of conversations, testimonies, and critical texts. The following is an excerpt concerning the non-fixity of the group and its participants' desire not to be "catalogued":

> Very quickly, these realities were called into question by the group. On 11 June 2013, I wrote: "Of whom is this group made? People who visit social centers? Not only. Perhaps we should decide never to foreground this specificity, since it isn't one. The group is composed of unique individuals, not 'samples.' According to their wishes, the people involved thus acted in their own name and not according to a social or cultural affiliation.[31]

Quite concretely, the effects of each person's "provenance" were discussed. What did it mean to be (a) representative(s) of a social center? What did the museum, the participants, the social center expect from the artist? What did the museum and social center have to gain from this communal activity? What were their motivations in instigating it? What effect did this have on the group's functioning? How did this assign us with a certain representation, a certain principle of equivalence among us as beings? Here, we returned to the fact that we could not address a "politically coherent group" and that the task was not to fix an identity for an emerging group.

31 Marie Preston: Le contre-pouvoir du commérage. In: *Commères. "Chroniques Muséales"*. Exhibition catalogue. Vitry-sur-Seine: MAC VAL 2015, pp. 6–14, here p. 8 (transl. from the French by Julia Zelman); see also pp. 6–7.

The starting point for our experiment was organized around the sharing of these lines of questioning as well as the reading of a text from a work by John Berger, *La Cocadrille* (1979). This excerpt concerned "gossip" [*commérage*] and its ability to create a living portrait of a village, of which each speaker is the author and which is constantly changing through its capacity to be transmitted and modified. Berger writes: "The true function of gossip, the oral history of the everyday, is to allow the entire village to be defined [...] The life of a village is a living, collective portrait in which each person is a portraitist."[32]
Although the text did not define gossip as a feminine activity (in contrast to ancient *doxa*), but since the group was exclusively made up of women, it led us to reflect on the place of feminine speech in public space. The functioning of our collective work was not that of a workshop assembling participants for a week or two, as is often the case. We met twice per month for a total of about forty sessions, which considerably extended the usual period that the Museum MAC VAL normally accorded this type of activity. The goal for the sessions was to conduct workshops in view of completing a communal artistic creation. Yet neither its nature, nor the deadline for its formalization, nor even the method for carrying it out was given in advance. The exhibition that marked the end of our collective work took place at the museum in March 2015.
During this period, and after each meeting, I composed several lines reporting what had been done or said. These texts, which I called "Gossip" and distributed by email, made up my journal. The following excerpt will help understand the polyphonic aspect of our experiment, which seems to me an entryway into the experience of being-with.

> 20 November 2013 with Aïcha, Alejandra, Arminda and Carine. The light dimmed slowly until night.
> We had met at 3 at the MAC VAL and set up in a ground-floor workshop. The group was smaller. Carine shares her research. Aïcha reads us a poem in Arabic. We explain to Alejandra where we were.

32 John Berger: *La Cocadrille*. Paris: Points Seuil 1972, 1992, p. 17. These sentences do not appear in the English version of the book: *Pig Earth*. New York: Pantheon 1979.

> We then decide to record Arminda and Aïcha's stories in dialogue format. After the sound recording, we discuss Alejandra's impressions with her. She speaks to us of "digested material," "autobiographical materials," of smoothing-over digestions, of the personal theatre she performed in Mexico, using real stories as sources. She speaks to us of "exhausting" her own story by repeating it, of objects to be invented, which would be charged with energy that helps us live. An object that has its own memory and that accompanies us. Aïcha speaks to us of the pebbles that her husband carved in prison, which he gave her every year for their birthday, the same date as their anniversary.
> What would happen if this text were given to children to draw? What does the filter of another subjectivity produce? What if the chaperons allowed us to listen to the story without seeing, which is so hard to tell with the eyes of others fixed upon us? Are stories easier to tell when they're sung?
> What is the meaning of these stories' convergence? I think that it's a way of seeing that these accounts are and are not ours. Fiction makes the game possible, an "I" articulated in multiple. I have the impression of being an attentive EAR. I am documenting the formation of the group. I am gossiping about the emergence of these characters.[33]

Part of our meetings consisted in sharing stories relating to our life experiences. These accounts were the point of departure for creating characters, which then led to collective works. The way these words travelled through us was the origin of graphic or performative shapes that we invented. Listening to them attentively also elicited effects of projection. It made what we had to do together resonate within us, revealing the otherness that we have in ourselves, making our inner voices, always in dialogue with another, perceptible. I return to Kester's argument concerning Jean-Luc Nancy's thought:

> dialogical encounters seldom involve a complete suspension of identity. Rather, identity is only partially transformed. These partial transformations can no doubt accumulate over time, and aggregate effect may be to radically transform subjectivity or identity.[34]

33 Preston: Le contre-pouvoir du commérage, pp. 20–21.
34 Kester: *Conversation Piece*, p. 157.

To reclaim expressions used by literature theoretician Mikhail Bakhtin, co-creation reveals the "irreducibly heterogeneous" state wherein being only exists in dialogue. Co-creation becomes necessary when the creation is meant to be anthropological and meta-discursive in relation to its own activity, inasmuch as "art and literature, forms of representation, are all the more effective when they are truthful, that is to say, when they resemble their object, the heterogeneous man"[35]. Beyond being uniquely constitutive of being, the Other is everywhere in our language. In contact with others, those most varied rich horizons, it is possible to touch this beyond-the-self. This is because:

> No member of a verbal community can ever find words in the language that are neutral, exempt from the aspirations and evaluations of the other, uninhabited by the other's voice. On the contrary, he receives the word by the other's voice and it remains filled with that voice. He intervenes in his own context from another context, already penetrated by the other's intentions. His own intention finds a word already lived in.[36]

In this sense, we had invited the storyteller Florence Desnouveaux to record a voice-over for one of the videos in *Les murs renversés sont des ponts* ("Toppled Walls Are Bridges"). The text that she was to read combined different utterances. On November 27, she explained her way of storytelling to us:

> [...] Florence speaks to us of how others' words travel across her body, Arminda's words emanating from the upper part, from her thorax, her heart, Aïcha's from her head, higher, and how the gossiping voices accompany movements of her neck and throat, following a gaze that crosses from left to right. She tells us how she seeks the greatest possible transparency, trying to erase her own intentions, making herself a passer, crossed through by the words of others. She speaks to us of a body work and of words' fluidity, their power, the worlds that they open up.[37]

35 Tzvetan Todorov: *Mikhaïl Bakhtine, le principe dialogique*. Paris: Seuil 1981, p. 123 (transl. by Julia Zelman).
36 Ibid., p. 77. Todorov citing Bakhtin: *Problemy tvorchestva Dostoevskogo* [*Problems in the Work of Dostoyevsky*]. Leningrad: Priboj 1929, p. 131.
37 Ibid., pp. 63–64.

The dialogical dimension of this experience was omnipresent. While conversation was, at all times, the point of departure for our creations and led us to experience what Bakhtin expressed above, dialogism also took shape through videos wherein one could literally hear several voices (*Devenir Commères* ["Becoming Gossips"]). One of such performances, for example, consisted of responding textually in public space by writing with chalk on the floor or on objects; these performances were attempts to create an account of our experience by using intentionally fragmentary forms and showing several points of view. If we deem that the term "experience," here defining what happens collectively, is used in John Dewey's sense, its completeness can only be achieved once it is communicated. Yet if the collective activity of co-creation as defined above makes being-with perceptible, what part of it can be transmitted? What part of it remains in the interpellation of a passing visitor or spectator who finds him/herself in the presence of works resulting from this creation process?

We should now proceed to analyze precisely the works themselves, indicating the gaps where thought can wriggle in, letting the "between as such" reveal itself, where consciousness of dialogism is possible, where sharing of the sensible is at work. Thus, the task is to distinguish between two moments: first, the creation process that is not public, in the sense that there is no spectator; no one is able to observe. This is the period of cooperation and group creation, the development of artistic collective work. It is also period of the experience that is later shown to the public through non-participative modalities, within the meaning that I use here. If they are indeed participative, it is according to Antoni Muntadas's usage: "Perception Requires Participation." Here I will linger over a particular proposition in order to show how points of view open, how mobility is suggested, and how the viewer is not encouraged to "create a work" but to put him/herself "to work," to quote a phrase by the artist François Deck.[38]

What happened with the "gossips" echoed a previous experience. Between 2011 and 2013, I had worked with visitors of social centers in Burgundy, aided by the Maison du Patrimoine Oral (House of Oral

38 Forum *L'oralité, le parlé*, MAC VAL, January 21, 2017. Part of a research program coordinated by Céline Poulin, Marie Preston and Stéphanie Airaud, "Héritages et modalités des pratiques artistiques de co-création." (Cf. http://www.arpla.fr/mu/creationscollectives (accessed February 17, 2017).)

Heritage) d'Anost-en-Morvan and the art center of Parc-Saint-Léger, on a project based both on life stories of those I met and collections of stories linked to my grand-grandfather, who also had lived in the Morvan. Objects (films, photographs, knitted works, texts, performances) were made from different cooperative endeavors, and were afterwards assembled for the exhibition *Le Pommier et le Douglas*. One of these pieces referenced the "bichos," works created by the Brazilian artist Lygia Clark. In 1983, she described these articulated metal sculptures, manipulable by visitors, made in the 1960s:

> This is the title that I gave my works of this period because of their fundamentally organic character. Moreover, the pliant element which links the planes makes me think of a spinal column.
> The placement of the metal plates determines the positions of the *Bicho* [animal], which at first seem limitless. [...]
> It's a living organism, an essentially active work. Between you and it, total, existential interaction is established. In what is established between you and the *Bicho*, there's no passivity, neither on your part nor on its. [...]
> The *Bicho* has its own circuit of movements, which reacts to the subject's stimulations. It is not composed of static independent forms susceptible to being manipulated indefinitely, at will, as in a game. On the contrary: its parts are functionally attached, as in a true organism, and the movements of these parts are interdependent.[39]

The idea of an active work that reveals interdependencies and infinite possibilities seemed like a fruitful accompaniment to our project. My first "bicho" was *Caroline et Henriette*, a photographic polyptych accompanying and supplementing the performance *Vieille Femme Salie* ("Dirtied Old Woman") by Caroline Darroux, an anthropologist and member of the Maison du Patrimoine Oral d'Anost. This polyptych was composed of twenty-two color photographs showing landscapes, a domestic interior, and objects, glued back to back to a sixty-centimeter-tall rigid mount. They were joined together on the vertical side by a flexible support. The organization of images and their articulation allowed an indeterminacy between the interior

39 Lygia Clark: *Livro-obra*. Rio de Janeiro, 1983. In: *Lygia Clark*. Exhibition catalogue. Marseille: Galeries contemporaines des Musées de Marseille 1998, p. 121.

and exterior of the object itself, as well as of what was represented in the photographs. Blank pictures provided punctuation between the photos and permitted the gaze to wander. When manipulated, its movement was fluid and produced a light rubbing sound. The form and nature of this object, like all those presented in the exhibition *Le Pommier et le Douglas*, emerged from a slow process of discussion, listening, and trial and error, leading to the execution that seemed best to each of us. With Caroline Darroux, we had to create a manipulable object for a performance that would take place alongside her account of her experience in ethnographic fieldwork. This performance comprised received and collected tales, stories from myth, and scientific conclusions from her study for the people concerned by it. The study regarded the real and imaginary figure of the "dirtied old woman" and was based on her thesis on the anthropology of narrative. Caroline Darroux describes the object in her journal thus:

> When Marie presented me with the object for the first time, I played with it lengthily in order to understand its logic. Then, little by little, my movements became natural. I had the impression of playing with something living, as if I saw before me the concept that I developed about narrative material. It helped me to see the form of my thoughts. I had the impression of knowing this object. I let myself go. Then, from one image to its hidden neighbor, apparition, disappearance, association of ideas, moving continuity, the meaning emerged ... I hadn't been able to tell the story of the dirtied old woman. Today, thanks to this object, I have found the structure of the story, in a few hours. It was so simple. This isn't an object, it's more. It's my crystallized thoughts.[40]

Caroline Darroux's gestures and her description of what they produced, as well as the imaginary that they facilitated, seemed to me to correspond to Lygia Clark's ideas on the *bichos*. However, from the point of view of the reception of this performances, what seemed fundamental and related to being-with was the way the spectator-group was immersed in observation and yet, at the same time, could project

40 Caroline Darroux / Marie Preston: La Greffe et le rejet. Ethnographie et création collective en Bourgogne pour un désir de transmission. Symposium "Discipline dissipées: expériences anthropo-artistiques" at University Paris-Ouest Nanterre, May 23–24, 2012. Unpublished talk.

itself into the experience of the other in order to complete what was shown. During the performances, the public sat around a table on which the photographic object was placed. No one could see all the images on the polyptych at the same time. The temporality of the tale they were hearing, together with the simultaneous observation of images 'in movement,' could evoke cinema. It was as though a film unfolded before the participants' eyes: its editing, if there was editing, was only carried out through the awareness of shared gazes on the same object. We saw each other, placed in a circle around the sculpture, looking at images that were hidden to us. This dialogic experience, I hope, allowed the visitor, friend, passer-by, watcher to create work in his or her turn and, perhaps, to brush against being-with.

In conclusion, Kwon's suggestion of conceiving of cooperative practices as collective praxes and temporary associations seems especially apt, particularly for practices involving creation by persons with different savoir-faire, respecting a certain principle of inequivalence. Engaged in these experiences, we feel being-with through the conjunction of provisionality, our interdependencies and common vulnerabilities, our activity and its shared dialogic process, listening, and the constantly evolving shaping and fragmentation of our polyphonies. Finally, if these experiences are particularly addressed to their own contributors, this raises the question of their transmission. I believe that this occurs between the narrative and the use of graphic forms, which embody the relationships involved and straddle gaps, facilitating the exercise of our critical thought and leaving the work open.

IV

Note / Lookout

Kai van Eikels

Performing Collectively, Performing Collectivity: What Does 'Together' Mean?

1. Exercises

In a famous sketch from the Monty Python's Flying Circus show, a military training officer demands that his recruits attack him with a banana, so he can teach them "self-defense." When one does as told, the officer shoots him with his revolver, then eats the banana to "disarm" the enemy. Adding to the absurdity, a discussion precedes the execution: The moribund argue for their lives, naming all the kinds of fruit that have been tried before in this exercise, desperately hoping that the arsenal of ineffectual weapons has been exhausted ... until the banana is discovered.[1] Grotesque and silly as it appears, the situation mirrors that of citizenship in a nominally liberal nation-state, where the sovereign power invites its subjects to be critical and even takes care to educate them in critical intervention techniques. Except that the means citizens are being provided with for challenging the regime are guaranteed to be no match for the nation-state's forces.

The imbalance between, on the one side, citizen's bodies equipped with nothing but the frailest makeshift armament and, on the other side, police or military squadrons armed to the teeth and backed by tanks, jets, ships, and missiles is so striking that this very disproportion generates a crazy faith in going on playing along: If we follow the rules,

1 For the full dialogue, see Monthy Python: Self-Defense Against Fresh Fruit. In: *Monty-Python.net*. http://www.montypython.net/scripts/fruit.php (accessed January 16, 2018).

perhaps we can fool the system into demobilizing itself as it sticks to these same rules, since after all they have been defined by the system. If our civic initiatives internalize statist logic, obeying all the terms and conditions deemed necessary for becoming a proper political player, then one day, owing to sovereignty's neurotic compulsiveness turning inward upon itself, the long series of expected defeats may come to an end. The secular equivalent of mercy will reward us for many years of allegiance, during which we have dutifully attacked our rulers with passion fruit, oranges, apples, grapefruit (whole and segments), pomegranates, greengages, lemons, plums, mangos in syrup, cherries red and black. Like the dorky officer in the sketch almost seems to, the sovereign will finally take the fiction he has created for real – and that's when we will start to matter.

Up against a gun, Aikido would not have been any more helpful than bananas, or so it appears. But maybe it would. Aikido instructs a body without anything in hand that, while useless as a weapon, looks and feels like a weapon. It advises a body that can only perform, i. e. move and bring about the effects of an action in the form of moves. This body is temporally naked, as it were, exposed to a moment whose present – configured through bodily awareness, focusing and unfocusing – is not determined by the triggerism of operating an apparatus. Rather than subjecting its motility to a technological or an institutional mechanism, the body that has learned to perform Aikido movements unreservedly inhabits the time-space within its reach: The reaction limits its own intervention to continuing the other's movement a little more in this or that direction. "Yes, and …," it says, like an improviser who knows that negation, in the material world, needs to adopt the form of a turnaround. It deflects, not the bullet as it is about to put a hole in your chest after the enemy has pulled the trigger, but the enemy's motion of firing at you. Techniques of a performative, temporally naked self-defense will not teach you how to turn your entire body into a gun (or a giant banana). They will inform that body on what can be affirmed in another body's movements, and then redirected using the other's power to disable the attack, and what cannot.

In 1972, Steve Paxton and a group of dancers developed a practice that would become world-famously known as Contact Improvisation. One of their sources of inspiration were East-Asian techniques of self-defense. They reconfigured the instant of *decision*, in which the skillful fighter brings the opponent to the ground by making them lose their balance with the help of their own propulsion, so as to open it up to a continuation. Disabling, in Contact Improv, may be converted into enabling. Two or more performers (or a single human performer partnering with non-human movements in the environment) learn how to perceive the other's movement as an occasion for continuing their own movement. With increasing popularity in dance as well as in rehabilitation medicine, psychotherapy, social work, and pedagogy, Contact Improv underwent an ideological softening. The 'flow' resulting from bodies keeping in touch in at least one spot virtually all the time makes it tempting to believe that the goal is to establish the smooth, harmonious whole of 'two bodies acting as one,' if that is what one desires. However, a closer look at Paxton and his partners[2] gives a quite different impression: Every sequence of their movements could equally plausibly belong to a fight as to a collaborative venture. Mutuality is visible throughout, but whether the subjectivities hosted by the bodies (riding them, one might say) are positioned with or against each other remains open to interpretation – and it remains *open throughout*, since no final gesture ever sums up the series of effective reactions. Where a movement sequence stops, information is there for anyone to take up, continue, further, alter.

Although Contact's vocabulary contains expressions like "giving" and "taking weight," mutuality means less the give-and-take of exchange than two or more lines of continuing that occasionalize one another. Touching is neither about overcoming separation, fusing, becoming one in a unified movement, nor does it refer me to the tragic-erotic experience of an unbridgeable gap between the other and myself (it is *not tender*, not subject to what Emmanuel Lévinas called "la régime de tendre"[3]). All sensitivity will be needed to acknowledge a concrete friction and assess its informative value, scanning-maneuvering a difference in time-space that narrows and widens, warps, fuzzes and solidifies, then fuzzes again. The irritation about bodies that keep on moving for quite a while, without being able to name anything in the movement that tells me whether these are friends' or foes' bodies, has

2 Their exercises can be seen in a recording at https://www.youtube.com/watch?v=9FeSDsmIeHA (accessed: September 10, 2018).

3 Cf. Emmanuel Lévinas: *Totalité et Infini. Essai sur l'extériorité.* Paris: Livre de poche 1971, p. 283.

a political point which makes Contact Improv a precious find in the Judson Dance Theater artists' search for *democratic movement*: The body participating in a democratic movement is not the body that bonds and is bound by the task of embodying an imagined community. Neither is it the isolated body, whose integrity is defined by the same sovereign power that guarantees its inviolability, a power that redefines the movements of that body as an execution of authorized or unauthorized acts. In their democratic realness, bodies are reacting bodies: bodies that allow themselves to be guided by reactions, for they know how to make decisions in the kinesthetic present tense of reacting; bodies on par with the presence of others, in situations where no single body gets to define or measure the present. Bodies, that is, that are trained to observe and treat anyone, from the most intimate person in the world to a stranger never met before, as a *body among others*. Specific, unique, and equal. Friendship and enmity perhaps, but no *politics of* friendship, no *politics of* enmity.

What would political life be like in a society where Contact Improv was practiced at school, as a regular part of the curriculum? Not much different, if the practice happened in Art, Theater, or Physical Education classes. Different, if it happened in Civics – if political debates were carried out in Contact communication instead of talkers sitting in circles; if criticality came to unfasten dissent from resentment in Contact arguing, adding No's instead of withholding Yes's; if synchronizing with multiple lines of continuing became the current concept of 'together,' whether in organizing a paper chase or in organizing protest. Very different, if the moving body was discovered as an object and instrument of study common to all these subjects. Even though, as long as private capital is the only alternative, the schools would do well to remain state-run institutions, students might learn there how to relate to one another in collective undertakings unmediated by a sovereign authority and still not falling for the lures of love- and hate-driven community imagination. "Tomorrow we have Continuation," a teenager might tell their parents with an expression of mild boredom which hides curiosity from those who would only ask for tasks accomplished. "There's no homework, except the things you do anyway and telling which of them helped getting on with last week's activities. It's easy. I might choose it as my major. It's all so fucking easy, this collective shit."

2. A thoroughly distributed power

One person can create and fashion a thing, but it will need many people to realize something by way of *praxis*. An action is volatile, attaining a reality that outlives the singular moment of its being performed only insofar as others, who happen to be around, let themselves be motioned to acknowledge the performed action in conveying its momentum via their own, multiple bodies. Therefore you cannot act alone. Hannah Arendt developed her entire theory of political action from this seemingly simple insight into the essentially collective disposition of *prattein*, acting, which Aristotle distinguished from *poiein*, producing, in his *Nicomachean Ethics*.[4] And she reminded her contemporaries, to whom "politics" meant a state management aimed at producing optimized living conditions, of the difference between the Greek verbs *archein* and *prattein*. Both mean 'to act,' but whereas *archein* stresses the moment of initiation, of envisioning and conceiving something, *prattein* shifts the accent towards the process of carrying out. Whatever has been conceived must become lived reality through series of reactions that put it into practice, and only in the loose, contingent networks of support will a political dimension unfold.[5] Practice, Arendt insists, should never be reduced to a mere implementation of concepts.

Anyone who has ever performed – on a theater stage or at some performance art venue, in a concert hall, or in a public square among passing pedestrians – will most likely confirm this: Practice should never be reduced to a mere implementation of concepts, as it has a dynamic of its own. *Prattein* dynamic is the collective *energeia*, the movement of becoming real, the real in-becoming, in its occasional textility of actualities communicating, synchronizing or corresponding. You know this when you've been performing, engaging in collective practice for some time. But how much recognition is given to this by our theories of the political? And how much recognition is given to it by our theories of art?[6] What demands to be recognized in a theory of collective

4 Cf. Aristotle: *Nicomachean Ethics*. VI, 1139a ff.

5 Cf. Hannah Arendt: *Between Past and Future. Six Exercises in Political Thought*. London: Faber & Faber 1961, pp. 165–166.

6 For an insightful discussion of this question's context, see Randy Martin: *Critical Moves. Dance Studies in Theory and Politics*. Durham / London: Duke UP 1998, pp. 1–13.

practice is not only the *practitioner's* freedom, the performer's freedom as distinct from (and sometimes opposed to) the freedom of the author, the director, the composer, the concept artist etc. It is also a *practical* freedom, which neither shares the authority of the creative act nor its liberty to put a thing into the world as though it were the direct materialization of an idea, of a pure possibility, and not the material transformation of something that had a different shape, a different complexion, and perhaps a different inclination until it was modeled to manifest the creator's will. The respect for the materiality of change requires the 'I' of theoretical discourse to renounce a certain type of power, namely sovereign power, in favor of another, thoroughly distributed type of power that is much less in sympathy with our traditions of employing language for the purpose of telling the world what it needs, whether in terms of order or in terms of inspirational chaos. A theory of collectivity that arises from practice, in politics and in art, implies a critique of the tacit pact the theorist-ego (and its rhetorical multiplications, where the text exchanges an 'I' for a 'We') entertains with the figure of the sovereign.

The relation between *archein* and *prattein*, between the focused, resolute (in modern times hysterically resolute) beginning and a dispersed, heterogeneous, intrinsically frivolous continuation, is a major power relation. Against Plato, who asserts that the initiator, due to his superior access to the *arche*, the original idea, must also be the *archon*, the leader, Arendt locates power in the decision to take up, continue, further, and thereby alter, an activity once it has been started and proposed to the public. Ingenious minds have a role in catalyzing sudden leaps, speeding up technological progress, sometimes with dramatic impact on the economic and the social state of affairs. But a truly political power only evolves with many people translating individual initiatives into collective practice. Nothing is *per se* political or not political. It is only through reactions that something will have become political. Neither the cadences of institutional governance nor the great proclamations, which historians quote to relate stories punctuated by events, ever fully capture the political because its reality remains suspended in this re-actuality.

Teaming up political action with artistic performance, like Aristotle, Arendt emphasizes that politics and art should *not* be connected through the assumption that the commonwealth resembles a work of art and that the political agent, be it a single person or a collective, is an artist-double who works with living bodies instead of paint or marble in order to produce it. As Philippe Lacoue-Labarthe has shown in *La fiction politique*, attempts to transfer the metaphysics of the created work to living together in the hope of turning the heterogeneous, chaotic, imaginably violent collectivity of crowds into the harmonious whole of 'the people,' from Plato to Heidegger, ended up in totalitarian, if not outright fascist, concepts.[7] It is the *weakness* of the performing arts, their incompetence to deliver a work that would be as compliant-resistant to time as an institution is (and hence would be apt to bond with institutions, enhancing each other's power), which brings them near sites of multitudinal political action.

For Arendt, politics and the performing arts share the temporal condition of their reality. Lacking a product to be separated from the process of production, political action and artistic performance are forever handed over to the scattered memory of "living on from one forgetting to another," as the German poet Jean Paul once paraphrased glory.[8] Rather than building on an institutionalized, Hegelian time, which selects and sublates but never lets a single incident pass unnoticed, politics and performing arts do well to assess reality from the likeliness of being forgotten. Politics happens in a world without a Homer, as Arendt puts it: No single poet will be granted the authority to save the past from falling into oblivion by virtue of a superior, outstanding work like the *Iliad*.[9] Instead, many voices will start and stop and sometimes start again and keep on telling things, performing narration in various disciplines and idioms, and memory will be *one* effect of this practice while forgetting will be another. Recalling Nietzsche's distinction between 'may remember' and 'must remember,'[10] being remembered, for the time being, will thus reflect the freedom, and not the obligation, to remember.

7 Cf. Philippe Lacoue-Labarthe: *Heidegger, Art, and Politics. The Fiction of the Political*, transl. from the French by Chris Turner. Oxford: Basil Blackwell 1990.

8 Jean Paul: *Ideengewimmel*, ed. by Thomas Wirtz. Frankfurt am Main: Eichborn 1996, p. 242 (transl. K. v. E.).

9 Cf. Hannah Arendt: *The Human Condition*. London / Chicago: University of Chicago Press 1998, p. 197.

10 Cf. Friedrich Nietzsche: *On the Advantage and Disadvantages of History for Life*, transl. from the German by Peter Preuss. Indianapolis: Hackett 1980.

3. How (not) to go on?

If official politics disregarded the value of *prattein* in Arendt's time – a period of strong liberal and authoritarian nation-states – the situation today seems more ambiguous. Something is happening from below. After the 20th century's mass movements played into the hands of dictators, today's local civic activism and global movements try to reinvigorate the liberating, anti-totalitarian power of the many, and where their bottom-up approaches were able to assemble millions within a short time these forms of extra-parliamentary opposition demonstrated how strong collective practice can be. Yet, they experience problems with continuing that, which at the beginning looked like an irresistible wave of change. Hopes that this wave would keep on rolling, carrying the 'energy' of revolt from the Arab Spring to European societies as well, were dashed. Indeed, the image of the wave – i.e. the metaphorical application of mechanics to self-organized collectivities – misconstrues political *praxis*. Reactions, however large in number, do not follow the laws of energy transmission. Disseminated information makes bodies react to one another, and the responses prompted by information's influences will be involuntary, even unconscious, to a large degree; still, terminology referring to energy is inappropriate for describing what human bodies are doing when they get involved in processes shaped by multiple reactions.

Prattein dynamics can neither be explained by a vectorial logic nor by force fields – and it should not be imagined in terms of energetic force because the idea that collective political agency is constituted and maintained through impulses that seize people like toppling dominos, or through particles caught in a Brownian motion,[11] further obfuscates the conundrum which any bottom-up collective undertaking will face sooner or later: How to go on doing this? And how to go on doing *this*, as the integrity of change cannot rely on a simple, unequivocal identity. Multitudinal reactions are not guaranteed, not even likely, to preserve an original impetus (hence the eminence of foundational myths). Presupposing that a political movement needs an extremely strong and spectacular kick-off in order to last long enough

11 Cf. Gilles Deleuze / Félix Guattari: *A Thousand Plateaus. Capitalism and Schizophrenia*, transl. from the French by Brian Massumi. London / Minneapolis: University of Minnesota Press 1987, p. 33.

for a chance to implement change, seems as ill-informed as the corresponding eagerness to believe the latest spectacular event is finally the true revolutionary fanfare.

Escalation – a moral-architectural interpretation of auto-attraction and -intensification effects – links the pleasure people take in doing similar things, and in doing them repeatedly, to an equally unhelpful pattern. Political persistence is neither tantamount to perseverance, nor to letting oneself be pushed and pulled up a flight of stairs in preparation for some big collective jump into the abyss. While excited, zealous participants may be crucial for a political movement's rapid growth, the movement's ability to survive a downturn following an upsurge will depend on the not-so-keen, the moderately committed, the also-rans. If they hesitate to join or quickly lose interest, this does not betray a 'lack of energy' (or a moral deficiency, which the physical short-windedness signifies), and so adding more pressure will not solve the problem. Time and again, history has belied allegations that an increasing level of physical suffering or moral insufferableness eventually thrusts people toward revolutionary action, as though by mechanical necessity. If political theory wants to counsel a sustained, persistent practice, it must learn to understand the vagaries of people's reactions – and to *appreciate* them, since an apprehension of the irregular, the "whatever" which Giorgio Agamben epitomized in *The Coming Community*,[12] can only come from an appreciative entanglement in its twists and turns.

Recent attempts to reintroduce a pre-Newtonian concept like Spinoza's "conatus" to political thinking, deriving an integrity of change from the immanence of life,[13] reveal somewhat honestly that physics really stands in for metaphysics in respect to explaining collective dynamics.[14] The inability to dispense with a metaphysical warranty for cohesion and connectedness-in-time is due to

12 Cf. Giorgio Agamben: Whatever. In: G. A.: *The Coming Community*, transl. from the Italian by Michael Hardt. London / Minneapolis: University of Minnesota Press 1993, pp. 2–3.

13 Cf. Jane Bennett: *Vibrant Matter. A Political Ecology of Things*. Durham / London: Duke UP 2010, pp. 2–4.

14 Karen Barad offers a critique of analogisms between physics and politics in the first chapter of *Meeting the Universe Halfway. Quantum Physics and the Entanglement of Matter and Meaning*. Durham / London: Duke UP 2007, pp. 3–25.

an incongruence between individual act and collective movement. Although every action has its reality of being carried out in some physical movement, only particular movements count as actions according to the normative ethical-juridical notion. For a motional complex to be deemed an action, it must be possible to attribute all the movements to a person (possible, not necessarily feasible). Personhood may expand across motions performed by multiple bodies as long as their unity has been established, for instance, through an institutional frame, a legal construct which allows a real or imaginary court to treat them as one in respect to their responsibility. Without a sufficient degree of institutionalization, what many bodies are doing can only be accounted for in terms of movement: If you and a hundred thousand others form no party or NGO, you will have been a movement. Outside of its juridical definition, collective action lacks a proper form; and understanding a multitude's non- or para-institutional reality with the help of a vocabulary alluding to movement has navigated concepts of collectivity in a gray area between apparent forms and their apparent absence.

Can political movement have a form, other than that provided by (quasi-)institutional representation? Can it adopt and maintain a *performative form*, a collective form that results from – or is, however indirectly, an effect of – the multiple *rhythmoi*, the spatiotemporal forms of material processes in which human bodies participate among other bodies when they are moving, and perhaps acting, together? Form, then, would mean *occasional* evidence, communicated over the course of performing, in and by doing, rather than something general applied by design for a specific enterprise and to a particular selection of people. The collective form would be performative in that it utilizes, in passing, some formal qualities already 'out there' in the orbit of occurrences – picking up stray relationalities on its way through a world that self-organizes into processes and thus manages its continuity (or rather, continuities), while this worldly maintenance includes subjective and inter-subjective modes of affective-effective involvement.

There is, in other words, a *material continuity* to be discovered, observed, analyzed, and then possibly employed with more dexterity. The immense efforts required for a correct representation of collective action have diverted attention away from this material continuity and its formal dimension. Activists become aware of it mainly in moments when the attempt to make a political movement resemble an institutional person fails. Failing institutionalization belongs to the genealogy of democratic political movements: With distributed, bottom-up activities, the institution-mimicry never fully succeeds. Discussions and negotiations trying to achieve a consensus on what the collective *is*, what it looks like, how it shall be represented to the inside and outside, are bound to be endless. They can only ever be interrupted, for better or worse. And whether agreeing or disagreeing with a General Assembly's final resolutions, people will continue to imagine the movement's form in many ways, partly diverse, incongruent, irreconcilable. If a political movement exists for a while, this is not merely thanks to a superb symbolic administration, but always to a certain degree in spite of it.[15] As people move on, some go on doing some of that which they are doing, and the letting-go exposes constellations that evolve from material consequences. Of what does this material consequentiality consist? When and where – if we abstain from attaching the universe to metaphysical ideas, of which actions derived from activities would be but actualizations – does *prattein* take over the generation of form? And why is *prattein* form so untoward, flirting with disaster rather than propelling a new world order, when our familiar political concepts discover events?

4. Leadership as collateral damage

Earlier theorists of the sovereign state, like Thomas Hobbes in his *Leviathan*, conceived of it as something principally reactive. The sovereign stood for the threat of harmful, possibly deadly retaliation in the eventuality that citizens displayed unruly behavior, attacked state officials or attacked one another ignoring the monopoly on the use of force. Michel Foucault defined this mercurial sovereignty as the

15 Cf. also Kai van Eikels: Consensus. The Togetherness of Those Who Would Not Wait for One Another. In: Geheimagentur / Martin Jörg Schäfer / Vassilis S. Tsianos (eds): *The Art of Being Many. Towards a New Theory and Practice of Gathering*. Bielefeld: Transcript 2016, pp. 61–66.

power to 'make' die and 'let' live.[16] With the 'biopolitical' redetermination of governance, whose onset he saw in the 17th century, sovereign power projects itself into productivity, aspiring to make live and let die. While this claims a much more comprehensive influence on the reality of people's lives, it also reveals a gap between two dimensions of the potentate's power: his glory and his reign; the potentially infinite, divine or divinely-sanctioned authority and the legislative acts that make up his actual regime.[17] A ruler's decrees often fail to achieve the intended results, provoking but superficial conformity on the side of the subjects or leading to unforeseen consequences as many individuals' obedience engenders something altogether different on a collective level. The sovereign hence needs a legion of mediators, of quasi-angelic agents who convert his decisions into measures capable of steering the social and economic processes concerned. And since these processes are interrelated, enmeshed in complex clusters of population dynamics, the translation is itself an interminable process, necessitating permanent supervision, analysis, and readjustment of regulations.

From this permanence emerges the professional politician. Politicians at first were executive officers, managerial assistants distinct from the sovereign they served – and well positioned for the task of putting sovereign power into operation because their position in respect to power was *not exactly* that of its source. In the modern nation-state, particularly in a representative democracy, however, the politician has come to incorporate both sides of the difference between sovereign act and managerial performance. In a formally democratic state, the sovereign's place, according to Claude Lefort, remains structurally empty.[18] Therefore the implementers, now turned representatives,

16 Cf. Michel Foucault: *Society Must Be Defended. Lectures at the Collège de France 1975–76*, transl. from the French by David Mackay. New York: Picador 2003, p. 241. The empirical activity of sovereign rulers was mainly warfare against others; and unto this day the military remains the prime expression of a sovereign's activeness.

17 Agamben has presented the relation between a sovereign God and an *oikonomia* managed by his army of angels as a model for the alliance between sovereign power and political economy. See Giorgio Agamben: *The Kingdom and the Glory. For a Theological Genealogy of Economy and Government*, transl. from the Italian by Lorenzo Chiesa. Stanford: Stanford UP 2011.

18 Cf. Claude Lefort: *The Political Forms of Modern Society. Bureaucracy, Democracy, Totalitarianism*. Cambridge, MA: MIT Press 1986.

must *perform the sovereignty part in addition* to the mediating part. They must *embody* that which their enactments translate into laws and administrative measures, and it is through this reduplication that they become *leaders*. The advancement of the state official to the rank of a civil *archon* can be seen as collateral damage by the 'democratic' nation-state's compromised design, which tries to align the principle of representation with sovereign power. Delegated by the people, descendants of the States-General deputies, the members of government and of the various committees that put parliamentary decisions on track are nonetheless expected by those same people to display leadership virtues. They serve insofar as they lead. After autocratic leaders ordained the 20th century's most atrocious and catastrophic measures, one could hope that the very concept of leadership would be banned from all democracies. But it remains essential for as long as a politician's professional profile entails providing a body with 'something sovereign' about it.[19]

As the mediators find themselves in the position of initiators, the political process, albeit formally representative-democratic, calls for *archon* qualities. It is being posited, and ultimately believed, that one can envision and construct collective reality. Policies of "citizen participation," which pretend to distribute the sovereign power of 'making live' among the governed, are socializing the biopolitical. What gets distributed, though, is not the authority (the state fashions scenarios of "empowering" its citizens, but hardly ever authorizes them to decide matters without keeping a firm grip on possible outcomes). Rather, people see themselves confronted with the challenge to *act as though they were able to create* the life they are living, including the 'together' of living together. In its neo-liberal epoch, biopolitical governance introduces a phantasm of the creative act to the dimension of 'together.' Promising to promote to the status of co-leader anyone who adopts an inventive and convincingly competitive stance

19 One could write a political history of *fat* and sovereignty, for example. Jane Bennett proposes to include foodstuff in political discourse – for one reason, because food shapes the bodies of the governed, and hence food production and distribution, food law, dietary programs as part of health policies, etc., all belong to a political economy which manages the population (see Bennett: *Vibrant Matter*, pp. 39–51). It should be instructive to look at the bodies of those who govern as well, after the King's two bodies have to fit into one.

towards life, the sovereign urges its subjects to be accomplices in pursuing *archon* power through creative initiatives. The centralized structures of sovereignty stay in place, if not intact; but the biopolitical generates a distributed, performative sovereignty, a set of values and behavioral evaluation routines programmed to reclaim every process of self-organization for the state-society-enterprise's augmentation.[20]

5. A chase for the creative

The phantasm of the creative act insinuates that reacting is not good enough. Where creativity becomes a biopolitical-social-economical paradigm that synthesizes speculations on change, innovation, and growth with hopes for stability and control, an archo-poetic notion of value affects how bodies understand time. Process time re-determines time-to-product. Although the word "process" has a more generous ring than "product" (it sounds like people are granted the freedom to try things out, fail, try again, reconceptualize their approach or even appreciate unplanned results), *archein*-oriented processual temporality signals to every participant that they are about to fall behind in the attempt to make it to the leaders' class. And even if process time gets the better of clock time, this does not mean the clocks stop counting. By equalizing all individual rhythms according to standards defined and supervised by national institutes in global collaboration, sophisticated chronometry upholds the modern chrono-sovereignty. In terms of time, nation-state and private capital have always been bracing each other, even through conflicts when, for example, around 1900 corporations pressed reluctant governments to introduce a time law because Fordism's top-down organization of labor aimed for total synchronicity.[21]

20 This also shows in media technology policies: With every new communication tool, an *archein* interpretation lays claim to the effects generated by its collective use. The invention of the technology, it is inferred, is also the invention of those practices. Hence the control you have over an invented technology (an engineer's sovereignty) can be extended to the collective dynamics of users' interactions.

21 Whereas modern science, namely the General Theory of Relativity and Quantum Mechanics, epistemically abandons time as a *singulare tantum* in favor of a relational understanding of temporality, nation-states and corporations work together in *producing* such a standardized time.

Post-Fordist management philosophies cherish the mutual synchronization of multiple rhythms in flexible teamwork, recommending that work performers should be "exploring the empty spaces" of groove-based collectivity like improvising jazz musicians.[22] But surviving in the co-competitive currents that make up "collective creativity" teaches freelancers or employees on short-term contracts to internalize the time pressure formerly imposed through the assembly line. In critical support of Theodor Adorno, who compared jazz's frantic, panicky rhythmicity to a pogrom, pop theorist Diedrich Diederichsen says that the hybrid jazz culture, which attains emancipation from white dominance by simultaneously defying and appropriating the oppressor's cultural norms, trains people to be competent performers both in the role of the one who is chased and in that of the hunting pack member. Jazz thus models time as an iterated chase with switching positions, and this temporal signature gets imprinted on the workday in post-Fordism.[23]

Post-Operaist philosopher Paolo Virno observed in the 1990s how the economic sphere absorbed abilities which would have been important for a civic political life: the rhetorical skills to convince or persuade others; the sense of balance between cause and relationships, strategic calculus and personal integrity; the susceptibility for *topoi koinoi*, commonplaces, popular opinions and sentiments.[24] Subjected to a socio-economic reckoning that accredits the generated surplus value only (or disproportionally) to those work performers who boast the added value of creative impulse in working together, this know-how never meets the present of *praxis* – a present, that is, right in the middle of things happening, on level with an ongoing day-to-day. The ambitious and the scared are working more and more hours because the temporal logic implied in the post-Fordist creativity values urges

22 Cf. Mary Jo Hatch: Exploring the Empty Spaces. How Improvisational Jazz Helps Redescribe Organizational Structure. In: *Organization Studies* 20:1 (1999), pp. 75–100.

23 Cf. Kai van Eikels: What Your Spontaneity Is Worth to Us. Improvisation between Art and Economics. In: Sabeth Buchmann / Ilse Lafer / Constanze Rum (eds): *Putting Rehearsals to the Test. Practices of Rehearsal in Fine Arts, Film, Theater, Theory, and Politics*. Berlin / Wien: Sternberg 2016, pp. 22–30.

24 Cf. Paolo Virno: Virtuosity and Revolution. The Political Theory of Exodus. In: P. V. / Michael Hardt (eds): *Radical Thought in Italy. A Potential Politics*. Minneapolis: University of Minnesota Press 1996, pp. 189–212.

them to *return* from their current state and its entanglements *to a first moment*, a Genesis Day One type of undiminished potential when the world was not yet formed, not yet populated, not yet glitched up with myriads of wrong decisions and knotty, complicated, pain-laden relations. The process's actual present is, in a way, already too late for creation, and continuing with what is underway would mean to admit this. The "collectively creative" teamwork operates in permanent denial of the second law of thermodynamics; disavowing material time, it tutors working bodies to incorporate a quasi-religious narrative, a creationism of becoming.

Under the spell of this chase for *archon* power, state administration merges with the commercial sphere in providing "services." Citizens are alerted that they need to take "pro-active" steps regarding their health, their employability, their finances. Pallid politicians and stuffy officials use the same "future"-spiked vocabulary as PR word-mongers. For want of their own sense of orientation, they copy corporate management, often badly and with an awkward mix of haste and delay. Sovereignty consists in a fiction. Working the legal construct of a political sovereign into the communicative reality of living together demands that institutions, institutionally-defined procedures and the people who execute them all pay service to this fiction. Technically speaking, no executive can afford to react. Committed to the *archon*, anything executives do must attest to the actual interaction between human bodies confirming a fictional relation, which configures and controls the possibility of their encounter. The *arche*-task of managing the conditions of possibility – in order to keep the real under reserve, reserving the right to grant or deny a reality status to the re-actuality of what many people are doing – is the common denominator between nation-state and service economy in the 21st century.

In an institutional context, a true reaction is always already on the threshold to corruption. And as far as records capture it, corruption seems to have been the most powerful form of self-organized collectivity ever since the sovereign empire or nation-state established itself as the standard model for governing a commonwealth. That is, because the agent of corruption *repeats* the archo-poetic gesture, turning it *against* the structures of institutional power: He or she does something which their office does not authorize them to do, responding to a concrete situation, recognizing or intuiting an opportunity for a deal (organization-wise, the horizontal arrangement of the deal emancipates the individuals, undoing or loosening the hierarchical, compartmental order – whence Friedrich Nietzsche's lore for corruption's individualism[25]). But on the scene of discreet negotiating, this agent performs like an alternate legislator who just *invented* an extra-law. Corruption brings forth little Napoleons, bottom-up monarchs. Following a parasitic pattern, corruption both attacks *and* reaffirms the host sovereign's power at the same time. Whether networks of corruption entertain a stable, symbiotic relationship with institutions or render them dysfunctional to the point of causing a whole state to topple depends on effects beyond the control of either side, since the competition between two beginnings, two claims to *archon* authority, disables any understanding on consequences. For all the cunning nepotists invest in playing politics, corruption offers no political *praxis*. The reality of corrupt deals weakens the sovereignty fiction; but the corrupt pact's impersonation of the sovereign act detains the practical just as militantly as the sternest institutionalism.

6. Reactionary reactions

Reality's role in representational politics is uncertain anyway. And the less appreciation a political system has for that which is being articulated through reactions, the more likely the real will crumble into a stupid, annoying interruption of the governmental proceduralism, which today seems advised by a mix of Machiavelli ('We must give the people a show, so they believe they have rulers who care about them') and McKinsey ('We must make the people work for the show, so they will more likely believe what it shows them'). Officials shake their heads, in honest frustration or cynical satisfaction, when manifestations of "the people's will" produce obstructive instead of constructive results. The only answer you get when you push the plebs for a reaction, it appears, is a stubborn No: to a building project in their city, or to EU membership, or to refugees. In referendums and elections, we see

25 Cf. Friedrich Nietzsche: *The Gay Science. With A Prelude in German Rhymes and an Appendix of Songs*, transl. from the German by Josefine Nauckhoff. Cambridge: Cambridge UP 2001, I/23, pp. 47–49. For Nietzsche, Napoleon is the example par excellence of a ruler who came to power through corruption, and whose every word expresses corrupt individualism (see ibid., pp. 48–49).

reacting take on a reactionary character. This should hardly come as a surprise after people's reactions in the name of 'the people' have been systematically denied the possibility of conveying anything beyond a thumbs up or down, in response to an imposed question. Cornered, like a child whose parents shout "So *do* you want this?," the electorate expresses an "I'd prefer not to," either by not voting at all or by spitting into the face of the political establishment.

As dumb as such chains of reaction appear, we should bear in mind that the dumbness of 'the people' is not the result of individual intellects added up (the procedure of counting votes must not fool us into assuming one can summarize people or what they are thinking). This dumbness is the very product of an economic-social-political apparatus that ignores the inherent richness of reacting, narrowing down the feedback of the governed to a choice between acceptance or rejection, Yes or No, A or B, wherever possible – and attributing everything better to the (fantasy of the) creative act. There is an almost absurdly wide gap between the image of creating a different, a better world, which has been planted in our minds fastening our appetite for change to the desire for a new, clean beginning, and the reality of reactions, cut off from the power to do anything but confirm or obstruct. Politically, there is no need for more creativity (or for a more thoroughly-creative creativity that would envision the radically different, the impossible, the utopian future). Rather, we ought to make an emancipatory *transvaluation of reacting* our goal. If democracy is to mean more than 'nation-state cum regular elections, and perhaps the possibility of referendums' – if change shall emanate from the power of the many, of people organized politically along the lines of their living together, then we better devote some knowledge and persistence to breaking loose the multiple actuality of reactions from the stupefying dichotomy of the confirmative-constructive and the reactionary-obstructive.

Persistence, that is to say, pleasure. On a systemic level, change always happens like an accident to some degree, compelling a society to adapt to unforeseen circumstances; and the political goal of bringing about the right, good change requires techniques of connecting wishes, wants and wills to that which is happening – techniques which are able to inflect it, giving its incidentality a direction-form. What Jacques Rancière called "le partage du sensible," the partition and distribution of the sensible,[26] implies reorganizing the pleasure we take in doing things, according to an understanding of where the activities entertained by this pleasure should make us go. Transvaluation of reacting, in this respect, means volunteering towards an *un-familiar* organization of pleasure. After the dissolution of the estate-based society, the predominant order of pleasure in politics has endorsed the logic of 'affiliation,' which replaces the biological with an institutional family identity: party, NGO, activist group. This conceptualizes commitment based on a father-son(s) relation: I stay committed to a joint undertaking because not persevering equals infidelity, and no matter how futile and frustrating the collective dynamics are, I would hate myself for being the disloyal one. Such an institutionalization of the political field privileges affects confirming that the institution is in charge of fashioning continuity. These affects bind multitudes of any size, up to millions, to the habit of reproducing Oedipal patterns, as Jacques Derrida analyzed in *Politiques de l'amitié*.[27] Insofar as "Stay with us and keep on doing this!" becomes the imperative reiterated by an institutional superego – and we must not forget that the institutional can always be imagined, and that the power of 'real,' 'objective' institutions also comes from their collaboration with our imagination[28] – keeping faith with political kin will have been my duty. Consequently, discontinuation will appear as the (more) pleasurable alternative, seducing me to let go, do more rewarding things instead, join the sexy enemy for a drink, with the voice of a cute little devil. Political reason is neither the rationality of planning imposed on the process of carrying out, nor a rationality of choice which but re-creates the planning situation during this process. As Aristotle's term *sophrosyne* indicates, political reason rather consists of a sense of orientation, accomplished and performed within ongoing movement.[29] Its

26 Cf. Jacques Rancière: *The Politics of Aesthetics. The Distribution of the Sensible*, transl. from the French by Gabriel Rockhill. London / New York: Continuum 2004.

27 Cf. Jacques Derrida: *Politics of Friendship*, transl. from the French by George Collins. London / New York: Verso 2006.

28 Cf. Cornelius Castoriadis: *The Imaginary Institution of Society*, transl. from the French by Kathleen Blamey. Cambridge, MA: MIT Press 1987.

29 And perhaps *the political* only exists in (and as) this particular form of reason. Definitions that relate politics to a certain field of affairs or (professional) activities tend to obscure to what degree the assumption that "political" means something

intelligence of redirecting an action while continuing becomes operative among multiple participants through widespread, broadly accessible knowledge about how to navigate praxis pleasures. The most superior level of insight will not replace or compensate for a lack of such know-how. Our personal histories pile up encounters with necessity that left us doing something else. Arendt rightfully criticized how easily this doctrine of the willing spirit and the weak flesh got accepted in political theory[30] – for it injects ethics with the worst of occidental metaphysics: an excuse, which fails to liberate the body and instead fortifies the regime that discourages the body from doing even what it can do.

7. **A world without comparison**

What it can do, for instance, is imitate. Thinking of how something someone started is being taken up and continued by others, imitation comes to mind first, and it should not be too quickly dismissed on the pretext that we know all about it. The mimetic has been extensively discussed as a mode of representation and as a topic of aesthetics. But investigating imitating as an organizational principle has only recently been evolving from vague, generalizing guesses to a more varied and detailed understanding. Gabriel Tarde, who was rediscovered by cultural theorists some years ago, declared in *Les lois de l'imitation*, published in 1895, that imitation is the vital principle of society. To figure out the power of an idea, a device, a form of acting or a behavioral pattern, he recommended that the analysis focus less on inventors, statesmen and military leaders and instead scrutinize the distributive processes of their popular pervasion via imitation.[31] A closer look at what happens when imitation organizes collective movement or action reveals that every imitative response effects slight alterations. Looped

more specific than "concerning the polis" is a modern conjecture and has no intrinsic historical link to democracy. There could be democratic living-together without politics – but hardly without practical consequences that verify the political, the effects of political reason.

30 Cf. Hannah Arendt: What Is Freedom? In: H. A.: *Between Past and Future*. New York: Penguin 2006, pp. 142–169.

31 Cf. Gabriel Tarde: *The Laws of Imitation*, transl. from the French by Elsie Clews Parsons. New York: Holt 1903, esp. pp. 59–88 (chapter III "What is a society").

and passed on among thousands or millions, those many slight alterations can engender a fundamental change of the performed action over time. This concatenation, without any discernible beginning or end, does not amount to collective creation. The numerous bodies involved never aggregate in any constructive effort; they might never even get to reflect themselves in an image that represents them as a collective-singular actor. The change in question often happens in the shadow cast by the bright images of change which the conglomerate of corporations, governments, journalism and its social network add-ons are promoting.

This change remains absent from a historical accounting of time, inasmuch as even a critical history willing to acknowledge a certain polychronicity seems to have no mode of attention for the *similar*, for that which is neither identical nor different, neither old nor new, neither before nor after x and t_x – and neither heading towards an (ideal point of) unification, which allows it to be treated as a sum, nor breaking up and rearranging sameness, which can be depicted in wave diffraction patterns.[32] Monitoring becoming in the spatiotemporality of the similar, we encounter *a world without comparison*. The experiential present of collective life, being "virtual all the way in,"[33] will never coincide with an instant that has you or me knowing how what you do is or is not what I do, or how what I do is or is not what I could do. For every period of time, from a split second to a century, only an "intraactive" evaluation which counts in the observers *as some among many* recognizes the collective dimension in performing actions, since the very reality of performing is distributive.[34] In such an evaluation, a reaction will not be an action the evaluator identifies as the effect of another action, interpreting this other action as its quasi-cause. Rather, the term reaction, if it is visited by theory in its dynamics of mattering, in material space-time, will indicate a genuine transference pertaining to anything done by anyone.

32 For the concept of diffraction, see Barad: *Meeting the Universe Halfway*, pp. 71–94. Barad is picking up the term from Donna Haraway, re-connecting her conceptual metaphor to research in physics that deals with the diffraction of light and various substances.

33 Alva Noë: *Action in Perception*. Cambridge, MA: MIT Press 2006.

34 For intraaction and its distinction from interaction, see Barad: *Meeting the Universe Halfway*, pp. 145–185.

8. Shall we reserve the right to react?

Tarde's social materialism succumbed to Émile Durkheim's more subjectivist approach, which calibrated sociology based on the relation between an exemplary individual and an abstract entirety called 'society.'[35] General by nature of its idealistic definition, the social was spelled out in norms, rules, customs and habits, and its proper concreteness was one of manifestation: a becoming-apparent *in* material reality, which still inscribed a tiny, technical transcendence, a slight shift between the general and its singular application, into the social situation itself. Although sociology focused on everyday life, it shared this 'general/singular' form for observing reality with the mainstream in Western philosophy and political science. And deliberately or not, it thus referred to the state as the most prominent objectivization of this form. Social norms, rules, customs or habits could resist, challenge, ridicule, oppose, and eventually bring governments to change laws, *because they were formally analogous* to the law.[36] The West German postwar sociologist Arnold Gehlen captured this constitutive analogy when he asserted that a person was "an institution in a single case."[37] A human body can respond to Louis Althusser's policeman's "Hey, you!" appellation, turning their head and in turn be defined as a subject to sovereign power, for the reason that their social specificity has been shaped primarily and predominantly by a generality intervening into every singular moment of life. Wherever two or more people hit on each other, each of their acts will but actualize patterns of speech and behavior, reiterating signs, quoting countless other moments, possible or real (nobody knows), of employing the same linguistic-performative stencils.

35 With the exception, to some extent, of the Chicago School, whose investigations of crowd behavior have resurfaced along with Tarde's concept of imitation.

36 The controversy between an 'ethics of the law' and an 'ethics of morals' in philosophy never got to the point of undoing this structural analogy. 'Law,' in these debates, means that the abstraction from material time and its influences between bodies is established top-down, whereas 'morals' means it is established bottom-up. The dimension of life that has bodies organize living together in ignorance of law and morals – not because the *persons* forget them, but because the *effective agent* is not the social persona – altogether escapes them.

37 Arnold Gehlen: *Die Seele im technischen Zeitalter. Sozialpsychologische Probleme in der industriellen Gesellschaft.* Reinbek: Rowohlt 1957, p. 118 (transl. K. v. E.).

As Judith Butler's political take on deconstruction has laid bare, the concept of reiteration, adopted from structuralism, does not relate to series of actual performances in the past which affect the present situation through material consequences (in the way e.g. of neurons firing repeatedly within a certain interval or ants organizing their foraging through stigmergy). Neither does 'reiteration' cue us to perceive in a present act the reaction to the presence of other bodies, the polychronicity of a world where you are never alone and where time is being measured by synchronizing and desynchronizing rhythms, human and non-human. In *Excitable Speech*, Butler's argument reveals how a deconstructive effect depends upon the superiority of the single person's relation to the general over actual encounters, over the participants' mutual impact on what takes place. The attacker who threatens me with physical violence must borrow phrases from the public archive of aggressive rhetoric in order to execute their intrusion. Insofar as they are executives claiming access to a sovereign power (bonding with the evil twin of the good, protective sovereign), I will be able to counter their attack by exposing its derivative condition: You are not the author of your words, and you will not be the author of your deed. Even if you shame me, beat me, rape me, injure or kill me, I will not recognize you as the bearer of that power – and therefore, no matter how severe the physical damage inflicted, you cannot touch me directly. The conventions of language, of society, always come in between us. What I say-do in response (maybe now, maybe later, much later) will defeat your strategy of imposing your definition of the situation on me, precisely because this saying-doing will not have been a reaction. Witnesses may record reflexes, resonances, fallouts on my part, but I reserve the right to a response that will be (or might be) different from a reaction.

Butler's deconstruction-as-defense targets a different moment in the confrontation than does Aikido. Leaving, nearly abandoning the scene of physical contact where the damage is being done, the deconstructive counter-measure meets the enemy at the point of our shared dependency on social recognition. No, your body and mine will not determine the present of this incident, this strategy insists. The infinite number of absent others, which make up humanity, have a say in this, more so than the finite number of those who *were* present but did not come to my help. Absence saves in the absence of help. Butler upholds the belief in a general sphere, common to all, where every concrete outcome may forever be submitted for revision. The situative evaluation in terms of material consequences is only ever provisional, awaiting a verdict spoken by a truly just meta-collective voice, a court of justice that is not of this world, yet is required by this world to remain inhabitable.

Like Jean-François Lyotard in his Kant-inspired *Le Différend*[38], Butler proposes the interminable continuation of a struggle over meaning and status as the theater for battle. The battle will thus be for *archein* authority. The possibility of lodging an appeal, which political deconstruction avers for opening up the present to a future, is crucial since it enables the weaker party to revisit the *archein* moment of the other's action: the moment when the action had not yet been carried out, when the violence was still vision, promise, phantasmatic lapse. Instead of addressing the thrashing, the material reality of violent contact, an interpretation of the event assumes two (plus *n*) bodies, each one properly assigned to a subject-agent, each of these subject-agents caught up in an interval between what they could do, would do, might want or desire to do, and what they will do in an instant, which never fully passes. Only founded on such an archeology of the performative can a philosopher who titled one of her books *Bodies That Matter* celebrate "vulnerability" as a political virtue. My vulnerability is what awaits future justice. It is inimitable – I can neither learn how to be this vulnerable, nor how to develop my vulnerability according to the technical requests of particular fights – because its humanness precludes imitation or any modulation from body to body. It can only be embodied.

What I have called a transvaluation of reacting might require that we stop reserving our right to react. Or, more precisely, that we learn how to react right here, right now, regardless of what the future may bring. Hope, first of all, needs to be forgotten. And any technique of reacting will instruct its practitioners in actively forgetting about what *would be* the right thing to happen. Certainly, a freedom to react can be founded in the freedom of not having to react right now; but

38 Cf. Jean-François Lyotard: *The Differend: Phrases in Dispute*, transl. from the French by Georges Van Den Abbeele. Minneapolis: University of Minnesota Press 1988.

insisting on this freedom reaffirms the political sovereign, transferring agency to a metaphysical institution that is merely a more just version of the state's institutions. A different, an-archic, performative freedom to react arises within letting it be real that *this is happening*, and happening on the time and terms of others, including myself as one (or some, perhaps many) among others. Performing collectively, and performing collectivity, does not endorse a metaphysics of presence when it embraces the actuality of what is happening without reservation. Rather, it acknowledges that the material reality of bodies, always more than one, defines and measures the present at any particular moment, in any particular place. If reactions are what constitutes collectivity, the freedom to react is to be found in people's ability to use the informative value of gravity, momentum, inertia and friction for redirecting each other's movements, thus altering the profile of their actions. Political activism can learn this from contemporary dance and performance art: how to become aware of the bodies, how to be less desperately obsessed with the symbolic and imaginary powers of embodiment.

List of Figures

Katia Arfara: *X Apartments*

Fig. 1: Akira Takayama's installations at the Larissis train station, *X Apartments Athens*, 2015. Photo Stavros Petropoulos. © Onassis Fast Forward Festival / Stavros Petropoulos, 2015.

Fig. 2: Lampros Moustakis in his tent with a participant, *X Apartments Athens*, 2015. Photo Stavros Petropoulos. © Onassis Fast Forward Festival / Stavros Petropoulos, 2015.

Narges Hashempour: Theatrical Performances in Today's Iran

Fig. 1: The Ta'ziyeh *Imam Hussein*, Tehran, 2009. http://anasr121.mihanblog.com/post/1073 (accessed September 20, 2016). © mihanblog.com.

Fig. 2: Hamid Pourazari: *U-Turn*, Tehran, 2010. © Published with the permission of the director Hamid Pourazari.

Bernhard Siebert: Survey on Stage

Fig. 1: Kate McIntosh: *All Ears*, 2013. Photo & © Robin Junicke, 2013.

Eva Holling: Lacanian Transference

Fig. 1: *Marina Abramovic Made Me Cry*, Screenshot. Source & © http://marinaabramovicmademecry.tumblr.com/ (accessed February 10, 2015).

Fig. 2: The Gorilla in Forced Entertainment: *Bloody Mess*, 2004. Photo: Hugo Glendinning. © Forced Entertainment, 2004.

Eliane Beaufils: Self-Play and Togetherness

Fig. 1: Looking at/like teenagers in Gob Squad: *Before Your Very Eyes*, 2011. Photo & © Phile Deprez, 2011.

Fig. 2: Angels of Disobedience in *Rhythm Conference Feat. Inner Splits*, 2014. Photo & © Maarten van den Abeele, 2014.

Marie Vandenbussche-Cont: Nature Theater of Oklahoma

Fig. 1: Nature Theater of Oklahoma: *No Dice*, 2007. © Nature Theater of Oklahoma, 2007.

Fig. 2: Nature Theater of Oklahoma: *Life and Times Episode 1*, 2009. © Nature Theater of Oklahoma, 2009.

Chloé Déchery: The Guest Performer

Fig. 1: Tim Crouch: *An Oak Tree* with Amy Griffiths, National Theatre London, 2015. Photo & © Greg Goodale, 2015.

Fig. 2: Michael Pinchbeck: *The Man who Flew Into Space from His Apartment*, 2014. Photo & © Julian Hughes, 2014.

Ivana Müller: A *Pas de Deux* You Cannot Dance Alone

Fig. 1: Spectators read the text of *We Are Still Watching* and enact the show themselves: a doing by reading and imagining. Ivana Müller: *We Are Still Watching*, 2012. Photo & © Ian Douglas, 2012.

Fig. 2: People go for a walk and spend hours, months in a forest conversing without endings ... The spectators accompany their reflections. Ivana Müller: *Conversations Out of Place*, 2018. Photo & © Bernhard Müller, 2018.

Fig. 3: The unseen and the unheard become the people in the center of the stage in *Edges*. Ivana Müller: *Edges*, 2016. Photo & © Bernhard Müller, 2016.

Leon Gabriel: Scenes of Plural Constellations

Fig. 1: Romeo Castellucci: *FOLK*, 2012. Photo & © Wonge Bergmann, 2012.

Fig. 2: Jacques-Louis David: *Le Serment du Jeu de paume*, 1791. Musée national du Château de Versailles.

Fig. 3: Kate McIntosh: *Untried Untested*, 2011. Photo & © Phile Deprez, 2011.

Fig. 4: Kate McIntosh: *Untried Untested*, 2011. Photo & © Phile Deprez, 2011.

Fig. 5: Kate McIntosh: *Untried Untested*, 2011. Photo & © Sam Verhaert, 2011.

Fig. 6: Kate McIntosh: *Untried Untested*, 2011. Photo & © Sam Verhaert, 2011.

This book was printed with the generous support of
Université Paris 8 (Laboratoire : Théâtre ; EA 1573) and
the ANR Program "Investment in the Future" (ANR-10-LABX-80-01).

German National Library Cataloging in Publication Data
A catalog record for this book is available from the German National Library:
http://dnb.d-nb.de

Cover Design: Marija Skara, image by Kerstin Krone-Bayer
Editing & Typesetting: Neofelis Verlag (mn / ae)
Printed by PRESSEL Digitaler Produktionsdruck, Remshalden
Printed on FSC-certified paper.
ISBN (Print): 978-3-95808-156-7
ISBN (PDF): 978-3-95808-204-5